SPEAKING TRUTH TO POWER

The LIFE AND TIMES of an African Caribbean British Man

The AUTHORISED BIOGRAPHY of Arthur France, MBE

by Max Farrar

HANSIB

First published in Great Britain by Hansib Publications in 2022

Hansib Publications Limited
76 High Street, Hertford, SG14 3WY, UK

info@hansibpublications.com
www.hansibpublications.com

ISBN 978-1-912662-67-8
ISBN 978-1-912662-68-5 (Kindle)
ISBN 978-1-912662-69-2 (ePub)

A CIP catalogue record for this book
is available from the British Library

Design & Production by Hansib Publications Ltd

Printed in Great Britain

To all those who have put their bodies, minds and souls on the line in the struggle for the full emancipation of us all.

Enjoy The read
One Love
Arthur MBE
30/1/23

About the author

Dr Max Farrar has been involved in grass-roots politics in Leeds, UK, since 1968. In the 1980s, he worked in further and adult education at the Harehills and Chapeltown Law Centre. He also worked for the Runnymede Trust in London and as a freelance writer/photographer.

His PhD examining the Black-led social movements in Chapeltown in the 1970s, 80s and 90s, was published as *The Struggle for 'Community'* (2002). Edited books include *Islam in the West: Key Issues in Multiculturalism* (2012) and *Celebrate! Fifty Years of Leeds West Indian Carnival* (2017), with Guy Farrar and Tim Smith, which includes his photos and text.

He retired from paid work in 2009 as Professor for Community Engagement at Leeds Beckett (formerly Metropolitan) University, where he taught and researched in sociology from the early 1990s.

Max Farrar is secretary to the Board of the David Oluwale Memorial Association, a registered charity which uses all forms of art and performance in communicating messages for inclusion, diversity and social justice.

See also: www.maxfarrar.org.uk & www.rememberoluwale.org

CONTENTS

List of illustrations

Arthur France with Max Farrar, Nevis 22.1.2016 © Jane Storr

Ebenezer and Olga "France Clan". Courtesy Arthur France

The Austin of England 1953, the model driven by Ebenezer France

Houses, old and new, in Mount Lily, 2017 © Max Farrar

Teacher Franklyn and Mrs Brown, at their home in Nevis, 4.3.2017. © Max Farrar

Sir Joseph France, receiving his Knighthood in 1996. Photo courtesy Ms Prudence France

"Sorry, No Coloured"

Wole Soyinka, in graduation costume, and his family in Nigeria

Arthur France, outside 15 Grange Avenue, Chapeltown, where he lived in the early 1960s, with his sister Elaine and her husband George Archibald, 24th March 2021. © Max Farrar

Arthur and his motorbike, 1960s. Photo courtesy Arthur France

The Leeds Technical College (later, Leeds Polytechnic's Engineering Department) c.1967. Photo: leodis.net

Arthur France, George Archibald and some of the UCA Supplementary school students, June 1974. © Dave Williams for *Chapeltown News*

Photo of front page of *Chapeltown News*

Mike Laxton, Kam Sngra, Veryl Harriott, Simon Horner, Dave Williams, Mike Standing and Norma Morgan. Photo © Leeds Library and Information Services at leodis.net. Courtesy Tom Williams

Vinod France, Tattra France, Prince Charles, Arthur France, with Brainard Braimah standing behind Tattra at Technorth, Leeds. Courtesy Arthur France

New housing in Ebor Gardens, Leeds, built by Wimpey, opened in July 1960

Arthur and Tattra outside Roscoe Methodist church, 21st August 1976. Photo courtesy Tattra France

Thousands of racist whites attacked Notting Hill's Caribbean citizens in the summer of 1956. *The Daily Herald*

Frank Worrell, Everton Weekes and Clyde Walcott, 1957

Arthur France and Maureen Baker, August 2003. © Max Farrar.

'Prostitution out of Chapeltown' demonstration, April 1975. © Max Farrar

Arthur France outside Leeds West Indian Centre, 24 March 2021 © Max Farrar

When Arthur met Mohammed Ali, at the Park Lane Hotel, London, 24 April 1984. © Hansib Publications. Courtesy Arthur France

Arthur France performing on the road at Leeds West Indian Carnival in 2015. © Guy Farrar

Carnival pioneers: L-R: Calvin Beech, Arthur France, Rashida Robinson, Ian Charles, Willie Robinson, at the 50th anniversary Carnival, 2017. © Max Farrar

Arthur and Mahalia France at LWI C in 1977. Courtesy Arthur France

1974 Carnival committee members outside Cowper street school, L-R: Vince Wilkinson, Hughbon Condor, Hebrew Rawlings, Arthur France, Kathleen Brown, George Archibald. © Max Farrar

Arthur France and Inspector Roy Exley at Leeds West Indian Centre, 1992. © Max Farrar

Carnival Queen with Arthur France at LWIC in August 1975. © Max Farrar

L-R: Susan Pitter, Cllr Bernard Atha (Lord Mayor of Leeds), Dudley Nesbitt, 2001. © Max Farrar

Members of the Nevis delegation to the 2017 Carnival celebrations in Leeds Civic Hall, including the Premier, Vance Emory, Abonaty Liburd (Director of Culture), Keith Scarborough (Premier's Ministry), Vernon Richardson, Dis and Dat (Calypso King), Nevis Cultural Group including the Sugar Hill String Band, Cllr Jane Dowson, Cllr Angela Wenham, Cllr Alison Lowe, Cllr Mohammed Rafiq, Rehana Minhas, Rashida and Willie Robnson, Calvin, Hyacinth, Angela and Karen Beech, Veronica and Tyrone Samlal Singh. Arthur France is in the back row. Photo © Sylvester Meade

Standing up to racism: Arthur France and Calvin Beech in 2017.
© Christian Høgsbjerg

Arthur France and troupe on stage at LWIC, August 2015.
© Max Farrar

The Big Breakfast: Tattra, Vinod, Mahalia, Arthur and Asha
France at Channel 4 TV, 1995. Photo courtesy Arthur France

Vinod, Arthur, Tattra and Asha France after Arthur's MBE
ceremony, 14th June 1997. Photo courtesy Arthur France

Some of the family in 2003, L-R (back row) Fritz, Vinod, Modassa,
Asha. L-R (front) Cathy, Tattra, Arthur, Mahalia with baby Halima.
Photo courtesy Arthur France

Arthur and Tattra France's Family Tree. Drawing © Sketch (Lloyd
Herah). Courtesy of Arthur France.

Map of Saint-Christophe and Niévès (St Kitts and Nevis) showing
location of Mount Lily

The map of Nevis in 1870, showing Mt Lily Village

Map illustrating the Triangular Trade

Hard labour in the cane fields of St Kitts, 1903. Source: USA
Library of Congress

A 'Bill'

PREFACE

I know it doesn't seem likely, but I first met Arthur France at a fashion show. It was a student graduation event held, for reasons that escape me now, in a marquee outside Harewood House. We were introduced by Fabian Hamilton MP, whose constituency, before they changed the boundaries, then included both Harewood and Chapeltown. I knew of Arthur of course, as a major figure in Leeds' West Indian community and the founding father of Leeds Carnival, but as I have got to know him better over the years I've come to realise he is also far more than that. He is one of those rare people who truly embodies what he believes and whose beliefs grow out of his own direct experience.

This was brought home vividly when my wife Diane asked Arthur to open an exhibition by the Antiguan artist Frank Walter in the Terrace Gallery at Harewood House, timed to coincide with the 50th anniversary of Leeds Carnival in 2017. Walter was a true eccentric, who lived the last fifteen years of life as a recluse in a remote hut on his native island, making over 5,000 paintings and compiling a massive 25,000 page autobiography, which included descriptions of his time in Leeds in the 1950s, working in menial jobs despite his qualifications, suffering from the unthinking and widespread racism of the time. Arthur spoke, powerfully and movingly, of his own experiences of Leeds at that time and how things had changed – for the better, he said, but still with room for improvement. Speaking of his own life, Arthur shone a light on Frank Walter's that no art critic, however eminent, ever could.

Arthur was also responsible for persuading my dear friend Geraldine Connor to come to Leeds. I worked with Geraldine to produce her epic piece of musical theatre, Carnival Messiah, in a huge big top in the grounds of Harewood House in 2007, part of the commemoration of the Bicentenary of the Abolition of the Slave Trade. Arthur's support and through him that of Leeds' Caribbean community was crucial to making this happen. After Geraldine's untimely death in 2011, I was proud to stand alongside him in urging the city to honour her appropriately. There was an emotional funeral service at St Aidan's in Chapeltown and an exhilarating Gala performance at what was then still called the West Yorkshire Playhouse.

Leeds Carnival has become a regular highlight of the year for me, always featuring Arthur's famously shoulder-juddering high-five greeting and Max Farrar's ritual photograph. Carnival has gone from strength to strength and it was very strange and very sad that 2020 was the first and let's hope the last time it hasn't been able to take place. Bad weather, prejudice, violence and lack of funding have all threatened it in the past and have all been overcome. But the corona virus has meant that all the things the spirit of carnival embodies – inclusiveness, camaraderie, a celebration of what brings us together, not keeps us apart – have had to be temporarily suspended. But I have no doubt that Carnival will be back, stronger and more vivid than ever, with Arthur embodying its heart and soul as he has for so long.

It is a privilege to know him and an honour to be asked to write this short foreword to Max Farrar's biography. May you continue to go from strength to strength Arthur – One Love!

David Lascelles, Earl of Harewood
December 2020

Chapter One

INTRODUCTION: THE SHOCK OF THE NEW

Arthur France is a radical citizen of Nevis, the Caribbean, England and The World. Now in his 80s, he still commands the scene with his strong physique and distinctive voice. I first met Arthur in Leeds in the early 1970s. I was overwhelmed by the force of his personality and politics. In truth, I was overawed, not least because I was a callow, white, revolutionary student experiencing the full force of Black people's demand for independence. I received, and often deserved, strong criticism from the supporters of Black Power. Over the following years we became good friends, but I never dreamed that one day he would ask me to write his biography. (Actually, it was his wife Tattra who first suggested this project, but Arthur embraced it wholeheartedly and read every draft with care.)

In telling his story, this book seeks to explain some of the contexts that have shaped Arthur's life, and it raids other publications to provide insight into the lives of other people of the African diaspora, particularly those who have visited or grown up in Leeds, UK, where Arthur settled in his twenties.

Born in 1935 in Mount Lily, Nevis, one of the smallest islands in The New World, Arthur's first shock as a young man was to encounter the fierce inequality of income and power, based on skin colour and class position. Then, in his 20s, there was the shock of finding out that The Mother Country was, in fact, a bad mother. A lifetime of struggle to reverse these injustices provided many more shocks, and several triumphs, as this story will tell.

Within a few years of leaving Nevis and arriving in Leeds – a city in Yorkshire in the north of England – Arthur France and his politically-minded friends set up the United Caribbean Association. This was in 1964 and there were around 2,000 other people from the Caribbean in Leeds. Most were from Nevis and St Kitts; there were Bajans and Jamaicans, and a few Trinis and Montserratians as well. Arthur's ambition for unity among people of African-Caribbean-Asian descent was evident right from the start. Later, each of the islands was to form their own associations in Leeds, including one for St Kitts-Nevis, but Arthur's brainchild was the United Caribbean Association. 'I don't want any of that petty nationalism, I want Black people to unite and fight for their rights,' is a paraphrase of his views then, and now.

Mount Lily in the St James parish at the north of Nevis is a small settlement off the main road that winds around that beautiful island, close to the shining Caribbean Sea. (There are maps of St Kitts and Nevis, showing St James parish, in the Appendix to this book.) There were about 12,500 people there when Arthur left in 1957, and there are about 1,000 fewer than that today. 'They're just small islanders' is one of the jokes among Caribbean people from the larger islands, but there's nothing small about Arthur France.

The (very small) Queen of England honoured him with the Member of the British Empire medal on 14th June 1997, in recognition of his major contributions to English society. She was probably thinking of his role in founding in 1967 the first Black-led, Caribbean-style carnival in Europe. But Arthur's bigger contribution, arguably, is his role as an organiser of manifold struggles for the rights and freedoms of people of colour everywhere. Yes, he's a member of the Empire, but he's a fierce critic of imperialism.

This book traces Arthur's days as a child and young man in Nevis; his student days in England; his work in engineering and in education; his activity in the Black Power movement and community organising; and his utter dedication for over 50 years to making carnival costumes and drawing hundreds of others into the arts and pleasures of carnival in Leeds. Arthur speaks movingly of his love for and admiration of his father Ebenezer, his mother Olga and his uncle Joe: family is a central pillar of his life, and the final chapter of this book speaks of the family he has established in Leeds.

Among the jokes and stories you hear in any conversation with Arthur you'll realise how, after more than 60 years in England, Arthur remains rooted in Nevis, with Africa at the front of his mind. To fully understand Arthur, you have to understand the slave trade and its impact on Nevis. This is a complex and deeply disturbing history. I've done my best to digest a range of sources and I've told it through the lens of the Caribs who were tricked and massacred, the Africans who escaped and rebelled, and the emancipated Nevisians and Kittitians who organised politically against the white, capitalist colonisers. This is the history in which Arthur has formed his identity. But not everyone will want to read this grim – but ultimately inspiring – chapter, so I've placed it at the end of the book as an Appendix.

The book is based on long, recorded interviews with Arthur that I conducted in 2020. Now in his 80s, he is still full of energy. I put his words in inverted commas when I'm using his direct speech. Mainly, I summarise him in my own version of the recorded words. I'm sorry that I can't capture his rich accent, which to this day bears the mark of his childhood in Nevis. You'll be able to imagine, though, how strong and resonant is his voice, and I hope you can feel the conviction with which he speaks.

For his early life I interviewed, in Nevis in 2017, some of his siblings, his cousin, his life-long friend and comrade Calvin Beech, and his main teacher, Mr Franklyn Brown. Their

Arthur France and Max Farrar in the cook pot in Charlestown, Nevis, 22.01.2016.
© Jane Storr

comments appear in early chapters. Sometimes I insert the experiences of other people, and I have added materials drawn from other sources so that we can see Arthur's unique life in a wider context of Black people's migration and settlement – too often, *un*settlement – in England.

Far too little has been written about these intrepid pioneers, and this book hopes to become a resource for people who want to understand how England has become a country of 'contested multiculturalism'. I try to achieve this by telling the story of one man who has done so much to contribute to the convivial, compassionate and equal society that so many of us believe in. The sources I have used are referenced at the end of each chapter to provide students and other researchers with some suggestions for further reading.

Shining throughout this book is Arthur's absolute commitment to the role of education in developing the individual and society as a whole. This is characteristic of all the people who have the courage to migrate and to bear the racism that meets them when they settle, even when it's the 'mother country'.

Charlene White, the first Black woman to read ITV's News at Ten in the UK, got a private education because of her parents' commitment to education. 'I've never known my dad to do just one job,' she said. Her parents did 'five or six jobs between them in order to send us to school'. (Her mother was educated in Britain: her experience of racism in school made her determined that her children would get a better deal.)

One of my sources, providing context for Arthur France's story, comes from another famous Leeds person, Spice Girl Melanie Brown. Mel B is part of the generation that was formed by the 1950s, 60s and 70s Caribbean pioneers. Her father was born in St Kitts, and settled in Leeds as a young adult. Melanie wrote this of her pride in her identity, and she spoke of her dreams:

I am – like so many British people – part immigrant. I have my mum's British blood and my dad's Caribbean blood, carried over the seas to the docks of Southampton along with so many others who came over in the 1950s on ships like [the] *Windrush*. I'm proud of that. Being an immigrant is all about struggle, survival and having a dream of a better life. It's in my blood, passed down from my grandparents. It's part of their past and my past, and it has propelled us all forward into a different future.

Melanie understands as clearly as Arthur that migrating from the Caribbean and settling in the UK involves perpetual struggle. People of mixed heritage, like her, have been steadily growing in number in Britain since the 1960s and they are as committed to social progress as Arthur, his children and grandchildren.

Two of the people closest to Arthur described him to me like this:

Arthur is very committed to whatever he puts his mind to. He's very honest. He's fun-loving, but he has a serious side. He was like this as a little boy – but he's improved a lot. He's all about people. Within reason, he'll do whatever you ask. He's not easily led by anyone else. He's very thoughtful. I might be biased, but I think he's a wonderful person.

Hyacinth Beech, Arthur's sister

Arthur's a person who is very much for Black people. And he's 'pro-Black' without being racist. He's very committed to making positive social change. In any social setting he's very lively. He's very warm-hearted – he always finds the right thing to say to people. And he's loyal. Once he's a friend, he's friend for life. He's got a lot of integrity and he's scrupulously honest. But he's not the most organised person in the world. There are a lot of people who would follow Arthur anywhere, wherever he would lead.

Calvin Beech, brother-in-law and oldest friend

In a profile for the BBC, Rob Dale wrote:

Arthur France has become not just a figurehead for the Black community in Leeds, but for Afro-Caribbean people across the UK. His work has been celebrated with multiple awards, his initiative has produced society-changing projects and his desire to improve standards in the community means he is heralded as a hero by those who have grown up influenced by his optimism and leadership.

That's a good summary. I'm one of those who have been much influenced by Arthur France. So I'd just add that he is not only committed to raising standards in the Black community: Arthur is committed to making the world a better place for everyone, whatever their skin colour. So he's a hero for lots of white people, too.

When, after hours of interviews, I asked Arthur to sum himself up, he said: "I've had a very good life, and when you

consider other things, I haven't got much to complain about."
Here speaks a man whose modesty, positive spirit, and
compassion for those less fortunate has driven a life of immense
achievement.

And who are you?

Arthur asked me to produce this book because he'd checked out
my writing over many years. He'd commissioned me to write for
his Carnival magazines in the 1980s and 90s, and, when I was
trying to make a living as a freelance journalist, Arthur had
helped me get some articles in *Caribbean Times* and *Asian
Times*, edited by Arif Ali. In the early 2000s my book about
Chapeltown's social movements was published and, in 2019, Guy
Farrar, Tim Smith and I published a book about Leeds West
Indian Carnival. So I bring some expertise to this book, along
with trepidation.

In recent years, white people have become more visible in
standing alongside Black people who, for so long, have been
struggling against racism. The term 'allies' is being used, and
contested. My own journey began in the early 1960s when I
became friends at boarding school in Liverpool with a Black boy
called Dave. His grandfather came to the UK from Trinidad in
the early 1900s to study medicine. His father, too, was a medical
doctor. Through him, I supported the African-Americans' civil
rights movement already taking to the streets in the USA. We
vowed to join the ANC and fight against apartheid in South
Africa when we left school. Reading the novels and essays of James
Baldwin embedded my values and developed my understanding.

Moving south, from 1966 onwards I was able to listen to, and
applaud, the orators of Black Power, particularly Roy Sawh, at
Speakers' Corner in London. It was when, from the early 1970s,
I lived in Chapeltown, the low-income area of Leeds where many
British people of African, Caribbean and Asian heritage had
settled from the 1940s onwards, that my learning took off. This
was my own 'shock of the new'. I realised that 'lived experience'

cuts much more deeply than books and media stories; the gulf between my privilege – based in my class, gender, sexual choices, Englishness and skin colour – and that of the myriad peoples of Chapeltown was vast. (The white people I lived alongside were from all parts of the UK and East Europe, and, however well-educated they were, their economic position was more precarious than mine.) However much I listened, however quickly I learned, the gap in experience remained huge. Nevertheless, through active support of the many campaigns and movements that erupted in this neighbourhood, and through working at the Harehills and Chapeltown Law Centre in the early 1980s, my understanding rapidly developed.

In the 1960s and 70s it was hard to find much to read in the UK about 'race' and racism. Key books for me were those written by Derek Humphry (a white journalist) and Gus John (born in Grenada, now a prominent activist and intellectual, and a friend of Arthur's). Ann Dummett and Ken Leach (associated with the Runnymede Trust) were other white people publishing important work who would now be described as allies. In sociology, Michael Banton and Sheila Patterson were white researchers whose work should have been better absorbed in the 1950s and 60s.

When I became a sociologist in the 1990s I decided to pick up on the study I had begun in 1972 of the Chapeltown Community Association. Much more writing on 'race' was available by then. Books, articles and talks by Zygmunt Bauman (Polish heritage), Avtar Brah (Indian and Ugandan heritage), Paul Gilroy (Guyanese heritage), Stuart Hall (Jamaican heritage) and Lynne Segal (Australian heritage) were particularly important in shaping my thinking. It's no co-incidence that all of these are migrants who not only help to build Britain, but who bring special insights to this country. The African-American writer bell hooks was equally influential. I benefited also from membership of the British Sociological Association's Race and Ethnicity Study Group, many of whose members were Black British sociologists. (I'm using 'Black' here in the old-fashioned way; some people now say 'people of colour'.) I hope this book will demonstrate some of the knowledge I gained in this period.

With Arthur, and the many others I got to know who saw beyond 'race' and were more concerned with what people have in common, bridges were built, and I could learn more deeply. In this book I refer to the work of CLR James, the Trinidadian Marxist. James's writing and political organising showed that, in capitalist societies, it was not just class exploitation that held people back. He saw that Black people and women were specifically oppressed because of their distinct identities.

James also noted that class identifications cut across those oppressions. Thus upper class white and Black people could substitute their class interests for their ethnic loyalties. (As Boris Johnson's Conservative government in Britain showed, people of every colour and any gender can willingly join with whites in exploitation and oppression.) Under some circumstances – when white and Black people have mutual respect and equal power – working class alliances against the ruling class can and will emerge.

CLR James's relative Darcus Howe, a leading member of the Race Today Collective based in London, taught me a great deal in the 1970s and 80s about the necessity, therefore, for Black people to organise autonomously, while making alliances where the struggle – simultaneously against capitalism, racism and gender oppression – required. In 1975 I joined Big Flame, the only British socialist organisation that understood the Jamesian philosophy and applied its insights.

I mention all this to give readers who are interested some idea of the 'position' from which this book is written. Stuart Hall taught us to read critically, taking note of the position from which an author writes. I am easily identified, or positioned, as an old, white, heterosexual, middle class man. I should add that I'm a sociologist with a life-long focus on 'race' and racism, and a political activist. Those identity positions will shape how I think, what I hear and see, the values I develop – and thus they will push all kinds of bias into my narrative. One that I readily acknowledge is my value commitment to the liberation of all of humanity from oppression and exploitation. But I know that this won't free me from the ignorance, mistakes and omissions that travel with me, buried in the baggage of my identities. I invite readers to take a critical approach to this book, as advocated by Stuart Hall, and to dissect it accordingly.

Professor Hall also taught us that identities are malleable, fluid, and syncretic. They are formed as we relate to other people, and as relationships change, so can we. We have agency, and we do not have to be fixed in the locations of our birth. I'd like to think that I sometimes slip out of the confines imposed by my class, gender, sexuality, colour and age – mainly because living in Chapeltown for many years provided so many opportunities to rub up with people of all colours, ages, sexualities, classes and genders, busy producing wonderfully diverse identities.

I can be reduced to my identity positions, but, on a good day, I can also float in other directions. It was in the process of slipping the knots of my birth that I came to realise that I had to work with white people in educating and organising against racism – we caused it, so we have to help solve it. I also realised how little I knew. Our work against racism and for social justice will be effective only if it is based in careful appreciation of the emotional, economic, social and political effects of the very long history of white people's exploitation and oppression of all those whom we have described as 'not white'. That requires a lot of listening and learning.

From a bumpy start in the 1970s, Arthur and I became good friends and political allies. I learned much from him, and this book is my tribute to an extraordinary man. In setting out his life and work, and placing it in the context of the history of his first island home and the obstacles that England erected in his path, I want readers to grasp his values, his altruism, and his sheer determination. He has so much to teach us. If this book turns into a resource for others to follow in his footsteps, I'll be a contented author.

Many thanks ...

I'd like to thank people who've helped me with getting this book into print. First of all, I'm more than grateful to Arif Ali, the Hansib publisher, for encouraging the book from the very start. Kash Ali has been very helpful too. I'm particularly grateful to Arthur's relatives (his sisters Janet and Hyacinth, Violet Jeffers Nichols, cousins Prudence and Floretta) and his brother-in-law Calvin Beech for the interviews quoted at various points in this book. Victoria O'Flaherty, Head of the St Kitts-Nevis National Archives, was very helpful in providing the records of Nevisians named France. Dr David Small provided me with a very useful reading list. Dr Christine Eickelmann's amazingly detailed research on a Nevis plantation is employed in this book, and she kindly gave me further advice by email. Dr Christian Høgsbjerg has provided me with extra sources and he made really useful suggestions and gentle corrections. Professor Karim Murji gave me pertinent advice on improving the introduction. Danny Friar dug out relevant press reports that I would never have come across without his help. Dr Tom Steele provided a vivid account of the Fforde Grene protest, included here verbatim. David Lascelles has enthused too, and kindly provided the Preface. Dr Emily Zobel Marshall and Colin Grant gave me good advice on finding a voice for my interviews with Arthur. Emily gave further advice and I'm very grateful to her, and to Professor Paul Warmington for the commendations they provided on the back cover. Jane Storr was totally supportive throughout, even during our holiday. Many thanks to you all.

References in this chapter

'The shock of the new' was the title of a TV programme by the art critic Robert Hughes.

Melanie Brown (with Louise Gannon), *Brutally Honest*, London: Quadrille, 2018.

Rob Dale, 'Gallic Flair – Arthur France is one of Chapeltown's favourite sons, due to the enormous contribution he's made to his community'. BBC (Leeds) 05.06.2009. Available at http://www.bbc.co.uk/leeds/content/articles/2009/06/05/people_arthur_france_feature.shtml Accessed 5.10.2021.

Max Farrar, 'Multiculturalism in the UK – a contested discourse', in Max Farrar, Simon Robinson, Yasmin Valli and Paul Wetherly (eds.) *'Islam' and 'the West' – Key issues in multiculturalism,* London: Palgrave, 2012. Available from https://www.maxfarrar.org.uk/writing/multiculturalism-in-the-uk-a-contested-discourse/ Accessed 9.10.2021.

Roy Sawh is well represented here https://soundsfromthepark.on-the-record.org.uk/people/roy-sawh/ Accessed 05.10.2021.

Charlene White: Ellen E Jones, 'A Little More Conversation, *The Guardian*, 01.02.2021. https://www.theguardian.com/media/2021/feb/01/charlene-white-on-loose-women-prejudice-and-the-poppy-row-it-still-upsets-me-now Accessed 06.02.2021.

Chapter 2

GROWING UP IN NEVIS: HAPPY DAYS

Thomas Arthur Benjamin France was born to Olga and Ebenezer France on 16th September 1935 in Mount Lily village in Nevis. The family had some status, because of Ebenezer's occupation, and the because of the family's productive, well-tended farm. Mt Lily is one of the clusters of houses at the north of the island, in St James Windward Parish. (The other villages in this parish include Newcastle, Rawlins, Fountain, Camps, Burnaby, Hicks, Brick Kiln, Whitehall, and Butlers.) Arthur France speaks of his early life in Nevis in the 1930s and 1940s with a mixture of awe, humour and delight.

In contrast, James Sutton, born in 1916, nineteen years before Arthur, described a very different life in Nevis in the 1920s. With his mother, known as Ma Kelly, and five siblings by three different men, none of whom stayed long, Mr Sutton grew up on the Rawlins estate not far from Mt Lily in a little 'Vora' house made of wood cut from the forest, thatched with sugar cane leaves, and a dirt floor. 'Very early in my life I became conscious of my mother's poverty and loneliness,' he wrote.

Mr Sutton's Christmas, with neighbours Punsy Liburd and Buddy Archibald, provided something of a feast for Ma Kelly and her children, because almost everyone owned a little land – they planted crops, and some kept some pigs and cows. They gathered together for the holiday celebrations, eating, drinking and enjoying carnival masquerades.

But it was a very hard life. With their bare feet and 'shirt tails' (short shirts and no pants), a highlight for Ma Kelly's children came when they managed to pull cane off a passing cart, escaping the driver's lash, for a 'sucking feast of sugar canes'. Moving to St Kitts when he was four, Mr Sutton described the labourers on Pond's estate as 'half starved for the rest of the year', but Christmas was a little better because the manager gave each man some flour, salt-fish and a bottle of rum. (The women got a headscarf or a piece of cloth.)

Arthur was better off materially, and he was happily ensconced with his mother, father and siblings. His father, Ebeneza France, was ever present in Arthur's life. He inspired awe, and it's striking how often Arthur's own core belief in discipline and hard work is illustrated with stories about Ebeneza. Ebeneza's brother, Joseph, later Sir Joseph, was also a formative influence on Arthur's later years on Nevis and St Kitts – stimulating his commitment to equal rights and social justice.

There is more about Sir Joseph in the Appendix to this book, outlining a history of Nevis and St Kitts which stresses the resistance of the Taino people and the Africans to white European power. A hint of that history has been provided by the novelist Monique Roffey, who was born in Trinidad. The Rain family, Roffey wrote, had 'bitten off' 2,000 acres of the small Caribbean island in which the novel is set.

> It was a land she [Miss Rain] knew intimately, girl to woman, land in which she had come to understand the heinous sins of the white men before her forefathers, and then their sins, the severe barbarity of their pious Christian souls.

That barbarity provides the overarching context for the whole of this book. This chapter, however, concentrates on Arthur France and his own family. Arthur is described by his siblings as a happy boy, and for every serious statement you hear from him today, you'll hear a lot of laughter too. He seems to have delighted in his childhood on that lovely island; his father's strict regime never damaged his sense of fun and adventure.

The other Frances in St Kitts and Nevis

Arthur's African ancestors arrived in Nevis in manacles. (For more history of this abominable trade, see the Appendix.) Prudence France, Arthur's cousin, told me that there is a story in the family that their surname derives from a child abandoned in the 18th Century by the French when they were finally forced off St Kitts by the British. This un-named child was, the story goes, found on the jetty in Basseterre and adopted by a family who called him 'France' because of his origins. Whether or not this is true, there's a message here that fits with the France family's long history of compassion and care for others.

Transported Africans normally lost their birth names and were re-named by their masters. Africans born in the Caribbean could acquire the name of the plantation where they worked; or, when the white owner had taken an African woman, the children might adopt their father's name; or perhaps a new name was implanted by a parent or an owner. Whatever the name's origins, we can track some of the Africans in St Kitts and Nevis with the name of France because, from the early 19th Century, the colonial rulers started making lists.

Victoria O'Flaherty, Head of the St Kitts-Nevis National Archives, kindly supplied the details she extracted from the slave registers of those people called France, born in the mid-1700s and registered in the first decades of the 19th Century. It is unlikely that any of these are actual relatives of Arthur's family, but this list does give us a picture of the terrible trade in Africans and the imposition of European names:

- A man named France, born in approximately 1757, nationality: Mozambique, owned by John Tyson on St Kitts, was registered in 1817.

- A man named France, born in approximately 1765, nationality given in the register as 'African (Black)', owned by Thomas Marr on St Kitts, was registered in 1825.
- A woman named Jenny France, born in about 1767, nationality St Kittitian, owned by the Honourable Lord Cranstoun on the island of St Kitts, was recorded in 1817.
- A man named France, born in approximately 1767, nationality St Kittitian, owned by William G Crooke on St Kitts, was registered in 1817.
- A man named France, born in approximately 1773, nationality African (Black), owned by George Clarke Forbes on Nevis, was registered in 1817.
- A man named France, born in approximately 1773, nationality given in the register as African (Black), owned by Thomas Marr on St Kitts, was registered in 1825.
- A man named France, born in approximately 1777, nationality Congolese, owned by William Wharton Rawlins on St Kitts, was registered in 1817.

The nations listed – Mozambique, The Congo – are the ones delineated by the colonial powers as they divided up Africa, and in several cases the census officials don't even bother to specify the nation, labelling them generically as African and Black; significantly, two were born in the Caribbean and thus acquired a Kittitian (UK) nationality. We have no idea if our branch of the France dynasty is linked to any of those listed above – Arthur's ancestors could be from the Congo, Mozambique, or, like the majority of captives, from Nigeria or Ghana.

Victoria O'Flaherty told me that the earliest mention in the government's other papers of a France in St Kitts was Ann France. In 1817 Ann was a slave registered as performing the role of guardian to Elizabeth Benners (who owned Ann France).

Ann must have been a slave who was held in the highest esteem by her owner, since Elizabeth made Ann France her guardian. Victoria O'Flaherty also searched the post-emancipation birth registers (started in 1859) and found a record of Frederick France, a merchant who was married to Christiana Thomas in 1855; they had their first child in 1860. By 1878 Frederick described himself as an Insurance Agent. In Nevis she found a carpenter and a shopkeeper named France.

Christine Eickelmann and David Small, whose extensive researches in Nevis are referred to in the Appendix, kindly supplied references to Frances in the records that they have compiled. They found these: Rebecca France from Westbury Village (Nevis) was buried on 9 May 1892, aged 98; and there are the Frances who were among 570 or so who signed the petition, dated 8th April 1902, by J C Taylor of Pollards Village (Nevis) to the King regarding economic distress: Alice France, Brother France, Emma France, Ephraim France, Evelyn France, Joseph France and William Francis. (David Small pointed out that people named France and Francis may well have been related.)

All this is intriguing but inconclusive as to Arthur's family's genealogy. We know a lot about the physical violence imposed by the slave owners; it's always worth thinking about the damage done by the symbolic violence of discarding the true name of your family and inserting a new one, which may or may not signify who your parents actually are.

Arthur's Family

Fortunately, Arthur France knew his immediate family very well and was loved by them. He has five sisters – Ernestine, Inez, Elaine, Marjorie, Hyacinth, and Janet. His brother Samuel died in 2018. Arthur's birth is registered in one of the huge books carefully stored in the registrar's office in Charlestown. Our Thomas Arthur Benjamin is there, alongside his father's full name, Azariah Ebeneza France, whose occupation was noted as

The Olga and Ebenezer France clan: Standing, at the left: Queen Mother Olga France. Sitting at front, according to seniority: Ernestine, Inez and Elaine. Standing at the back, from right to left: Marjorie, Arthur, Hyacinth, baby brother Samuel, and baby sister Janet. Photo courtesy Arthur France

'chauffeur'; their home is listed as Mt Lily, St James Parish, in the north of the island. His mother is inscribed there too: Olga Vera France, née Jeffers.

Alongside Arthur's birth details are the other babies born in Mt Lily around September 1935 and each parent's occupation gives us a picture of the social structure of their village. Rebecca Iris Nisbet, mother of Edward, was a shop-keeper at Brick Kiln; Edward Addison Jeffers was a carpenter at Mt Lily, who, with Malvina Mahallah Jeffers, née Hanley, had a son called Samuel; David Brown was a trafficker [a dealer in livestock] at Liburd Hill who had a daughter called Marjerie *(sic)* with Eulicia Brown née Maynard; Angelina Clarke, a labourer at Mt Lily, had a son called Cedric; and Hubert Maynard, who was a labourer at Butlers, had a daughter named Helena with Catherine Maynard (née Bussue).

When he was three years old, Arthur went to the nursery at George Maynard School, about five or ten minutes' walk from home. The children would sit under a tree and play and write with a slate and pencils (not a chalk) – the pencils made a white mark. "It was fun," Arthur said. "You had your peer group to play with – my friends were James Skeete (T was his nickname) and Rodney, and a girl whose name I can't recall."

Ebeneza's occupation in the registry does little justice to the roles Arthur's father actually performed. No mere chauffeur, he was the manager of the Nisbet coconut plantation which stretched from the main circular road to the northern coast of the island – Nisbet's Beach Resort is the trace of that estate today – close to Newcastle. Ebeneza's other role was to drive the owner, Sir Arthur Lees, on all his official business around the island in a large grey 'Austin of England' car. Everything had to be absolutely punctual. Ebeneza and his brother Joseph were born in Mount Lily. Thomas France, their father, worked on a road gang, supplementing his meagre income by growing vegetables. Ebeneza and Joseph fared much better than their father; he too must have been a good influence on his sons.

Arthur's father got on very well with Sir Arthur Lees, his wife and the whole family (they had a daughter called Mary, Arthur remembered). The Lees family embodied the British upper-class way of life, wearing their jodhpurs and spurs as they rode their horses around the countryside. Indicating the respect Sir Arthur had for Ebeneza, he was allowed to use the car when the Lees didn't need it, so Arthur and his siblings acquired prestige as they drove around with their father. Arthur has fond memories of being in the Austin; it symbolised the island's

The Austin of England saloon — The 1953 model driven by Ebeneza France

connection with England and his father's pride in that link. His Dad became known and respected across Nevis by white people and Black people alike. "The big merchants in town still talk to me about my father when I'm back home."

Ebeneza had another occupation: farming. This was crucial to the family's livelihood. It took a lot of hard work, cultivating the land that his father owned. "I can never remember a day when the sun rose and father was in the house." Karen Fog Olwig has researched a Nevisian family she calls The Smiths, who lived in a place she calls Richmond Village. She wrote: '[Richmond] village emerged on abandoned sugar fields when the old English plantocracy finally gave up sugar production in the early twentieth century and sold parcels of land to their former, landless labourers, the Black descendants of slaves freed in the 1830s'. Ownership of land meant the Smiths could sustain 'a respectable, well-kept independent home' – 'a great accomplishment'.

This land has been described as 'worn out' after 300 years of mono-cropping but it was fertile enough to allow Black families to significantly improve their conditions of life. 'Lisa Smith' said this to Professor Olwig about her life in the 1950s in Nevis:

> I know that my mother and father had it tough. My father used to work the land at home and at [a nearby estate]. He was up early in the morning to work. My mother would go down there, but she would get something for us to eat before she left. They didn't have much in those days. We ate things from the land and the animals. Sweet potato mashed into milk. Sometimes we got bread and some kind of relish, cheese or eggs, because we had a lot of fowl. We lived on the ground provisions and the farming – milk from the cows and eggs from the fowl.

This portrait of home life and work is familiar to all Black Caribbean islanders living in rural areas. They were not rich, they worked extremely hard, and for long hours, but they were able to eat nutritious food that they cultivated for themselves. Importantly, Olwig pointed out that land ownership and farming meant that people could develop their social identity 'as proper citizens', supported by living according to the requirements of their Christian faith.

Ebeneza's family farm had three sugar-cane fields, a cotton field, and a field for vegetables. It had sheep, pigs, three horses and a mule. Arthur learned how to labour in this farm, under his father's watchful eye. (Ebeneza would test the ground to see they had watered everything properly.) Arthur's work ethic comes from his Dad: "I did the farm work before school and after school."

According to his close friend Calvin Beech, Ebeneza was a canny businessman. "Arthur didn't inherit that skill," Calvin smiled, "He never cared about money. The business brain went to his sister Hyacinth." Hyacinth was too modest to agree, but she didn't disagree with her husband. Those were long days for the young Arthur. "There wasn't much time to play. Dad was very strict about our school work and on the religious side of our education. We all sat together every night and did bible reading, after the work in the field, after school work."

The days of the big sugar plantations had come to an end by the 1930s but there were small producers like Ebeneza, and the government still had a factory on Nevis. Between January and August the France children would help the five men Ebenezer employed to do the heavy harvesting of the cane, and it would go to be processed into sugar at the government factory. They would also do the fertilising of the cane fields after harvest, spreading the leaves so they would rot, in preparation for next year's crop. When he was about 14 years old Arthur learned to milk the cows and his job included looking after the animals and taking the milk to market – the government bought all they could supply.

Ebeneza often played the organ at Combermere Methodist Church. The family were keen members of the church and its

Sunday School. Ebeneza's important role in the church gained him further respect from the community. His faith was strong. His Christian values no doubt informed his practice of giving a lot of the family's produce to those less fortunate. He'd say to someone he thought needed some assistance: "Send your grandson down for a bottle of milk," and give away the milk for free.

"Dad would butcher the animals and give meat away. People thought he was wealthy but he wasn't. He and mum were very generous." Farming is seasonal but he found work for his labourers throughout the year. A lot of the money he put aside he gave to other people. "I once asked him why he did this – he said I wouldn't understand. But I do now. I inherited lots of my father's attitudes. I learned from his example. I'm very much like him."

I had the privilege of visiting some of Arthur's family and friends in their well-appointed homes in Nevis in 2017 when I was researching this book. They showed me Mount Lily and the plot of land where his family house stood. Nearby were simple wooden houses like the one Arthur grew up in. Several of his relatives now live in new houses nearby. They gave me their impressions of the young Arthur France.

His sister Janet is a lot younger than Arthur. She told me: "I don't remember much of his early years on Nevis, but I do remember he was a good cook. His favourite dish was coconut porridge – he'd make it for the whole family. No one could cook it like he did." And: "Arthur was caring and loving and he mingled with the whole community. He would always assist others in whatever they needed. He loved his sisters and his brother."

Arthur's relative Violet Jeffers Nichols remembered him like this: "Arthur was very jovial and very outspoken. He always called a spade a spade. He was always very talkative. Anything he knew, he liked to expound upon it." Some people might well say he hasn't changed much since those early days. Arthur used

Houses, old and new, in Mount Lily, 2017 © Max Farrar

to go around with Violet's brother in Mount Lily village. "They never got into any real trouble – just childish pranks."

Arthur's cousin Floretta has a wonderful house and garden where she cultivates all kinds of different fruits. It's close to the top of the island, not very far from where she grew up on Mount Lily. She's quite a bit younger than Arthur and doesn't remember him well as a child. But she does remember their father. "He was strict. Too strict." Elvie Jeffers, who went to school with Arthur, said his father was "very strict, very disciplined." Arthur remembered getting "cut arse" from his Dad when he tried to get out of going to church by removing a button from his shirt.

I talked to Arthur's sister Hyacinth and her husband Calvin, one of Arthur's closest friends, on the breezy balcony of the Lemongrass restaurant on Bay Road in the heart of bustling Basseterre. Hyacinth agreed that their father Ebeneza was very strict – "thinking back, using the strap might sound a bit cruel" – and she thought their Mum was perhaps a bit too submissive. But she was full of praise for their father, too. "He brought us up to start work early, to pray and to be kind and think of each other." And she added that Ebeneza was "a bit of a comedian, too." Maybe Arthur gets his advanced sense of humour from his Dad?

"We were equally formed by both our parents. The day started at 5am with prayers and then we had to do our chores. We hated the early start, we wanted to sleep, but now I'm so grateful for that. Start early, pray, think of each other – that's what we were taught." On Sundays after church they would visit their aunts, and their Dad would tell them stories when they got home. "We had a very nice upbringing. Our family was very close. Daddy said we must always be kind. I used to wonder why he was so strict, but we turned out pretty good, because of our upbringing."

It's no accident that the Frances were, then and now, committed members of the Methodist Church. Methodism's founder, John Wesley (1703-1791) regarded slavery as 'the sum of all villainies' and he published a searing indictment of the system in 1774 in a pamphlet titled *Thoughts Upon Slavery*. Wesley was a mentor to William Wilberforce, who steered the first legislation against slavery through the UK parliament in 1807. Methodism spread rapidly through the British Empire as its preachers followed its colonists around the world.

Hyacinth said that even as a little boy Arthur was both fun-loving and serious, very thoughtful and helpful. Calvin said that Arthur wanted to be an individual from early on. He said Arthur put a shoe on his donkey, even though his father called him "one fool" and said no one did that. Everyone laughed at his donkey-with-a-shoe clip-clopping along the road. "Arthur just wanted to be different." In 1960, just about to be 18 years old, Hyacinth arrived in Leeds, England, joining up again with Arthur, to train as a nurse. "Daddy told Arthur to make sure I had everything I need – he knew I was in good hands."

Arthur's cousin Prudence France is the daughter of Sir Joseph France. She's a senior executive in the bank at Basseterre. She remembers Arthur being an enthusiast for the 'mini-carnival' on Nevis and crossing to St Kitts to join a troupe at 'Sports', the colloquial name for carnival. "Everyone here knows Arthur," she told me. Apparently he once had an open-topped vehicle in which he ferried kids around. She remembers him always saying "Keep your head high. You're a proud African."

Hyacinth told me that their mother Olga's kindness was legendary. Arthur described his mother, who died in September 1998, aged 90, as loving and caring. She was a school teacher until she had children. She used to say: "Manners and good behaviour carry you around the world without costing you a penny." Arthur couldn't understand what she meant, "but I do now." Another of her sayings was "Talk with your mouth shut". He didn't understand that till much later either – it's sometimes better not to say anything at all.

Their mother Olga was the only Black woman with a horse and saddle. It was a white horse called Kate. She would ride the seven miles into Charlestown to see her sister. She was reasonably strict but less so than Ebeneza. Arthur remembered her giving him a beating in the yard with a coconut branch when he was about 14. He tried to protect himself and his mother said "Wait till your father come." It was going to get worse.

Arthur gave me a picture of a happy childhood working with the animals, always in the context of strong discipline. Much as he enjoyed himself, things could go wrong. A sow and her piglets would continually run away from him. He would only be able to catch them when they got stuck in the bushes. There was more trouble when he took the sheep to the pool to drink water. One day Ebeneza's best breeding yew tried to escape. Arthur chucked a small coconut at it to try and slow it down. Calamity: the coconut projectile broke the ewe's leg. Arthur feared the wrath of God. So he told his Dad that a ram had broken the ewe's leg. This time, he got away with his small lie. "If he knew what I'd done, I would have got a good cut arse. When he beat you, you got three good lashes with a belt or a stick. I would only get three lashes but you wouldn't want a fourth one."

"I'm keen on discipline myself, but I detest that kind of strong discipline. I'm more relaxed than my Dad was, because that's how it is today." On the other hand: "We're drifting backwards nowadays. Without discipline you're not going to hit the targets that you should."

Arthur's memories of his childhood are sunny. The Nisbet Estate was bounded by the sea, and Arthur and his friends would spend lots of time at the beach. His Dad taught them all to swim so they were safe. Sometimes they would take the horses, and even the cows, into the sea to clean them and to play, riding on their backs as they swam. And although they worked hard, they could make a few pennies by gathering coconuts on the estate. They got 4 pennies for every hundred they collected – and they could spend their earnings on sweets.

Going to School

The importance of education was instilled in Arthur and his siblings by his parents. This is characteristic of so many of the people of St Kitts and Nevis. As 'Yvette Smith' told Karen Fog Olwig: 'School was a must. No matter how much work [on the family farm], we had to go to school. My mother and father were not totally illiterate, but they wanted their children to do more. They insisted on school.'

When he was 5, Arthur went to Combermere School a bit further down the island, towards Camps. The building is still there – it belongs to the Methodist School. Head teacher Miss Cross was very strong on discipline. She was very friendly but there was a thick red line you didn't cross. All six teachers were Black; the class spanned children from five to 16 years of age. Teacher Enid (her full name was Enid Martin from Butlers on the east side of Nevis) was his first year teacher. In his third year it was Teacher John (Maynard). Arthur remembers them all: Teacher Burt from St Kitts, Teacher Walwyn from Rawlins Village on Nevis, Teacher Glery from Newcastle and Felton Skeete. Teacher Inez (Morton) from Gingerland was another teacher – she was related to the Frances. They were all friendly but serious. It was "the worst thing" if a teacher singled you out.

"Teacher Inez was hellfire." She'd say "If I have to call you up here you will fall asleep crying."

Felton Skeete left teaching to go to work as a sailor – he ended up in Leeds, England. "It was amazing how he changed. He was highly educated: but the only job he could get in Leeds was labouring in factories. It was so annoying." Anticipating some of the themes of the next chapter, Arthur said: "If people who left Nevis for England knew what they coming to they would never have left home. Felton actually got less money in England than he did on Nevis."

I talked to Mr Franklyn Anderson Brown, known to everyone as Teacher Franklyn, to learn more about Arthur as a schoolboy. From the age of 14, Teacher Franklyn was a pupil-teacher at Combermere School in St James' parish. He went on to study in Barbados and in England, bringing his additional skills back to improve schooling in Nevis. He taught English language, arithmetic, geography, history, science and botany. Arthur was about nine or ten when Teacher Franklyn joined the school. He doesn't recall Arthur doing terribly well at school, but

Teacher Franklyn and Mrs Brown, at their home in Nevis, 4.3.2017. © Max Farrar

he was always willing to learn. "Arthur was a boy in a family with a lot of sisters, so he was fairly awkward," Teacher Franklyn said in the voice of a man who just told it as he saw it, without fear or favour. He thought that the absence of male siblings put Arthur at a disadvantage when it came to games: "He wasn't willing to play cricket and so on." But his behaviour was good – "It had to be; he had a very strict father."

Teacher Franklyn said that there was little or no work on the island for boys in the 1950s. "The sugar and the cotton industries were failing. People were going away. It was said that the Queen of England invited people to come and everybody was hoping to get there." The 'Smith' children in 'Richmond Village' in Nevis interviewed by Professor Olwig came to the same conclusion: because work opportunities on the island were so limited, 'out-migration for economic opportunities abroad seemed to be the only viable way ahead for most of them'.

But that wasn't the case for Teacher Franklyn. As his name states, he had a profession: "I loved teaching, I loved home and I always felt I could make it on this island." Teacher Franklyn added: "I'm proud of Arthur. Many others who left Nevis have not achieved much, but he has."

Arthur enjoyed school and looked forward to going each day. He'd have his exercise book with his homework all done. (His parents insisted on that, and uncle Sir Joseph would check too, when he visited.) Now he wonders how the teachers coped with 20 children in the class, on their feet all day, marking all the homework. They got their initial training session in Charlestown and then more professional development in Antigua or Barbados. Teachers were highly respected.

Standards were maintained by the inspectors, all of whom were Black, led by Inspector Joseph. "The teachers were scared of them," Arthur recalled. "If you saw a car passing you wondered if Inspector Joseph was coming. He gave the school no notice." He would check the headteacher's documents. Then he would walk around the whole school unaccompanied. He would watch a lesson and then take over the class, inspecting your exercise book. Arthur still remembers his sarcastic remark to a girl named Marjorie. He looked at her book and asked her if her father "still living on that hill? "Yes teacher," said Marjorie. "So I have no need to look at your book. I can just look at the hair on your head and tell you he is." Her hair was untidy, and so was her book. It was a tough regime at Combermere.

Nevertheless, very few children left at 14. Almost everyone stayed till they were 16. "We got quite a good education. We'd cry when we left. We would sing the hymn, 'Our school days passed and gone and yet we linger here'. It was very painful to leave." Those who got the Seven Standard Certificate would become assistant teachers. They got sent back to teach younger ones as substitutes for teachers going off to other islands for training.

First employment

When he left school, Arthur went to train as an apprentice cabinet maker and joiner. Johnny Howell, the best builder in the island, was his boss and teacher. He was a Black man who specialised in making furniture, coffins and cartwheels. After five years, an apprentice became skilled and could branch out on his own. "Mr Howell would price the job for you and let you take some of his workmen and then you would share the income." His son Welton Howell and about nine others worked there. Yet again, his family background made a difference: "My Dad was well known and respected so that's why I could get one of the best apprenticeships on the island." He was proud to be earning money and in his spare time he could continue to help his parents with the animals or working in the fields.

There were only about 100 white people on the island. Arthur recalled Mr Gossley Benn who ran a big merchant's shop in Charlestown. There was Wildey who had a shipping business and Garnett Stevens who had a garage – he introduced motor vehicles to Nevis. "When I went home, these men would always remember my Dad and say good things about him." These were rich, powerful white men, but Arthur spoke of them warmly.

When he was about 20, he crossed the short stretch of water to St Kitts. He decided to leave the countryside to go to the larger town of Basseterre because there was more work and better pay at the St Kitts' sugar factory. His job was to lag the steam pipes, and he did part-time carpentry work as well. He lived with Uncle Joseph, who by then was General Secretary of the St Kitts-Nevis-Anguilla Trades and Labour Union. (Anguilla seceded in 1980.)

Joseph France was born in 1907 in Mount Lily, Nevis. A senior member of the Workers' League, he was a prominent leader in the 1935 strike by the workers at the St Kitts sugar factory. Prudence France told me that her father was fearless in the face of the planters – one of whom had killed three protesters, including James Archibald, at Buckley's estate in January 1935 – telling his children much later that he had no time to think about his own safety, knowing he would be protected by his people. Paul Foot wrote that 'Nowhere in the West Indies were the planters more resistant to change than in St Kitts. Consequently perhaps, nowhere were the sugar workers more courageous in their support for their trade union and labour leaders.'

Joseph was elected General Secretary of the Workers' League in 1938. The Workers' League transformed itself into the St Kitts and Nevis Trades and Labour Union in 1940, later becoming the St Kitts-Nevis-Anguilla Labour Party, under the leadership of Robert Llewellyn Bradshaw, with Joseph remaining General Secretary. Joseph France was a Minister in Paul Southwell's government, when the St Kitts-Nevis-Anguilla Labour Party came into power in 1961. Bradshaw became Chief Minister in 1966 and Premier in 1967. (He died in 1978.)

Uncle Joseph was offered the job of Chief Minister when St Kitts and Nevis became independent in 1983, but Arthur said he was the thinker, the man with the pen, and he preferred not

Sir Joseph France, receiving his Knighthood in 1996. Photo courtesy Ms Prudence France.

to be the leader. In 1996 Joseph became a Knight Commander of the order of St Michael and St George, dying a year later as Sir Joseph France, KCMG, CBE, JP. (There's more about his political work in St Kitts in the Appendix.)

In Chapters 6 and 7 we will see how this party and union, in which Sir Joseph France played a central role, influenced Arthur's political work in England. In particular, he subscribes to Sir Joseph's view that each person has their own specific talents and should develop them accordingly – there are always 'horses for courses'.

It takes a village ...

Nevis demonstrated the African proverb that it takes a village to bring up a child. The island is very small; it is actually possible for families to be so interconnected that they can take care of each other. In the 'History of Nevis and St Kitts' chapter (in the Appendix of this book) the point is made that the colonial rulers allowed their enslaved Africans on Nevis to live in clusters of family groups, and, much later, allowed them to grow fruit and vegetables, keep animals and engage in trade. This was the basis for both social solidarity and some economic independence.

These are among the reasons why the Nevisians and Kittitians in Leeds are so closely inter-woven.

The message that Arthur transmits from his early life on Nevis is that people did look after each other. His parents emphasised this and he's always taken it to heart. What might seem (to metropolitans) like too much scrutiny and too much control is described by Arthur as a useful way of keeping people on the straight and narrow. He recalled the trouble he was in when someone reported to his parents that he'd been laughing at a woman using bad language while she disciplined her child. And when a teacher saw him and his friends misbehaving on a beach during the holidays, they spent their first day back at school "head down, ear cocked." Sure enough, at the end of the day they got three stripes with the belt. The school and all the parents – his in particular – made sure that everyone behaved well.

School was important, but Ebeneza was the big figure in Arthur's development. "From my Dad I learned about time-keeping, about loving your family and friends, and to keep smiling." His father died in June 1965, aged 64. "I end up crying thinking how hard my father worked and what he did for me. I dream of sitting down to thank him, but I never managed to."

Arthur repaid his father by his life-long embodiment of his father's values: hard work, discipline, education, and looking after others. As the next chapter shows, he put all this into practice from the minute he arrived in England in 1957.

References in this chapter

Paul Foot, 'Twenty years of pirates, profits and blood', *Socialist Worker*, 19.0.4, 1969. https://www.marxists.org/archive/foot-paul/1969/04/windies.htm (Thanks to Christian Høgsbjerg for this article.)

Karen Fog Olwig, *Caribbean Journeys – An ethnography of migration and home in three family networks*, Durham & London, Duke University Press, 2007.

Monique Roffey, *The Mermaid of Black Conch*, Leeds: Peepal Tree Press, 2020.

James W Sutton, *A Testimony of Triumph: A narrative of the life of James Sutton and family in Nevis and St Kitts, 1920-1940*, Scarborough, Ontario, Canada: Edan's Publishers, 1987.

John Wesley: Wikipedia entry at https://en.wikipedia.org/wiki/John_Wesley

Chapter 3

ENGLAND: THE BAD "MOTHER" COUNTRY

Arthur France was 22 years old when, on 13th September 1957, he took the bumpy crossing from Nevis to St Kitts, where he got a plane to Barbados. He boarded the SS Soriento en route to Genoa in Italy, then he went by train to Paris, and then to France's coastal town of Calais. He still remembers the excitement of being on a train for the first time. A ferry took him to Dover.

Academic books call it 'chain migration'. Not the chains of slavery – they mean the invisible chain that links one migrant to another as they make their decision to move. Arthur France was in a family chain: to be specific, his sister Elaine had migrated to the north of England, to Leeds, in the county now called West Yorkshire, a couple of years before Arthur took that momentous trip to the same place.

Why Leeds? Caryl Phillips, now a Professor of English at Yale University, was born in St Kitts but he arrived in Leeds with his parents as a baby. Growing up in Leeds, he was always aware that he didn't really fit in, always thinking of his Caribbean roots, even though his parents didn't talk about their own history. When, as a young adult, he went back to St Kitts to investigate his origins, he saw something which answered the 'Why Leeds?' question. In an interview with Professor Bénédicte Ledent, Phillips said this:

Walking through the sugar fields in St Kitts one day, many years ago, I came across the small sugar cane trains that snake their way through the fields. And I'd always wondered why so many people from St Kitts settled in Leeds; I'd never really figured this out. And as I was walking through the sugar cane fields I looked at one of these trains that was parked up, and it said on the side of it: 'Made in Hunslet'. Hunslet is a part of Leeds; it's an industrial hub of Leeds. And I realised, some guy from Leeds had to come out to service this train; if they make these engines and wagons in Leeds somebody would have had to come out from Leeds to maintain the system. Eventually people in the villages will have grown to associate England with Leeds. They will know England is Leeds, so when you migrate to England and get off the boat-train your first thought might well be to go to Leeds, which is England! Of course, it's not that simple, but that's the general picture. As a colonial subject, your knowledge and your understanding is, to a certain extent, tied to where the people are coming from at the colonial centre. So, the umbilical cord between the Caribbean and England has always interested me.

The 'umbilical cord' between St Kitts-Nevis and Leeds is strong (and it makes us think of the Mother), particularly when you have a sibling in the city to ease your path away from your own mother in the Caribbean.

'Edwin Smith', a member of a Nevis family researched by Karen Fog Olwig, was also in the 'family chain'. 'Edwin' travelled first to Oxford, in 1961, where his sister was about to marry a Kittitian man already settled in Oxford. He later moved to Leeds with his girlfriend 'Syvilla' from Nevis, because he wanted to live among a larger community of Nevisians. Edwin had no money and no prospects, but 'I was determined to show [Syvilla's parents] I could look after her ... and I worked hard' to prove his worth to her parents. They regularly sent her parents money, so that their child 'Roger' could be properly looked after by his grand-parents. 'Roger' joined them in Leeds later.

Arthur was one of many adventurous, forward-looking Caribbean people to take this long and challenging journey. The 'Windrush generation' were the pioneers, about ten years earlier, but this was still a path not well-trodden. To get a flavour of this experience, it's worth hearing what others had to say about the migration they undertook. For example, Archippus Joseph arrived in Plymouth from Monserrat three years earlier than Arthur, in September 1954. He described his experience to Colin Grant:

> When we stepped off the boat a lot of people cried because you'd formed friendships; you're living with people you don't know before, and from other countries as well, you formed this bond, and naturally enough you feel sorry when the boat has stopped. At Paddington [in London] we stood there and thought, 'Where are we? What happens now?' Believe it or not, we had no one to come to, and we land on that platform – and in those days a lot of West Indians who came over before used to come down and welcome ... or to see what's going on, probably just nosing around. It was nice to see them, but they can't help you.

Fortunately, Mr Joseph's cousin Joe West was there and he took him and his two friends to rent a room at £1 a week (£28 in 2019 UK pounds) in a house in Hackney (in London) owned by 'a black man from St Kitts married to a German woman named Woodley'. He continued: 'I cried after a while, not straight away. When you're on your own and have to look after yourself, more or less, washing and cooking and so on, a few tears shed, until you get used to your surroundings.'

These pioneers had heard a similar story to that which Alfred Williams told Ray Brown: 'All my life Jamaica people is telling me, "Come to England. Come to Mother Country, it flow with milk and honey ... There is no bare foot, no more torn off nail." This must be a good country, I think.' Eventually, Mr Williams settled in Leeds.

The sociologist Sheila Patterson provided a vivid description of the scene she observed as a ferry arrived in Folkestone in February 1956 – she captured the profound shock the West Indian travellers felt:

It was one of those days when the sea and sky were a menacing grey, the wind cut to the bone, and the rain was almost sleet. The Channel boat had docked almost two hours late after a rough passage, and its few ordinary passengers had come ashore and settled with relief on the waiting train. On board, some six hundred West Indians of both sexes and all ages awaited in pathetic misery for someone to tell them what to do. Some leaned over the rail or against the windows, staring with unbelief at the unimaginable prospect outside; others, overcome with [sea-sickness], lay back with their eyes shut. Almost all wore sandals or light shoes, straw hats, and pastel-coloured summer clothes, now stained and crumpled after three days of train and sea travel from Genoa. Several had wound towels round their necks or heads, or had put on two or more jackets, in a vain effort to keep out the dank chill.

This dejected mass of humanity was finally moved down the gangways into the waiting train. The train had no restaurant car, but most of the migrants had only a pound or two in cash. They had either spent their meagre capital *en route*, or locked it into their trunks – these, it now emerged, had not accompanied them from Genoa and would not arrive for several days. A few of the men brought out rum bottles and a certain animation developed in their vicinity. But the majority of the migrants remained frozen in apathy or apprehension, unable to give more than a bare account of themselves and their plans to the West Indian officials who now moved up and down the train, ticketing those students who were to be met by the British Council, and the women and young people who were travelling alone and had no contacts nor a precise destination. Some had the addresses of friends, but most of these, reflecting village patterns, were confined to surnames and streets – welfare officers would be kept busy seeing that the newcomers, if they were not met, got to the right Mr Smith in the right King Street in London. Others had been told that it was best to take a taxi on arrival and had to be dissuaded from taking taxis from the London terminus to Manchester or Birmingham ...

I remember two comments which I overheard in a number of groups: 'I still can't get over how strange it looks to see the white people working on the railway line, doing the dirty jobs, and cleaning out the toilet; and the white porter, he call me "Sir".' And, as the train reached South London: 'Look at all those mean little houses and the hundreds of chimneys giving out that black smoke. I never think London she look so old and dirty and poor and so different from the way I picture.'

Arthur France also felt these shocks. He got a train to London and he too was given advice. Some time later he arrived at the old train station in Leeds (known as Leeds Central, not far from the current station in New Station Street). This journey from home had taken him the best part of a month. A taxi took him to the neighbourhood known as Chapeltown just north of the city centre – to No. 1 Hamilton Avenue to be precise – where sister Elaine had been living for a couple of years, having married fellow-Nevisian George Archibald. This is the area that was already becoming known as the 'West Indian' part of Leeds, since the majority of the small number of Caribbean people in the city were linking up with family and friends who were already settling in that part of Leeds.

The actual numbers were very small, but such is the legacy of Empire that the new arrivals, British citizens who happened to have brown skins, were already attracting attention. Since the context for much of this book is white racism against these Brown and Black Brits, and the struggle by Arthur and countless others to combat that scourge, we should examine some of the relevant figures, and note just how few Black people there were.

Anthony Richmond recorded that in 1960 there were about 250,000 'coloured' people in Britain. That was 0.5 per cent of the UK population. Of these, about 150,000 were from the West Indies and about 50,000 each from India and Pakistan. (The total population in 1961 was 52,370,000. West Indians thus formed 0.28 per cent of the population.) Along with Arthur, 22,000 Caribbean people were estimated by the government to have arrived in 1957. In 1960, 42,000 landed in Britain. In contrast, 10,000 had arrived in 1954. By any rational assessment, this was a very, very small percentage of the UK population.

Dark Strangers is the title of Sheila Patterson's study of the West Indians who arrived in Brixton in the mid-1950s. She took the view that there was a 'sense of differentness and strangeness felt by hosts and newcomers alike'; she wrote that the dark skins of the West Indian newcomers provoked a cultural norm of 'mild xenophobia or antipathy' in the 'insular, conservative, homogenous' host society. She argued that this norm of antipathy to strangers had recently also been applied by the 'insular' British 'hosts' to the post-war migrants from Eastern Europe.

But her book is testimony to the peculiar social power of the colour of a person's skin; it throws into question her assertion that British xenophobia is 'mild'. Patterson, a liberal-minded sociologist, was honest enough to admit that she too was shocked when she encountered Black people. When she started her fieldwork in Brixton (London) she wrote: 'I was immediately overcome with a sense of strangeness, almost of shock ...'

She continued:

> [W]hat struck one so forcefully was that, apart from some shopping housewives and a posse of teddy boys in tight jeans outside the billiard hall, almost everyone in sight had a coloured skin ... At least half of the exuberant infants playing outside the pre-fab day nursery were *café noir* or *café au lait* in colouring. And there were coloured men and women wherever I looked, shopping, strolling, or gossiping on the sunny street-corners with an animation that most Londoners lost long ago.

Between 1954 and 1960, the number of Caribbean people in Britain had increased by 32,000. In 1961, they represented less than 0.3 per cent of the population. The hostility they received was not mild. In 1958, white racists and Nazis had attacked Black settlers in Nottingham and Notting Hill (in London), setting a scene that would steadily unfold throughout Arthur's life. (These 'race riots' will be described in Chapter 7.) The moral panic about 'race' that was then stirred up in the 1960s by Conservative MPs such as Patrick Wall and Enoch Powell resulted in large protests about the small increase in the number of 'coloureds' in the post-war period.

Rational people said Britain desperately needed this new labour force; they pointed out that less than 1 per cent of the population being 'coloured' was of little or no significance. But racism is irrational. Instead of campaigning against rising racism, the British government made concessions to the racists: its 1961 Immigration Act began to close the doors to British citizens with black or brown skins.

The migration figures for Chapeltown, where Arthur made his new home, reflect the national picture: the proportion of

Black people in Leeds was tiny. In 1955, Leeds journalist Derek Boothroyd obtained some estimates of the numbers of Commonwealth citizens in Leeds and suggested it was 0.2 per cent of the city's population – 'not a frightening proportion!' he concluded. Christopher Duke's study of housing in Chapeltown stated that, in 1969, 15,000 people lived in that part of the town, of whom about 3,000 were 'born in the Commonwealth' (he meant Africa, the Caribbean or South Asia). (The actual boundaries of Chapeltown are a matter of dispute.)

My book about this neighbourhood included the statistics for Leeds at this time. In 1961 the number of Caribbean people in Leeds was only 2,186. Since there were only 1,700 South Asians in Leeds at this time, if Duke's '3,000' figure for all Commonwealth citizens is correct, a high proportion of the Caribbean people must have been living in Chapeltown. By 1967 there were around 6,000 Caribbean people and about 500 Black people who had migrated from Africa. In 1961 the total population of Leeds was 715,000. People from the Caribbean therefore formed 0.3 per cent of the city's population in 1961, and 0.8 per cent in 1967. Even if you add in the migrants from South Asia who settled in Leeds, the percentage is only 0.7 in 1961. If racism had been expunged, the settlement of Black and brown British citizens would have been straightforward. That would have taken political courage by each of the parliamentary parties; too few MPs were willing to rise to that challenge.

A 1993 book about Africans, Asians and Caribbean people in Leeds, ironically called *Land of Hope and Glory?*, recorded 1991 census figures showing 6,807 Caribbeans, 1,362 Africans and 2,722 Black 'others' in the city. That makes the proportion of Black people in Leeds in 1991 only 1.5 per cent. If South Asians are added, the proportion rises to 4.6 per cent. Still not an integration problem if Britain had seriously tackled its slave-based colonial history and the racism that it produced in the post-war period.

The 'bad mother' country

It was quite a shock for Arthur, arriving in England. Everyone who has migrated from the Caribbean mentions how cold it was. White Brits think October is quite warm, but nothing prepares someone from the regions of real sunshine for the pallid skies and chill winds of Leeds in autumn. Arthur saw the benches on the side of the road and he couldn't think what they were there for. Why would anyone sit on a bench in this cold weather? "It's ridiculous."

But the real disappointment was the contrast between what he had been taught about England at school in Nevis and the reality he encountered. As soon as they arrived in London, his companions on the journey from the Caribbean dispersed all over the country, while the English were rushing to and fro without a word.

"We had a British education. I enjoyed reading English literature and learning about the Royal Family. We were told this was the Mother Country. But when I got to Leeds the dream was slashed. It was cold and people were unfriendly. You expected people to be normal, but they weren't." Normal in Nevis is a friendly greeting to everyone you see; that civility disappeared from English cities long ago.

'Edwin Smith', from Nevis, told Professor Olwig that 'We had heard fantastic stories about England, like how money was growing on trees in the backyard ... Or the streets were paved with gold. People were very disappointed when they came here [to Leeds].' His girlfriend 'Syvilla' said: 'When I came here, it was a horrible place ... The houses were disgusting; England was filthy. I cried for months to go home. I was depressed. It was easy to get in, but hard to get out'.

Mr Pennycook had come from Jamaica to Leeds a few years before Arthur. He owned one of the mansions on Chapeltown Road (No.148), once lived in by the newly-prosperous English middle classes who built this neighbourhood towards the end of the 19th Century. Lots of the new arrivals could find a room to stay at 148 Chapeltown Road with Mr Pennycook while they sorted themselves out. Arthur said "Pennycook's was such an important house for the Black settlers that it should have been preserved." People who had been here for a while would then help others to find a place of their own.

But Arthur was able to go straight to sister Elaine's. He shared a room with George and Elaine for a week, and then got a room of his own at 1 Hamilton Avenue, a house owned by Oliver Gaskin from St Kitts. There were five bedsits – while not as big as Pennycook's, the houses in Hamilton Avenue are substantial, late-Victorian terraces with large rooms.

The others living there were from Caribbean islands – "very friendly" – and they looked after Arthur and made him feel at home. "We had lots of visitors because it was a Black man's house." He was too young to be with the big men and too old to be with the children, so Mr James Condor, known as Major, one of the older generation, would always make fun of him for being "in no man's land." As usual, Arthur was amused each time Mr Condor repeated his joke, which was quite often, over many years. (Sadly, Mr Condor passed away in 2020.)

On his first Saturday night one of the guys visiting them said he had been here for two years; another said he'd been here for four – "I thought they must be crazy." Already Arthur was thinking he wanted to go home. He remembered another guy saying "England is like an open prison. They don't call you but you can't get out."

Arthur thought he was quite right. "Everyone was saying they are going back home." He said he didn't regret the decision to move to England, but it "Seemed to be a very funny system." He found that he could cope with this strange system because he was living with other West Indians, who were very friendly and helpful, even the ones he didn't know from back home in Nevis.

A revealing account of how white people in Leeds responded to the newcomers appeared in an article in *The Yorkshire Post and Leeds Mercury* in 1955. Derek Boothroyd interviewed a 'plump, good-humoured looking woman' in her garden at an unnamed location (which is very likely to be in Chapeltown). Her use of the N-word is immediately shocking to today's readers, as Boothroyd reported:

> 'Coloured people!' she said, ironically. 'We're the United Nations up here. We've got Czechs, Rumanians and Italians, as well as Egyptians and niggers. There's even a Chinese family at the top.' I said it was the negroes – and I emphasised the word – whom I was particularly interested in. What sort of people were they? 'Oh, the niggers are alright,' she said. 'They're not noisy or anything like that. We don't have any bother with them at all. What their houses are like, of course, I dread to think.' ... 'Oh no, I wouldn't go in.' ... 'You can't expect us to be overjoyed at them can you. I mean they've ruined the district.'

This seamless move between 'They're alright' to 'They've ruined the district' points to a deep ambivalence among some of the white working class towards these 'dark strangers'. But Boothroyd then summarises this interview and others he conducted as follows: 'All she says is that black is black and white is white and never the twain shall meet'. No ambivalence there, just deep and irreconcilable division, according to this journalist.

Boothroyd then added that this lady feels 'It would be much better all round if the black people did not want to come to this country in the first place. Having come, however, they must be tolerated with as good grace as possible.' The failure of the white British to resolve these contradictions set the context for the rest of Arthur's life in Britain.

Orville Byron, from Trinidad, told Chris Mullard some of the things that Arthur heard in his first few days in Chapeltown, but he put them even more strongly:

After travelling to various parts of the world, I thought it was time to visit the so-called Mother Country known to us as England. I arrived here in 1960 and found, for the first time in my career, that I am a Black man. This shocked me deeply because the impression we have in the West Indies is that we are welcome in England any time, since we are supposed to be Commonwealth citizens; how wrong we were ... It is hard to think that the people who has taken away everything from us even our own language and our culture is telling us now they don't want us. This is sheer madness.

Arthur's sister Hyacinth was equally unimpressed when she arrived in Leeds in 1960. She told me (on the balcony in sunny Basseterre): "It was awful. The weather! I just wanted to go back home. I cried and cried, especially at holidays: there was no beach, no picnic, no fun." She went to sleep hoping to wake up in Nevis. But Arthur said there was no going back. She kept in touch with the family and friends in Nevis by writing letters. Hyacinth had friends in Leeds whom she'd known from her school-days, and she made friends with some white women who taught her to knit and took her to the movies. "I learned to integrate, and I became happy."

Their sister Janet arrived in 1964, when she was 14, to link up with Arthur and her sisters Hyacinth, Marjorie and Elaine. She went to the FE College to learn secretarial skills. She worked her way up two large firms (B Norman, the furriers, and Empire Stores, a mail order company). Talking to me in Nevis, near the house she grew up in, she said: "Yes there was racism, but I didn't take it to heart. I could mingle with anyone. I was flexible – I worked in lots of departments, including where the computer terminals were. I got a few more Black folks into that company." This ability to withstand racism and get on with everybody is a notable feature of the France family.

Arthur's friend Wilmot James arrived in Leeds from St Kitts in October 1959, a couple of years after Arthur. He wasn't as fortunate as Hyacinth and Janet. Colin Grant recorded his feelings:

> Personally, me, I never really liked Leeds, but I stayed here because my siblings was here. I always find that Yorkshire people was racist. Still is now; 60 per cent of the guys who around my age, they would tell you the same. Because the Yorkshire people didn't like Black people ... As long as you this colour, you have to be extra good to achieve, to reach where you want to be; and then at the end of it all you still get knocked back ... Back in the sixties, they wouldn't exactly say they don't like you, but with their actions you can read the small print.

Elvie Jeffers, who went to school with Arthur in Nevis, migrated to Birmingham to be a nurse in the 1960s. In 2017, she described her experience to me. "The notices in house windows said 'No Irish, No Coloured, No Dogs'. In the hospital the white people would say 'I don't want to be black like you' when you touched them." One patient said of a Jamaican nurse "I can't understand what she's saying". Another one said to this

Notices in a window, 'Sorry no coloureds'

nurse: "Turn around and let me see if you've got a tail". The Jamaican nurse was so angry she was going to "Box her down ... But we stopped her – she would have lost her job". She added, anticipating the content of Chapters 6 and 7 of this book: "Arthur and Calvin [Beech] did a good job in opposing this racism. We would come up from Birmingham to support their events and demonstrations."

Edward Pilkington wrote of two Black women's poignant responses to the hostility meted out to them. Interviewed by the *Daily Mail* in 1958, one said: 'I don't mind the fights. We have had enough of that back home. It's the hate I can't stand'. Another said: 'If you ostracise me because of my bad manners, I can mend my ways. If you shun me because of my ignorance, I can learn. But if you slam the door in my face because of the colour of my skin, I am lost'.

There is no single narrative of the migration and settlement of British Caribbean people who arrived in the UK in the 1950s and early 1960s. But no one has ever described 'The Mother Country' as a 'Good Mother', not even a 'Good Enough Mother'. Growing up extremely poor in Jamaica, and settling in Leeds, Alfred Williams, shortly before his death in 1990, told Ray Brown: 'When I think of my life I think I been sucking salt through wooden spoon. Try to understand that life: when somebody give you salt jar, put wooden spoon in, other end of spoon go in your mouth. Then they say, 'Start sucking!' Now I nearly 70 and I been sucking that salt every day of my life.'

Arthur's life, thankfully, has turned out differently. He is an individual and this book tells his story – but he is also a devoted member of a particular community, and he wants everyone to understand how many different Caribbean stories there are that deserve to be heard. And he's never heard anyone say that the Mother Country reminded them of their own mothers.

Going to work and some play

The difficulties of (un)settlement did not go away, but Arthur quickly got a job. His sister Elaine was a secretary at Union Cold Storage in Hunslet. She had contacts and she got him a job at British Railways. Each day he'd report for work at Leeds station and they would send him to Huddersfield to work as a relief porter. He packed containers and loaded the delivery lorries. He was the only Black person in that workplace, but the station master was a nice man and the other workers were quite friendly. "They were welcoming and we had a good laugh." He particularly remembers a white guy from the Meanwood area of Leeds who was unusual in not admiring Winston Churchill. His reasoning was that Churchill had told everyone to fight while he sat far from the front line in his office. The man made him laugh about "shitting himself" in the army during the war when he saw dead bodies.

It's likely that Arthur's friendly nature and his unfailing ability to see the funny side of life, along with his willingness to work hard, made it easy for him get on with the white people at the railways. But there's no doubt that, overall, there was a great deal of prejudice against Black people at that time.

For example, in 1956, journalist Tom Baistow reported Lloyd Rainford's experience when looking for accommodation: 'It's very difficult for us coloureds. Sometimes they smile very nice like and say "Sorry". Other times they just shut the door in your face.' Like so many others, Lloyd had fought for 'The Mother Country' as a corporal in the Royal Air Force. Now he and his wife were bus conductors, living in a ten-roomed house in Brixton, London, containing 30 residents. Most of his white work mates were fine, he said, 'But sometimes someone says "Why are you darkies coming over to pinch our jobs?"' Another Caribbean person told Baistow: 'Some white people look at us as if we were animals. When we cut don't we bleed the same blood?'

Nobel Laureate Professor Wole Soyinka was a postgraduate student in the English Literature department at Leeds

University in the mid-1950s. He arrived in 1954 in what he has described as 'the homeland of a colonial power that ruled with violence in parts of Asia and Africa'. In his poem *Telephone Conversation*, 'the record of an exchange with a landlady,' he sets out one of many 'trite encounters with British racism'. He went on, describing racism in Leeds in some detail:

> On public transport, for instance – admittedly I *enjoyed* having a seat to myself in a filled-up double-decker bus, it made the turning of the abnormally broad pages of *The Yorkshire Post* much easier but – could I really not notice, or fail to be stung by the fact that a boarding passenger had traversed the length of the bus, seen one empty seat next to me and climb upstairs to search for a vacant seat? That same passenger came down again – no standing allowed upstairs – and chose to attach his or her arm to a strap-hanger sooner than take that empty seat?

Even more blatantly, a white person on a seat next to the one where Soyinka was about to sit would immediately stand up and move away. 'Incidents like these, even in the mid-fifties, were

Akonwande Oluwole 'Wole' Soyinka was at the University of Leeds from 1954 to 1957. In 1975, he became Professor of Comparative Literature. He was awarded the Nobel prize for Literature in 1986.

mind-numbingly commonplace.' 'In shops, you turned invisible', he wrote, and if you protested that you were being ignored, you received an 'oiled, hypocritical ... *Oh, so sorry, are you next?*' Referring to the 'thick, regional accent' of Yorkshire, Soyinka reflected that this somehow made the encounter worse because 'irrationally, one somehow expected the country yokels to be more human than their cosmopolitan sophisticates'.

The humanity he hoped for was absent in these moments. Soyinka was being kind when he described these experiences as 'trite'; he admitted they 'stung'. And they numbed his mind. But white people's conscience was sometimes pricked. Lincoln Crawford, the son of a Trinidadian welder and a seamstress, who later became a prominent London barrister, arrived in Southampton in 1967 with £3 to his name. Searching for a job, he walked five miles for an interview, to be told that the vacancy had gone. The manager then noticed that Crawford's boots were held together with glue, took pity, offered him a job and took him home.

'Such acts of kindness made a profound impression on Lincoln, contributing to his wish to build bridges between races,' wrote Anthony Speaight QC. For many, the hostility cut to the quick. In 1969, a Leeds West Indian woman asked student journalist Dave Durman: "Why do you white people do it? Why?" In Chapter 7 we will examine the horrific experience in Leeds in the 1960s of Wole Soyinka's fellow-Nigerian, David Oluwale.

All migrants are searching for a better life. As Caryl Phillips has pointed out, Leeds was built by white people (initially from Scotland, Wales, Ireland, and the countryside of northern England) who had been attracted to the work opportunities provided by a metropolis expanding just as job opportunities where they lived were disappearing; from the 1870s Eastern European refugees from anti-Semitic violence arrived and they helped build the Leeds clothing industry, while Irish migrants were already building the UK's roads, railways and bridges.

The Caribbean migrants of the 1950s and 1960s were no different. They migrated because Britain needed their skills and their energy; they, in turn, needed to improve their lives when their islands were being plunged into economic decline.

There was an acute need for workers in post-war England. Paul Foot quoted a Labour Exchange official in Smethwick, in the West Midlands, who stated in 1954: 'Shortage of labour is the concern of almost every employer in the town'. There were 641 vacancies and only 22 people unemployed. In 1955 the Smethwick Labour Exchange manager reported: 'Coloured labour from the Commonwealth is greatly easing the labour shortage', but there were now 920 vacancies and only 23 unemployed. Dilip Hiro quoted Hugh Gaitskell, then leader of the British Labour Party, who pointed out in 1961 that there was 'an almost precise correlation between the movement in the numbers of unfilled vacancies ... and the immigration figures'.

In her book about the Jamaicans who settled in Leeds in response to the call to work in England, Susan Pitter wrote of the Leeds nurses who came to train in the National Health Service: 'They were given the most menial tasks, were denied job opportunities enjoyed by white nurses, and endured patients' racist abuse, even as they cared for them – and still they cared'. Francis 'Grace' Williams, who worked as a chef at Leeds General Infirmary in the 1960s, said: 'They called me "monkey" and "baboon". Many times I went to the toilets and cried and said, "Father, I'm just asking you to give me courage". I cried and I prayed'.

Jean White (née Mounter) came to England from Barbados in 1960 to train at Leeds's St James's Hospital. In the booklet edited by Palorine Williams, subtitled 'Black Women Talk', Mrs White wrote of her experience:

I was the first Black woman on the female side [of St James's nursing staff]. In those days they called the racism 'the colour bar' and I came across a few instances which were labelled as 'chips on the shoulder'. But I was able to bounce back from every chip, because of the quality of my nursing and because of my belief in myself and my determination to change the system ... But when it got to that bit for promotion, well then it was different ... I got a reply almost by return of post which said it was felt I was not yet up to the required standard. I didn't know I had it in me, but I went to see the doctor in charge of the unit. I looked straight at him and I said, "I would like to see the standard that is required so I may achieve it" ... [The doctor went to speak with the ward sister and] things were rather quiet on the ward for a while. And that was my first opportunity to speak up for myself, because I knew I was not an inferior person ... Then in 1972 I was given my blue uniform to be in charge. When I put it on I felt, at last, I'm here.

Jean White also joined the Labour Party and in 1995 she was elected as councillor for the Moortown ward in north Leeds. Throughout her progress to these elevated positions in work and in civic life, her husband Owen was always at her side.

Leeds' Black women are nothing if not resilient and resourceful and one of their many achievements is set out in a book they produced in 2000 telling the story of the Chapeltown Laundry-Cop. In the introductory chapters they wrote about their early experiences in the city. Myrna Tyrell arrived from Nevis at about the same time as Arthur – the intense cold, fog and smog were a terrible trial: 'If I could have run back to my lovely island I would have done'. But when her son said they should move out of Chapeltown she told him 'No matter where we moved to, he would still be a Black person'. When her children were young she worked hard in tailoring factories but later she attended night school, learning sociology, secretarial skills and book-keeping, as well as taking up several roles at Roscoe Methodist Church.

Frances Skelton came from St Kitts to Chapeltown, 36 Francis Street to be precise, in 1958. It was so cold, and there were so many rebuffs when she asked for a job that she wished she could go home. Eventually she got a job in a glass-grinding factory, then at 'Soapy Joe's' on Whitehall Road (it became Elida Gibbs in 1971) and finally at John Waddington's, the games manufacturer.

Mary Saddler's arrival in 1959 was, like Arthur's, made easier by moving in with a friend, but she had to take menial and badly-pad jobs – 'You had to work to survive'. While living in Chapeltown was 'quite congenial', having to wash the clothes in the bath and build a coal fire to dry them out was a real burden. Her council house in Cowper Street was damp and the 'slow wheel of repairs' turned year after year.

Millicent Francis arrived in the 1960s to join friends in Chapeltown and got a job straight away at Burton's clothing factory in Harehills. She loved the community feeling among the West Indians – 'people cared for one another' – but, looking back, she felt 'We were all white-washed to believe people would accept us'. Nevertheless, 'though we are yellow, black or white, we are precious in God's sight', she wrote. She never let the racism and sexism get her down, 'But what we accepted, the young would not take: the racist names, the abuse by everyone – teachers at school, on their street ... there was always somebody ready to start something. Our colour was the main target'.

Joe Harriott, who settled in London and had relatives in Leeds, was unusual among the migrants in the 1950s; he became a highly-regarded innovator in jazz. He had learned to play various instruments at the children's home in which he was brought up – the Alpha School in Kingston, run by Catholic nuns. Invited to England in 1951 to join Ozzie Da Costa's band, his talent was soon recognised and for the next twenty years he made his living from jazz.

Leading his own band, Joe Harriott is credited with inventing (in the early 1960s) free-form jazz, developed out of his interest in abstract art. He was also the first jazz musician to promote the merger of classical Indian music with jazz. The fusion idea was brought to him by the Calcutta-born violinist and composer John Mayer – Joe readily embraced it because he was highly intelligent and open to new ideas. Fortunately, Mayer and Harriott had access to a recording studio which was equally pioneering.

Nevertheless, even in the progressive world of jazz, racism was to blight Joe Harriott's career. Finding spurious relief in alcohol, he died of cancer and tuberculosis in 1973, aged only 44. *Jazz Journal* failed to mention his passing, but his friends, including the successful Caribbean-born musicians Shake Keane and Coleridge Goode, and well-known white jazz stars like Chris Barber, Ian Carr, Annie Ross and Norma Winstone held a memorial concert for him.

Harriott was by-passed by the jazz establishment, but at least his exceptional music was lauded. Most Black immigrants' talents were not recognised. Dilip Hiro cited a survey of West Indians in London in 1958-9 which found that 55 per cent of them were obliged to take jobs of a lower skill level than they had performed at home. A Caribbean skilled in welding was quoted as saying he would do 'anything which take me off the dole'; searching for jobs, he would jump off the bus wherever he saw a factory chimney. Eventually he got a job as a porter at a Lyons restaurant.

The national survey conducted at the end of 1966 by W W Daniel showed a 'staggering' reduction in status of people who, at home, had held white-collar occupations: 90 per cent of them were, in England, relegated to blue-collar manual work. When he surveyed 540 West Indians' reasons for being refused a job, 45 per cent said it was because of racial discrimination, and almost all of them could provide convincing evidence that racism was indeed in play.

This was particularly the case among those who were well qualified. 33 per cent of the West Indians in the survey had avoided the possibility of being discriminated against by only going for job interviews where they knew Black people were already being employed. Only 8 per cent of them said they were 'uncertain about the existence of discrimination'. Only 5 per cent said they didn't think there was discrimination. Daniel concluded that, 'in view of the extent of discrimination we have uncovered in our research' this 13 per cent had lived 'sheltered and protected lives'. I suppose we should be pleased that some Black people could find shelter and protection.

Beryl Gilroy came to Britain in 1952 from Guyana, where she had graduated First Class in 1945 from her teacher-training college in Georgetown. Despite several years' class-room experience, she was systematically rejected for a job at each London Primary School to which she applied. Then she was refused again when she applied for administrative posts in London businesses. After one rejection, a young man who had seen her arriving for the interview said: 'I bet she said the job's gone. Well, that's Mary Busby for you. Just because you're Black – nix for you.' She finally landed a job at Multi-Choice Mail Order Stores. Noting the surprise on the face of the woman who met her at the door, she heard a voice inside the office say 'I don't mind coloureds or blacks. They're the same as us'. It was the boss, so she got the job.

But one of her colleagues made his hostility plain, topping his many racist barbs with this: 'I know your sort of black, wearing a bit of toffee-nose civilisation. It's all on the top. I can scrape it off like paint.' Beryl Gilroy's women colleagues, however, declared that they would back her up in future. After another altercation, he apologised, saying 'I went too far'; Beryl Gilroy wrote 'I felt all the hatred of him going out of my heart'.

When she got jobs in infant schools from 1954 onwards, she noted innumerable examples of racism already embedded in white children by their parents. This is the reaction she received when she walked into her first classroom:

When I opened the squeaking door and the class came face to face with me, there was a gasp of terror, then a sudden silence. A little girl broke it with a whimper. Some children visibly shook with fear, and, as I walked across the room, the whole lot – except for two boys – dived under the tables.

While Beryl Gilroy met white people (most especially the man she married) who valued her talents and treated her with great respect, even when she became a deputy headteacher in 1968, racism was a regular experience. One child told her she couldn't come to school because her father 'didn't like blackies'. She became a headteacher in 1969, but this didn't stop the abuse. A child's grandmother came to school to tell her she should be on the TV with the 'Brooke Bond chimps'. The grandparent's remark on leaving was that 'the bleeding blacks' were 'getting above their station'.

Anthony Richmond's study of the British population around 1960 concluded that 'One third is tolerant of all coloured people, one-third is mildly prejudiced, and one-third is extremely prejudiced'. Maybe Arthur had the good fortune to meet up with some of the unprejudiced one-third; maybe he was able to overcome the 'mild prejudice' of the other third; my guess is that there were members of the miserable third who kept their mouths shut when Arthur was around.

All the migrants worked long hours in tough conditions. Spice Girl, Melanie Brown wrote this about her father, Martin Wingrove Brown (1953-2017), who migrated from St Kitts and settled in Leeds in the early 1970s:

I have never loved a man like I loved my dad. I used to watch him out of my bedroom window going off to work on his bike. It took him forty minutes to get there and forty minutes to get back – and he did that journey every day for thirty-five years. He worked as a welder at Yorkshire

Imperial Metals. It's brutal work, long hours, and when I was a kid he'd do double shifts (sixteen-hour days) for years so we could all go on holiday camping in Abersoch for two weeks, or have a Barbie house for Christmas.

I didn't know how he could do it. I used to cry sometimes when I watched him with my nose pressed against my bedroom window, getting on that bloody bike at the crack of dawn on a freezing-cold, grey day in November, January, March – take your pick. Even at the age of seven I'd think, as I watched the wind and the rain crack at his navy anorak, 'Why does my dad have to do this every day? There has to be a better life'.

Yorkshire Imperial Metals, echoing its imperial name, employed lots of Caribbean and South Asian workers in Leeds – it was always known as 'the copper works' – until it shut down in 1980.

For his entertainment in these early days in Leeds, Arthur would go with Elaine, George and their friends to the Forum Picture House on Chapeltown Road to see films. His Meanwood friend on the railways would go to the City Varieties in the town centre where they had Folies Bergère dancers showing their all – he'd make Arthur laugh describing them and he tried to get Arthur to go too, but he never did.

His fun was mostly self-made: visiting friends in the bigger houses and socialising there. In those days no one asked which island you were from, they just got together as Black people. Arthur doesn't drink alcohol – one experience with rum on a boat near Nevis put him off for life. But, at Christmas, the railwaymen would take him to the pub for a party where there would be a piano and lots of singing. He said they were friendly and he enjoyed being part of the crowd. He realised that in those days the pub was the hub of the white community, not just a place to get drunk.

A new type of play – with an underlying emancipatory purpose – emerged in 1966 when Marlene and Veronica

Samlalsingh and students at Leeds University organised a carnival fête at Kitson Further Education College in Leeds city centre. This prompted Arthur to set up the Leeds West Indian Carnival in 1967, the first Caribbean style carnival in Europe, created and led by Caribbean people.

One of the first young women to be crowned Queen (in 1971) was trainee nurse Linda Edmeade, born in St Kitts, and raised in the nearby island of Montserrat. Her prize was a trip to the Caribbean. In her interview with *Zodiac* magazine she captured the mix of pleasure and pain she felt in England: 'I'm longing to see my grandmother who lives in Montserrat. I can hardly tell you how excited I am. I love England, but it is natural for people to want to go back to where they came from, even if it is only for a visit'. (Chapter 8 provides the full story of the founding of carnival in Leeds.)

A place to stay

Housing was one of the mechanisms of racial discrimination in Britain. Arthur was lucky: he had a family home to move into straight away. It was harder for Alford Gardner. He told Colin Grant that he came from Jamaica to Leeds for a training course during the Second World War before serving as an engineer and motor mechanic in the Royal Air Force. He returned to England on the Empire Windrush in 1948 and attempted to find somewhere to live in Leeds. Like so many others, he was excluded, time and time again. His solution was to club together with four other West Indians and buy a house of their own.

The Chapeltown houses where West Indians lived in 1954 have been vividly described by a young student, J Russell Moston, in the book *Roscoe Methodist Church Leeds: A Unique History*. Moston was training to be a Methodist Minister at Wesley College in Headingley, a suburb on the north western side of Leeds. He had been asked by Reverend Harry Salmon, the Minister at Roscoe Place Methodist Church (the original Roscoe, on Chapeltown Road) to help him draw the newly-arrived West Indians into his church. Moston's diary for 1954 recorded many doors being shut in his face as he was told that the people he was asking about are not at home. Moston recorded: 'A sense of fear, filth and indifference seemed to be everywhere' in Chapeltown.

On Saturday 20th November, one house reluctantly let him in. The door was 'unlocked, unbolted and unbarred' and he asked 'a coloured man' if he could speak with 'Mr Thomas Scrocope'. In a small room so hot and thick with cigarette smoke he nearly fell down the step, he saw five 'coloured' men playing dominoes, a woman and a small child. Calor gas and paraffin heaters were ubiquitous in these houses. 'A rough looking man said "Huh, they's two fellows, not one – a Mr Thomas and a Mr Procope".' Moston was taken up the stairs. 'Clouds of dust [were] coming from the moth-eaten carpet under our feet. The place was filthy and reeked terribly.' This must have been a rented house, in multiple occupation, where the early migrants less fortunate than Arthur were forced to live.

All the bedrooms had doors painted in bright red 'and had catches on the *outside!*'. A 'well-dressed and educated' man came out of one of the rooms and said, apologetically, that neither Mr Thomas nor Mr Procope were at home. But the next day, 'an Irish lad' living in the same house introduced him to Mr Procope. His room 'was no better than the rest of the house ... poorly furnished ... wireless blaring'. His father was the editor of the *News Daily Bulletin* in St Kitts. Moston invited him to the church in Roscoe Place, and there he was at the evening service, with another man named Poole. Now there were '*eight* coloured people present in the Service'.

Aggrey Housing Limited was formed in Leeds in 1955, by a solicitor who specialised in housing law, Mr J C Charlesworth, in response to the council failing to provide good accommodation for the new migrants from the Caribbean. He named it after Dr James E Kwegyir Aggrey (1875-1927), the Ghanaian educationalist who had argued that just like the black and white keys on a piano, 'black and white people living and working together could create harmony in society'. Specifically responding to the housing needs of the Windrush generation, one of the parts of Leeds in which it provided good quality housing for rent was Chapeltown. Reverend Salmon assisted Mr Charlesworth in the Aggrey Society. (In 1979, this company merged with other providers to form the Leeds and Yorkshire Housing Association.)

Meg Merrylees was one of the early campaigners in the national movement for decent rented accommodation. In 1958 she wrote this in the *Times Weekly Review*:

We can and must all do something, and the burden that falls upon our particular shoulders is that of helping to ease the housing situation. The answer, 'but our hands are full with our own housing problems' is not acceptable. The housing of immigrants is our problem, because racialism is a germ that, festering inward, ultimately kills the social system that harbours it.

If they wanted to settle down and form families, it was safer for the new migrants to marry someone who shared their heritage, because, for those who didn't, problems were going to arise. British-Nigerian Gabriel Adams told me that, in the early 1950s, he used to go to the Mecca Locarno (now a shop called Reiss in the Victoria Quarter in the centre of Leeds) with his fellow Nigerian David Oluwale, Abbey Sowe (from Gambia) and the other West Africans in Leeds. (There's more about David Oluwale in Chapter 7.) When they asked white girls to dance, 'their' men would start trouble. Gabriel said that the man playing the records averted fights by setting up an 'excuse me' routine, where he would stop the record and the Black man would ask permission for a dance. The men were forced to concur if the girl said yes. That went well for Gabriel and Abbey: they met their future wives at one of these dances.

In the mid-1950s, The Mecca in Leeds was too low-class for Hilary Alderson, so she and her friends would instead go to the Majestic on Wednesday afternoons on their day off. She told Colin Grant that the Black students who danced there were, unlike the stowaways at the Mecca, obviously well-off – 'They were very well-spoken'. (Perhaps Wole Soyinka was among them.) She was reluctant to dance with them because everyone would think it was 'infra-dig, a bit beneath you'. When she did agree to a dance, to avoid hurting his feelings, 'I still felt awkward because it was such a new experience and I worried that everyone would think: "God, she's dancing with a black man"'. Arthur remembered those dance halls in the 1960s, saying all the Black men got dressed up in their suits and ties and had a good time.

Romance progressed well for Alford Gardner, mentioned above, until he went to ask for his future-wife's hand in marriage. Alford's intended's father said, 'What's he doing here? Get him out of here!' But she defied her father and moved in with Alford. 'The mother was alright. I mean, I couldn't care less. I was the first one in the family to have their own house. The rest of the family, we got on alright.'

Caryl Phillips arrived in Leeds from St Kitts in 1958. He has described his parents' early housing conditions like this:

My parents arrived in Leeds towards the end of the fifties, carrying me as hand luggage. They had heard that opportunities for employment were greater in the North of England, and somewhere in the back of their minds they had hoped that should they find work and make a home then perhaps, one day, it might be possible for their son to achieve an education in this northern city. They found a house on a cobbled street where people hung their washing out to dry as though their vests and pants and bras were some kind of celebratory bunting ...

Neither of my parents came from wealth or privilege – far from it – but, on the long journey across the Atlantic

Ocean, it never occurred to them that they might find themselves living in such dismal conditions ... Their stinking privies were located in the middle of the block [of back-to-back houses in the Whinmoor area of Leeds], and my whole childhood seems to have been dominated by olfactory assaults.

Phillips is now an internationally-acclaimed writer and academic so his parents' dreams for his education were realised, but the memory of his tough start in Leeds has never faded.

Another successful British-Caribbean, the poet and writer Benjamin Zephaniah, was also born in 1958 (in Birmingham). His mother (a nurse) came from Jamaica and his father (a postal

Arthur France, outside 15 Grange Avenue, Chapeltown, where he lived in the early 1960s, with his sister Elaine and her husband George Archibald. 24th March 2021.
© Max Farrar

worker) was from Barbados. His autobiography provides a vivid account of all the conditions of life that those Caribbean pioneers experienced. He recalled his mother filling the tin bath in the yard with kettles of water so he and his five siblings could be washed in the open air, sharing outside toilet with neighbours, sharing a bed with one or other of his brothers.

Arthur's socialising was within quite narrow boundaries – east of Chapeltown Road, including Spencer Place, Leopold Street, and Harehills Avenue pretty much set the geographical limits for their social lives. These were the small number of streets where Black people could get accommodation. The other side of Chapeltown Road – the Mexboroughs and the Saviles, named after the aristocrats who once owned the land on which Chapeltown was built – were "out of bounds".

When Nevisian Conway Walwyn broke through the invisible line and bought a house in Mexborough Street he was stopped by a policeman and asked what he was doing in that area (at the time, only white people lived west of Chapeltown Road). The policeman followed him to his new home to check his story. An African doctor bought No. 10 Grange Avenue in the heart of Chapeltown because, despite his high status, he wasn't able to buy a house in a more prosperous, and therefore white, part of Leeds.

Arthur wasn't personally affected by this type of discrimination, because Elaine and George were able to buy No. 15 Grange Avenue some time around 1962, despite prices being put up when a Black person attempted to buy off a white owner. Arthur moved into that large house with them. Apart from the example of Mr Walwyn being followed, Arthur said there wasn't any real trouble at this time with the police. "Black people are very law-abiding. I can't remember anyone being arrested. We went to work, and on Sundays we went to church. White friends laughed at us when we said we were off to church while they were off to the pub." (But West Indians did pick up "bad habits like smoking and drinking from their white friends.")

Anthony Richmond provided important evidence in 1961 on race discrimination in the housing market at the time that Arthur and his friends were finding their place in Leeds. He cited a survey in 1952 which showed that 85 per cent of London's landladies were unwilling to let a room to 'very dark' West Indians or Africans. Dilip Hiro referred to a poll in 1956 which showed that only 15 out of 1,000 Birmingham landladies would rent a room to a 'coloured' person. In Liverpool, despite having had a population of African descent for half a century or more, Richmond found evidence that showed that Black tenants were paying more rent than whites in equivalent properties.

In relation to the new migrants, Richmond commented:

The first experience of discrimination which a coloured colonial immigrant in Britain has to face is almost invariably in his search for somewhere to live. Whether he wishes to rent furnished rooms, with or without board, to take an unfurnished flat, to buy or lease a house or flat, or obtain temporary accommodation in a hotel, he is liable to find his colour a handicap to him. This is true irrespective of his social status. He may be a stowaway recently arrived from the colonies, a skilled worker or a professional man, a student, politician or member of the African nobility; it will make no difference.

This is why Arthur and the others settling in Chapeltown in Leeds went straight to their family members, or to friendly people from Caribbean islands, to find somewhere to stay.

But, as the Pennycock and Gaskin houses indicate, this was crowded accommodation. It was the same wherever the newcomers lived. Hiro cited a 1963 survey in Notting Hill, London, that showed that 60 per cent of Black households (a couple with children) had the use of one room only. A study of housing in Chapeltown in the late 1960s by a team led by Christopher Duke and including George Archibald, Errol James,

Maureen Baker, Allan Herbert and Eulalie Procope – all significant figures in the emerging Caribbean politics of Leeds – quoted a 1968 report from *The Times* newspaper: 'All too many coloured people are crowded together in the decaying twilight areas in the centre of cities'.

Duke's report, published in 1970 by the influential Institute of Race Relations, recommended increased access to decent council housing. Leeds City Council had recognised in the early 1950s that the large houses at the south end of Chapeltown Road (around Louis Street) were in very poor condition and were let to multiple occupiers, often Irish or Eastern European. Initially the council planned to refurbish them. Because it was run-down, this was an area where it was easy to find accommodation – one of the reasons why Black people had been accommodated there when they arrived in Leeds.

The quality of these houses in the south end of Chapeltown was very poor. A resident in Leopold Street wrote in a complaint to the council that her house had dangerous steps, mice, and a cellar full of water. Duke goes on to record a family of six living in one room in 1966 without access to proper hygiene facilities; another where the mother says she will go mad with the insects crawling out of the wall onto her baby; a third where mice are jumping over the children, rooms that were wet and other rooms where the floor was collapsing. These were the housing conditions of some of the Leeds working class, white and Black, in the 1960s.

After the first phase of clearance, the Black people who lived in the new houses built on the site were very satisfied with their new council houses, and his study exonerated the council of 'blatant discrimination', but, Duke suggested, Leeds (indeed, all cities) must escape the pattern of thought that its 'coloured' area was a 'ghetto'.

Trinidadian Orville Byron, quoted above, had this to say to Chris Mullard about employment and his effort to buy a house in England in the 1960s:

Having a little talent [as a professional dancer] I was able to flit around the Night and Working Men's Clubs, so that I can eat and live decently. The North East being a small place, my rounds of the clubs was soon exhausted and I had to find a regular job so I went to a certain foundry and steel works in Newcastle, seeing that I had some experience before I left home. They took me on. After working with them for five years I found they would lend their long service employees various sums of cash for mortgages and so on, after speaking to the relations officer he said to me you of all persons will surely get it on service and plus you are never late. When I went upstairs to see the big boss I was told that the particular money lending scheme is finished, I know he was lying and I told him so, because two of my white friends had gotten this two weeks ago. I was chased out of the office and told if I didn't watch my step I'd be sacked.

Arthur was always up for an adventure, however difficult were the times. In the mid-1960s he got himself a 500cc motorbike. Some other Black male friends got one too. Charles Brooks got himself a 500 cc bike, as did Ballick, and Rumpel got a 250cc. They put fish-tails on their exhausts to make the bikes sound more powerful. They zoomed around Leeds and occasionally got into races with white men on bikes. Arthur recalls a memorable contest with a man on a 750cc bike. "He was faster than me on the straight, but I was much more daring. We were coming into a double bend and I banked right over and took him on the first bend. On the second bend there was a double-decker bus coming towards me, so I just swing it and bust off. I had nerves of steel." This race might be a metaphor for his whole life.

At the same time that Caribbean people were making homes to live in, and finding ways to enjoy themselves, they were forming relationships and settling down to family life. Arthur's sister Janet told me that, by the time she arrived in Leeds in

Arthur and his motorbike, 1960s. Photo courtesy Arthur France

1964, Arthur was already at the centre of community affairs. "He was a very outgoing person. There were girls chasing him, but he was more interested in the problems the youth were going through." It wasn't until 1976 that he married Tattra. Arthur said that up to then, he was more interested in politics, organising cultural events, and hanging out with the boys than anything else. "I was always attracted to women, but they came down the list."

Tattra Sembhoo came from Mauritius to Grassington, in North Yorkshire, to join the National Health Service as a nurse. Grassington is a beautiful small town, but it's almost entirely white and the night-life can't compare with Leeds, only 30 miles away. Tattra and the other nurses would travel to the events Arthur and boys were organising. "When your head is full of carnival and cultural events it's very hard to pin you down – but Tattra did. We just seemed to click in a very funny way."

Roscoe Methodist Church

Even the Chapeltown churches reflected some of the prejudice so prevalent in Britain. St Clements was a Church of England place of worship at the south end of Chapeltown Road. Enos Harris, from St Kitts, was C of E, and when he arrived for his first service he was told to cross over the road to go to the original Roscoe Place Methodist Church opposite – "because that's where your people go". "How racist is that? Lots of Caribbean people are Church of England," Arthur said. Enos never went back; eventually he was the choirmaster at Roscoe, the church to which Arthur and his family belonged.

By contrast, Fay Comrie, a member of the Chapeltown Black Women's Writers Group, went with her family straight to Roscoe Methodist church at the south end of Chapeltown Road. She wrote: 'Now, we are spirit filled people and we shout hallelujah. They had a dedicated minister there and we shouted, "Hallelujah". And everybody started looking around because they have never heard it before. But the minister was so nice.' Roscoe was a beacon of hope for the Caribbean people in this part of Leeds. This didn't happen by chance: a far-sighted Methodist Minister made all the difference.

In the *Unique History* book, Reverend Harry Salmon, Roscoe's Minister from 1954 to 1958, summarised the situation like this: 'We visited these multi-occupied houses to welcome the new arrivals and invite them to Roscoe. We also became acutely aware of the hardships suffered during these early months of living in this country. Exploitation of immigrants was rife, racial prejudice was often encountered and only the least desirable jobs were available'.

On Sunday 13 November 1955 Harry Salmon conducted a special 'Anglo-West Indian Service' attended by 210 West Indians. Roland Lunn recalled in the official history of Roscoe

Church that the Revd Salmon also established the 'Anglo-West Indian Fellowship Meeting every Sunday evening after the service, attended by 50 or 60 people'. Among the West Indians, J Russell Moston recorded, there were 'a good number of English people'. This was an important stage in overcoming the 'fear and indifference' he had detected in his first days in Chapeltown. The role of Roscoe in providing solace and genuine community for the West Indians in Leeds can never be over-estimated. (Other Christian churches in this part of Leeds later also played a significant role, but it was at Roscoe where the welcome was strongest.)

As we saw above, these hopeful moments were thanks to the efforts of Reverend Harry Salmon and the student J Russell Moston, who became Roscoe's Minister in 1958. Like Revd Salmon, Revd Moston was engaged with civil society in Leeds, including the Leeds International Society (formed in 1955), Leeds Council for Social Services (chairing its study group on the 'employment and social welfare of coloured people' (1959) as well as the Aggrey Society.

Allan Herbert, who came to Leeds from Charlestown, Nevis, in 1955, described to Asher and Martin Hoyles what the original church (built in 1862) was like:

> The old Roscoe was a big church in the tradition of its day, with beautiful stained glass windows and upstairs balconies. However, in order for it to be warm on Sunday mornings, the coal-fired boiler would have to be lit on Saturday morning. Unfortunately, as the houses around Roscoe were demolished, the church was broken into frequently and items, especially those made of lead, would disappear.

The current Roscoe Methodist Church was opened in 1974. What it lacked in majesty, the new building resounded in functionality. It hosted its first wedding, Miss Gloria Simmonds and Mr

Hughbon Condor, on 12th October and one of its innovations (the idea of Revd Ian Lucraft) was to host a branch of Leeds Citizen's Advice Bureau.

By 1978 it extended its social remit by providing space for the newly-formed West Indian Family Counselling Service, with financial support from the Methodist Church Social Responsibility Committee's 'fund for multi-racial projects' and the Rowntree Charitable Trust. Its first staff member was Mr S Emmanuel Kebbe (from Sierra Leone) and in 1981 the redoubtable Mary Saddler became the co-ordinator. Congestion in the building was greatly eased when Willow House and Roscoe Hall were added to the building, opened on 25th July 1981 by the Lord Mayor of Leeds, Cllr Patrick Crotty OBE, LLB, a Conservative councillor who was one of the most ardent supporters of the rights of Black people in Leeds at the time.

In 1985, Roscoe demonstrated its deep commitment to all aspects of life in Chapeltown by forming the Roscoe Methodist Church Youth Steel Band, steered by Gloria and Hughbon Condor, Myrna Tyrell, Allan Herbert and, of course, Arthur France. Its constitution derived from the Leeds Brotherhood of Steel, which included lots of girls and young women, despite its title. It initially had much support from the Roscoe Girls and Boys Brigades, but it folded after a while. (In Chapter 8 we'll see how Arthur soon formed the New World Steel Orchestra.)

Arthur's early days in Leeds were eased by the services and the social life at Roscoe Church. He has fond memories of Revd Harry Salmon. Arthur said that Harry didn't care about your religious denomination – he visited everyone. He would just open your door without knocking and everyone made him welcome whenever he turned up. Another white man, Mr Mulligan, was an insurance salesman. He would come to the West Indians' houses where there might be ten adults to sell insurance at 10 shillings (50 pence) per week – and he would do good business. But it wasn't just the money – whenever you had a problem, Mr Mulligan would come and help you out.

The Roscoe Steward, Mr Lunn, another white man and his family were, Arthur said, "very genuine". He organised trips to seaside resorts like Blackpool and Scarborough. They went to Trentham Garden, the stately home in Staffordshire and to Gretna Green on the Scottish Borders where people go to get a quick wedding. "At Gretna, I got mock married to Elsie Plum, a white woman in Roscoe church – I'd do anything for a laugh." Often, Arthur said, he and his West Indian friends had a good time, and he let out that large laugh once more.

In the next chapter we look in more detail at Arthur's occupations after he left the Railways. Again, we will hear his laughter, and his seriousness.

References in this chapter

Tom Baistow, 'I don't ask at white doors any more. Colour Bar in Britain, Part Two of an Enquiry', *News Chronicle*, 9.10.1956. (The *News Chronicle* supported the Liberal Party, but was merged with the *Daily Mail* in 1960.)

Melanie Brown (with Louise Gannon), *Brutally Honest*, London: Quadrille, 2018.

Chapeltown Black Women's Writers Group, *When Our Ship Comes In: Black Women Talk*, Yorkshire Arts Circus, 1992.

Derek Boothroyd, 'Black is Black and White is White', *The Yorkshire Post and Leeds Mercury*, 8.12.1955. I am grateful to local historian Danny Friar for finding this article.

W W Daniel, *Racial Discrimination in England*, Harmondsworth: Penguin, 1968.

Nicholas Deakin, *Colour, Citizenship and British Society*, London: Panther Modern Society, 1970.

Christopher Duke, *Colour and Rehousing: Leeds*, London: Institute of Race Relations, 1970.

Dave Durman, 'Leeds Immigrants' *Union News*, (Leeds University Student Newspaper) 31.9.1969. I'm grateful to the local historian Danny Fryer for supplying this article.

Max Farrar, *The Struggle for 'Community' in a British Multi-ethnic, Inner-city Area: Paradise in the Making,* Lampeter and New York: Edwin Mellen Press, 2002, with a Foreword by Stuart Hall.

Paul Foot, *Immigration and Race in British Politics*, Harmondsworth: Penguin, 1965.

Millicent Francis, Mary Saddler, Frances Skelton and Myrna Tyrell, *Where's the Water Gone? The Story of the Chapeltown Laundry Co-Op*, Sunshine Press, 2000.

Beryl Gilroy, *Black Teacher*, London: Faber & Faber, 2021. (First published by Cassel & Co., 1976.)

Colin Grant, *Homecoming – Voices of the Windrush Generation*, London: Jonathan Cape, 2019.

Dilip Hiro, *Black British, White British*, Harmondsworth: Penguin, 1973.

Asher and Martin Hoyles, *From Nevis to Chapeltown*, forthcoming. Extract kindly supplied to me by Martin Hoyles.

K L Little, *Negroes in Britain – A Study of Racial Relations in English Society*, London: Kegan Paul, Trench, Trubner & Co., 1947.

Meg Merrylees is quoted in the website of the national organisation of Black-led housing associations: https://bmenational.co.uk/about/ Accessed 22.5.21.

Chris Mullard, *Black Britain*, London: George, Allen & Unwin Ltd, 1973.

Karen Fog Olwig, *Caribbean Journeys – An Ethnography of Migration and Home in three Family Networks*, Durham & London, Duke University Press, 2007.

Sheila Patterson, *Dark Strangers – A Study of West Indians in London*, Harmondsworth: Penguin, 1963.

Caryl Phillips has several essays about growing up in Leeds, and about the city itself. The 'housing' quote in this chapter is from 'Northern Soul', in Caryl Phillips, *Colour Me English*, London: Harvill Secker, 2011. For his emphasis on the role of the River Aire and the canal in making Leeds a truly international city, see Caryl Phillips and John McLeod, 'The City by the Water', *Interventions*, 2015, 17:6, pp. 879-892. Phillips' first novel imagines a couple travelling to England in the 1960s from a small Caribbean island (bearing much resemblance to St Kitts) with their baby. See Caryl Phillips, *The Final Passage*. London: Faber and Faber, 1985.

Caryl Phillips, in conversation with Bénédicte Ledent, 'Encountering Chapter One', the First Eccles Centre Plenary Lecture at the 43rd Annual *Conference of the Society for Caribbean Studies* held on 3 July 2019 at the University of Central Lancashire. London: The British Library's Eccles Centre for American Studies, 2021. bl.uk/eccles-centre

Edward Pilkington, *Beyond the Mother Country – West Indians and the Notting Hill White Riots*, London: IB Tauris, 1988.

Susan Pitter (edited for the Jamaica Society of Leeds) *Eulogy*, 2020, purchasable from https://coloursmayvary.com. Accessed 22.5.2021.

Alan Robertson, *Joe Harriott – Fire in his Soul*, London: Northway Publications, 2003.

Anthony H Richmond, *The Colour Problem*, Harmondsworth: Penguin, 1961.

Roscoe Methodist Church: A Unique History, compiled and published by Roscoe Methodist Church, Leeds, 2011. Introduction by Revd Mark Harwood. ISBN 978 0 957 00490 0.

Woke Soyinka, *You Must Set Forth at Dawn – A Memoir*, London: Methuen, 2007.

Anthony Speaight, 'Lincoln Crawford: A trailblazer for Black barristers, he campaigned for race equality and conducted many enquiries', *The Guardian*, 14.8.20.

Jean White, *When Our Ship Comes In – Black Women Talk*, edited by Palorine Williams, Pontefract: Yorkshire Arts Circus, no date, c.1992. ISBN 0 947780 83 1. (Other Chapeltown women featured in this booklet are Fay Comrie, Agnes Hinds, Odessa Stoute, Elaine Davis, Katie Stewart, Georgina Webbe, Joyce Bernard, Carol Comrie.)

Alfred Williams and Ray Brown, *To Live It Is To Know It*, Leeds: Normal Productions, 2003; originally, Yorkshire Arts Circus, 1987. ISBN 0 9544997 0 0.

Benjamin Zephaniah, *The Life and Rhymes of Benjamin Zephaniah – An Autobiography*, London: Simon and Shuster, 2018.

Mohsin Zulfiqar (ed.) *Land of Hope and Glory? The Presence of African, Asian and Caribbean Communities in Leeds*, Leeds: Leeds City Council, 1993. [Roots Project team: Paramjeet Singh Bhogal, Chris Booker, Max Farrar, Joseph Mills, Kobi Yagmaiepour, Mohsin Zulfiqar] ISBN 0 9521557 0 2

Chapter 4

IT'S ALL ABOUT EDUCATION

A rthur France came from a family that was passionate about education and he has never lost sight of its fundamental importance. Like so much of Arthur's way of thinking, he sees its value both for the individual and for society as a whole. His parents insisted that their children did their homework and succeeded at school. (His schooling was described in Chapter 2.) But learning didn't stop with the school. Bible study was extra-curricular learning for all of Ebeneza and Olga's children. And Arthur and his siblings were taught how to work the family's farm. He learned basic social values from his parents: each of us is part of a family and part of a wider community; at all times we must think of the needs of others, not just our own.

He often tells a story whose content used to puzzle me. One day his father was driving Sir Arthur Lees' famous Austin of England car (see Chapter 2). The car was packed full of Ebeneza's children and others when they passed a friend of Arthur's called Everley walking beside the road. Arthur asked his Dad to stop and pick him up. He was no doubt thinking that everyone should care for everyone else, and Everley needed some help. His father stopped, turfed Arthur out of the car, and took Everley on board. Arthur had to walk several miles home, on his own.

He tells this story with his customary big laugh, but it sounded a bit harsh to me, and I didn't get its moral. I thought

Arthur seemed to be doing the right thing, offering help. But his Dad was providing an important lesson, Arthur said: "Think before you speak; all your actions have consequences." At the root of all of this learning was a set of practical values: the deep significance of time-discipline, reliability and hard work. Later, when Arthur was setting up the Supplementary School and campaigning to reform state schooling in Chapeltown, Leeds, and when he became a teacher at Technorth, this early formal and informal learning in Nevis, steeped in social values, guided his work, as this chapter will show.

Further Education in Leeds and Erith

In the early 1960s Arthur enrolled at the Further Education (FE) technical college opposite Leeds Infirmary to study building construction. (Later the building was adopted by Leeds Polytechnic's Engineering Department.) Picking up on his apprenticeship in Nevis, the course, validated by the internationally-recognised City and Guilds London Institute, started with woodwork and then moved on to general construction and management. Those were the days when employers offered more generous conditions of work, and British Railways (where he worked at the time – see Chapter 3) allowed Arthur to be released from work, on full pay, for a day each week. He had classes in the evenings too.

Arthur's ambition was to be an architect. He saw the study of building construction as a step in that direction. He obtained a National Diploma in Structures and Management and became a member of the Institute of Building Management. Some time after his construction course at the technical college, around 1972 or 1973, he decided he needed to study building economics. For reasons he can't recall he enrolled at Erith College in Kent. Today it is the National Construction College South, still in Erith, which is now part of Greater London. I suppose if you've moved from Nevis to Leeds, a couple of hundred miles to Erith in the south of England is not much of a challenge.

The Leeds Technical College (later, Leeds Polytechnic's
Engineering Department) c.1967. Photo: leodis.net

He arrived in Erith on a Sunday with nowhere to stay. Yet
again, solidarity among this first generation of African and
Caribbean migrants came into play. Arthur accosted a Black
man walking by, who promptly helped him out by giving him
the address of a Black family in Erith. Soon after, Arthur
knocked on the front door at that address. They weren't terribly
friendly but they rented out their attic room and that was all
he needed to knuckle down to his studies. He was there for two
years, taking breaks from the course to visit friends in central
London.

He had saved up enough to carry him through two years of
frugal living in Erith. But it was not easy. One day he was totally
broke when £2 arrived in the post. (About £30 in UK sterling in
2020.) It came from a Jamaican guy he knew who was studying
at Leeds University. This fellow, another hard-working and
ambitious young man, had gone to Hull (on the coast, about 60
miles east of Leeds) for a part-time job cleaning fish. He knew
Arthur was struggling and he sent him two pounds out of the
blue. Well, being Hull, it was probably out of the grey.

Commenting on this random act of kindness, Arthur said:
"What was yours was mine and what was mine was yours – that's
how we lived in those days." After a hard slog in exile in the
South, Arthur graduated with a Diploma in Building Economics.

He still wanted to be an architect, but the cost of another five year course was prohibitive.

Enrolling at FE College provided Arthur an opportunity for another layer of his education, outside of the construction curriculum. He was the only Black student on his Leeds course, but there were other Black people studying other subjects, such as law and accounting – some from the Caribbean, others from Africa. There is a long and important history of Africans coming to Leeds to study. Nobel Prize winning writer Professor Wole Soyinka graduated in 1957 from Leeds University (some of his experience was described in Chapter 3), and Professor Ngugi wa Thiong'o was writing his ground-breaking novel *A Grain of Wheat* in 1964 while studying for his Masters in English in the same university. Ngugi wrote this in a 1964 letter to a friend about his first impressions of Leeds:

Leeds shocked me, threw me into bewilderment from which I am slowly recovering. It seems to be a city that – mushroom fashion – had sprouted without a planning hand. Black soot seems to be the only clothes the buildings wear to fight off the cold.

In a 1966 interview with the *Leeds Union News*, Ngugi went beyond physical to political impressions:

I found Leeds absolutely depressing. All those houses crouching like old men and women hidden in the mist. Then there is the question of what I had expected ... the way Colonial Education made you think of England as the ideal. Well, I was not here for long, before I realised that things were not all 'rosy', that all this idle talk about freedom of the press, freedom of speech, etc, has to be seen in the context of an economic and political life dominated by a very few rich men. The whole system is basically wrong. Just a small thing – I would never have believed before I came here that policemen in Britain could be so violent and that they could manhandle peaceful students demonstrating in the streets of Leeds ... On the whole [Leeds University students are] very disappointing. Some so naive that they believe everything they are told in *The Daily Express, The Daily Telegraph* or *The Daily Mirror* about Russia, China or Africa. But [there are a] few who are really active and broad minded. In this respect I am glad that I came to Leeds. There is a strong radical tradition here which of course helps every 'colonial' student who comes to Leeds in a way that places like Oxford or Cambridge cannot do.

Despite the shock of soot, cold, and having his expectations contradicted, James Currey observed that:

The University of Leeds was the right place for Ngugi to go. They did realise the importance of this young African writer. The publication of *The River Between* [another novel by Ngugi] was celebrated on 25 January 1965 by a party at the University of Leeds with a cluster of professors across the disciplines present and leading booksellers from the town.

Ngugi had pointed to another 'plus' factor: the radical, anti-colonial students (white and Black) that he was meeting at Leeds University. Given that Nigerian-British David Oluwale was at this very time sleeping rough on the streets of Leeds (he was hounded to his death by two Leeds policemen in 1969, as we shall see in Chapter 7), it is worth recalling these positive experiences for Ngugi.

A Leeds West Indian Students' Association, including students from both the Further and Higher Education institutions was formed, and Arthur was its President from 1969 to 1972. They joined up with the African Student Society at

Leeds University, led by Enos Chikowore, and in 1974 they took over the majestic Court of the University's Parkinson Building on Woodhouse Lane for their Pan African Festival.

I remember Enos from my days as a student at this conservative institution (1968-71 and 1972-74) and I was swept away by his charisma and intelligence. He was a leading representative in the UK of Zimbabwe's liberation movement (ZANU). I was later told he had left Leeds to join ZANU's military wing and had been smuggled back into Zimbabwe, crossing a river in a barrel. This possibly imagined story was just the thing to fire my admiration for the anti-imperialists of those militant days. (Enos subsequently became a minister in Mugabe's government, dying young in 2005, aged 69.)

The Parkinson was, and still is, the university's flagship building, with its 57 metre high clock tower and huge internal Court leading to its impressive circular library. It had been the site of the first Leeds student occupation in May 1968. Jack Straw, then President of the Students' Union and later Home Secretary and Foreign Secretary in Tony Blair's Labour government, claimed to be the leader of this occupation, and was roundly accused of selling it out. (Dr Christian Høgsbjerg has described this sit-in in an article that captures the spirit of 1968 in Leeds – see References at the end of this chapter.)

The African-heritage students fully understood the power of occupying the heartland of the university, filling what was normally a white space with Black bodies. Arthur remembered Black students taking over the Court with some glee. Their celebration of Pan Africanism filled him with enthusiasm – not least because the book stall provided by Jessica and Eric Huntley's pioneering Bogle L'Ouverture Publications demonstrated Black scholarship and creativity. *Leeds Student* (formerly *Leeds Union News*) failed to report on this important festival, but we published this in *Chapeltown News* (No. 15, March-April 1974):

Pan African week at the University and the Poly[technic], organised by Enos Chikowore with the help of many others was a big success. Notable contributions came from Darcus Howe, editor of *Race Today*, who showed how each landmark of revolutionary activity in the Caribbean has occurred when Asian- and Afro-West Indians had been united, and from Farrukh Dhondy, who showed in his discussion on education how Black youth leaving school are making a conscious political refusal to work – if 'work' only means low-status service jobs.

The children from the Saturday Supplementary School at Elmhurst entertained us with their dancing at the Cultural Evening and Errol Imruh Caesar's play 'So What If They Die' had a tremendous impact.

At the end of the conference telegrams of solidarity were sent in support of the Trinidad Sugar Workers, the New Jewel Movement of Grenada and the movement to liberate Dhofar and Oman. Lack of space makes a fuller report of the week impossible, but it provided much political stimulation for future action.

The 'many others' who supported Enos Chickowore included Arthur and the members of the Leeds University and Polytechnic West Indian and African Students' Association. As we will see in Chapter 7, Arthur's political education was in full swing by this time and this was another opportunity for him to develop his knowledge of African and Caribbean history and to see the impact that large public gatherings of Black people could have. In this commitment to overtly radical political education he was breaking away from the gradualist, reformist strand in Black politics in the UK.

Over the following years Leeds University did make some progress towards inclusivity, but even in 2011 there remained issues only too familiar to Black people in Britain. Joe Williams, born in Leeds of Jamaican heritage and a friend of Arthur's, said this:

I attended Leeds University in 2011 [on a Masters course] and I was still intimidated, and in awe. As a Black person I definitely got the feeling I didn't belong. I definitely felt from certain students who I don't know, you know you meet just in passing, just the surprise on their faces, 'oh, should you be here?' It is almost like they want to show you to where the cleaner's room is. But I think a good way of challenging that is through narrative.

Nevertheless, Joe has never given up engaging in educational work in unusual settings, just as Arthur would advocate. Through his lifetime's work as an actor, director, writer and historian Joe has worked tirelessly to change the dominant Euro-centric narrative and create a new perspective that celebrates Black history and achievements. One of his ventures is Heritage Corner, in which he and his colleagues research the many and varied signs of African knowledge, culture and struggle in the city of Leeds, manifested in publications, artefacts and in buildings; he disseminates this research through plays, his website and guided walks around the city.

Changing the education system in Leeds

In 1971, Arthur was a main mover in setting up the Saturday Supplementary School for Black children in the Chapeltown area of Leeds. The United Caribbean Association (UCA) (to be discussed in Chapter 6) had a keen concern for the education of the children in local schools. They could see that they weren't making the progress their parents expected.

Paul Warmington's research has revealed how extensive has been the work of Black British intellectuals in challenging the educational system. He quoted from the flyer produced by the North London West Indian Association (NLWIA) in 1969:

ALL WEST INDIAN PARENTS ... YOUR CHILD'S FUTURE IS THREATENED. It's time to get up NOW. We are ambitious for our children. No mountain is too high. Some people think we are too ambitious.

SO WE HAVE TO DO SOMETHING ABOUT IT. The Haringey Education Committee proposes to introduce changes which will affect YOUR child:

- Children are going to be 'banded'
- Children are going to be 'streamed'
- Black children will be dispersed.

UNITE AND FIGHT FOR YOUR RIGHTS

The NLWIA included Waveney Bushell, Jeff Crawford, John La Rose, and Hazel Walcott. La Rose, with his partner Sarah White, had already set up New Beacon Books in Finsbury Park, north London, in 1966, making educational materials with a Black and international focus more widely available for the first time in Britain. La Rose went on to form the Black Parents' Movement, with a branch in Manchester led by Gus John, both of whom were part of the Race Today Alliance in the early 1980s. (Gus John later became Director of Education in Hackney, London, and to this day forcefully campaigns for Black children's rights and a proper education system.)

Grenadian scholar and activist Bernard Coard had published in 1971 his coruscating pamphlet titled *How the West Indian Child is made Educationally Subnormal in the British School System*. Lambasting both the prejudices of white teachers and the class and race bias in the testing of intelligence (IQ tests were one of the means by which Black children were excluded from mainstream education), Coard placed the blame on the educational system instead of the child. In a section titled 'Things we can do for Ourselves', he wrote:

(1) We need to open Black *nursery schools* and *supplementary schools* throughout the areas we live in,

in Britain. Our nursery schools should have Black dolls and toys and pictures, and story-books about great Black men and women, and their achievements and inventions. Our children need to have a sense of identity, pride and belonging, as well as mental stimulation ... These [supplementary school] classes can be held on evenings and Saturday mornings. We should recruit all our Black students and teachers for the task of instructing our children ... (2) Parents must make it their duty to visit the schools that their children attend *as often as possible*. This will keep the teachers on their toes, and make them realize you mean business where the education of your child is concerned.

Beverley Bryan, Stella Dadzie and Suzanne Scafe wrote that London-based organisations like the Black Unity and Freedom Party and the Black Power Movement took up the issue of 'the mis-education of Black children in schools' and this drew lots of Black women into the radical movement, inspiring demonstrations and 'sit-ins [by Black students] ... study circles, supplementary schools'.

It was in this spirit that Arthur France, Calvin Beech, George Archibald and others decided to form an independent school on Saturdays, open to Black children of all ages who wanted to learn more, both to improve their chances in mainstream schooling, and to understand their own history and culture. They obtained permission to use Elmhurst Middle School on the edge of Potternewton Park in Chapeltown, and they recruited teachers from among the Caribbean students at Leeds University. As they explained in an article they wrote for *Chapeltown News* (No. 18, July 1974):

The setting up of the United Caribbean Association Supplementary School in 1971 was not a sudden happening. It was a gradual realization that something

was terribly wrong with the education of Black children
... [Parents'] complaints like 'My child is ten years old
and can hardly read. My boy is 12 and cannot add or
subtract. My little girl told me that the teacher had called
her a black bastard. My teacher says that Chapeltown is
filthy, therefore nothing good can come out of it. My
teacher is always putting me out of the classroom.' One
can go on and on.

These reports were the result of a survey the UCA activists had
conducted, and they had been astonished by how bad the
situation was. 'What was more astounding,' they wrote, 'was the
feelings of helplessness amongst Black parents'. They had made
repeated complaints and nothing had been done. In the case of
the Joseph family, the child had been 'shuttled between the
school, the Education Department and the educational
psychologist for about a year'. While they recognised that their
supplementary school is not 'the ultimate answer to the mis-
education of Black children in Leeds or anywhere else', it was
a start. It ran from 1.00 to 3.30pm each Saturday. There were
160 children on the register and about 80 attended each week,
ranging from five to 13 years of age. The curriculum centred on
maths, Afro-Caribbean history and English; there was a dance
group; and they organised outings to 'airports, zoos, museums
and other places of interest' in London and elsewhere.

Crucially, the Black teachers were able to supplement the
standard school curriculum with African and Caribbean history
and geography and the achievements of Black scientists, writers,
political leaders and others throughout the African diaspora.
Leeds University had students who were headteachers in
schools in Caribbean islands – Arthur remembers one from
Antigua who was "a joy to watch". Clifton Ali was a university
student who taught at the school. Eddy Bain from Trinidad was
another teacher who stood out – "He was so patient with the
younger ones," Arthur recalled. It made him think back to his

own school days, wondering exactly how he learned his arithmetic.

Arthur, George and Calvin ran the Saturday School for about five years. They gave it their full commitment. The Black students who did the teaching would walk to Chapeltown from Boddington Hall, in Lawnswood – about four miles – such was their dedication to the all-important cause of education. "The students were essential, but we [the UCA leadership] drove the organisation of the Saturday School." Vincent Caesar from St Kitts and Mark McWatt from Guyana were among the most committed teachers. But Mark had not been impressed with this time in Leeds. "He said he'd sooner sweep the streets than stay in England, he was so fed up with the racism he experienced here."

As they explained in *Chapeltown News*, the Supplementary School was not the ultimate solution. Recalling that work in 2020, Arthur said: "We were annoyed with the education of Black children. It was miseducation. We realised we had to take responsibility and make sure the state schools were changed."

Arthur France, George Archibald and some of the UCA Supplementary school students, June 1974. © Dave Williams for *Chapeltown News*

Parents often attended the consultation evening events organised in Earl Cowper Middle School, where most Black children aged nine to 13 were pupils.

Earl Cowper had owned the land that was transformed into Cowper Street, where, as well as large houses, a huge Board School had been built for the prosperous English middle classes who lived in Chapeltown in the late 19th Century. As the middle classes moved out and were slowly replaced by the Jewish refugees from Eastern Europe, beginning to prosper from the 1930s onwards, Cowper Street School was for a period a predominantly Jewish school, achieving good results.

By the end of the 1960s, however, Black parents were beginning to see that the teachers were not expecting their children to achieve high standards. Arthur, George and Calvin would inspect the children's homework books and they could see the problem. "They thought our kids were going to become labourers or coal-miners, so they thought there was no need to teach them proper maths." The UCA wasn't going to stand for that.

They organised a series of meetings with the headteacher, Mr Buckle, and with the senior officers of the council's Education Department, to discuss their concerns. They invited Mr R S Johnson, the Director of Education, to meet with the parents in Chapeltown. Education being such an important issue for the Black parents, the hall was packed. "Johnson talked to them. But everyone could see he was lying."

When the parents' leaders had been to the Education Department in the town centre they had been treated with disrespect. Officials in his office had pretended to be RS Johnson, trying to fob them off. "After lots of these meetings we realised the Cowper Street head was a racist crook. We could see that RS Johnson wasn't going to make any changes. We had had enough. We decided to take the bull by the horns."

They set up the Chapeltown Parents Action Group (CPAG), led by Mrs Odessa Stoute. Mrs Stoute shared their politics and was one of the older parents at Cowper Street School who commanded a lot of respect. Mrs Stoute had arrived in Leeds in 1961 and quickly got a job as a machinist at the huge Burton's tailoring factor in Harehills, adjacent to Chapeltown. In 'Black Women Talk' she wrote that she had no intention that her daughters would work in factories but 'the struggle had just begun for in those days to educate Black children was a very hard thing'. She continued:

I remember when the system changed in 1974 where some schools were changing to comprehensive to give the children a better chance. But we had a very big struggle to get the right change in Cowper Street School so we had to form what we called Chapeltown Parents' Association of which I was one of the committee members. Being a group we were able to get all parents together so that we could confront the education authorities and complain. But somehow being Black they took no notice of us, so we decide to be seen and heard. We would do something positive so we call a strike. Anyhow we did get a bit of attention.

Arthur said: "We involved Mrs Gertrude Paul, too, because she was the one Black school teacher in Leeds. But she kept in the background." The CPAG held a public meeting on 10th June 1973 to set out their case. *Chapeltown News* (No. 8, June 1973) reported the applause Violet Hendrickson received when she explained that Black people came to England to do the jobs white people refused. 'They were promised a better life, but we were disillusioned, it was nothing like we expected.' Schooling here 'Seems like a deliberate attempt to hold people back'. Errol Caesar (later, Imruh Bakari) said that people had to make their up own minds about the meaning of life. 'If a man's mind is messed up, he can only fit into the people's idea of what life is about, and that is making money for other people ... We must change our whole way of life.' Mrs Crombie told the meeting that

Chapeltown News (the home-made community newspaper) reported in June 1973 that the Chapeltown Parents Action Group was planing a pupils' strike at Earl Cowper Middle School.

their children's education could be improved by attending the supplementary school, reading to them and providing educational toys. Parents should visit Earl Cowper School and they should talk to teachers and demand that they provide better teaching. Mrs Crombie called for a strike at Cowper Street school to enforce that demand. The meeting agreed to the strike, and to write to the Education Department to demand that the headteacher was removed from the school.

On 25th June 1973 they withdrew all the Black children and took them for a day's education at the Church of God's premises near Chapeltown Road. "We didn't tell the Minister what our plans were, we just asked if we could use his hall. When he realised what we were doing he said he didn't support our radical stance at all," Arthur laughed. "There were parents who dismissed us as young hotheads, upsetting the apple cart."

Chapeltown News (No. 9, July 1973) started its report of the strike with the list of demands that had been announced at a public meeting called by the Chapeltown Parents Action Group on the previous day (Sunday 24th June). Mrs Louise Crombie had read out this list:

1) To de-class the school from a Middle to a Primary.
2) The removal of the Headmaster Mr Buckle.
3) More Black governors who are interested in their own people.
4) Better contact between the Headmaster, parents and staff.
5) Improved internal facilities in the school.
6) Attempts must be made to slow down the fast turnover at the school.
7) More Black teachers.
8) Members of the Black Community to be invited to speak to the children to give them more motivation.
9) Facilities and staff for extra teaching for the children in the evening.

About fifty Black people picketed Cowper Street School on Monday 25th June 1973. There were almost no Black children in the school – they had either been kept at home or, if their parents were working, they marched off in procession to the church hall. *Chapeltown News* reported: 'They returned to the school at 3.30pm and marched round the school shouting, with obvious delight, "Buckle Out, Buckle Out"'. It turned out to be a strike only of Black children simply because the white parents refused the CPAG's invitation to take part.

This was Black Power in action. Two days later, R S Johnson made this announcement at the CPAG meeting in Elmhurst School, as summarised in *Chapeltown News* (July 1973):

· The school will be re-modelled and re-equipped.
· Domestic science and craft facilities will be installed.
· More posts for senior teachers will be created, allowing

promotion of staff within the school, thereby (they hope) reducing staff turnover.

- A new experimental, relevant curriculum will be introduced, employing outside specialists and experts.

At the meeting Calvin Beech repeated the demand for more Black governors, which Mr Johnson accepted. But, as the CPAG Secretary said, the headmaster was still in place. Other parents offered further complaints against Mr Buckle, which Johnson fended off by asking them to come to his office for further discussions. Those discussions, with the ever-present threat of more strike action, led to the decision to remove Mr Buckle. *Chapeltown News* (No. 11, September 1973) reported that 'reliable sources' suggested that he would leave at the end of that term. These sources proved correct. Mrs Stoute later wrote: 'The school was still not up to the real standard but it was a little better than it would have been'. And her own daughters went on the get their 'O' and 'A' Levels.

In February 1974, *Chapeltown News* included an interview with Mr Brian Clarke who had taken up the post of head of Earl Cowper Middle School the previous month. He said he would ensure that parents, staff and children had a belief in their school. Clarke was seen to have made some improvements in the school's curriculum and its ethos, but, when Rodwell Gentles was badly injured on a school trip in June 1974, his father's enquiry about the school's manner of dealing with this resulted in him being 'treated discourteously [by Mr Clarke], as if the matter was of no importance, and [Mr Gentles was] eventually shown the door' (*Chapeltown News*, No. 18, July 1974).

The next step in the campaign to improve Black children's education in Leeds was to put pressure on the council to appoint Mrs Gertrude Paul as headteacher of Elmhurst Middle School when the post became vacant in 1976. By now the council was beginning to understand how much community power the UCA could exert. Mrs Paul was duly appointed and she was only the third Black female headteacher in the UK. Lauri Johnson's research into Black and South Asian headteachers in Britain noted that Clifton Robinson was the first male Black head, appointed to this position in Leicester in 1968. Yvonne Connolly also became a head in 1968, founding the Caribbean Teachers Association to promote leadership among Black teachers in the UK.

Beryl Gilroy's autobiography reveals just how tough it was for Black teachers in British schools at this time. In 1969, just before the start of her second term as headteacher of an infants' school in Camden, London, her anxiety was so great that she had come out in a rash. 'I was afraid to go to school,' she wrote, 'I was bound to encounter bigots of all sorts, the child who would always test me, and teachers who would be inhibited by my colour'.

Professor Johnson has pointed out that 'Black and Minority Ethnic' people are still 'woefully underrepresented' among head teachers in British schools. In 2015, only 3 per cent of heads were Black or Asian, whereas 14 per cent of the population have those heritages. Johnson described Mrs Paul as a director of the Supplementary School and quoted an interview with her in the *Yorkshire Post* (11.5.1978) where she emphasised the need for 'children to know their background and their origins so they can become aware of who they are'. Prof Johnson included Mrs Paul among those heads who were advocates for their community's rights.

Arthur and his colleagues applied for and were awarded in 1976 a £30,000 grant from the Commission for Racial Equality to provide a building as a base for the Supplementary School. A large property was acquired in Hall Lane in Chapeltown. This building, named United Caribbean Association House, initially became a school for dance, rather than pursuing the broad curriculum of the original Saturday School. In 1977 there was vigorous opposition to the way that UCA House was being developed under the leadership of Mrs Paul from the group that had taken over *Chapeltown News* after the Bonfire Night Trial in the summer of 1976 (see Chapter 7). Reflecting on these controversies in 2020, Arthur said he was sorry to see the Saturday School curriculum being reduced at UCA House, but he did not agree with the attack on Mrs Paul.

Teaching at Technorth

In the early 1980s, Arthur developed a new role as a teacher in a new type of educational centre called 'Technorth'. It was created by Leeds City Council in response to the violent urban protest led by Black youths in the Chapeltown and Harehills areas of Leeds in 1981. Politicians and journalists who want to portray these turbulent events as merely criminal actions carried out by hooligans call them 'riots'. The Labour leader of the city council, George Mudie, realised that these were actually protests about the conditions facing Black people. His response was to open a dialogue with Black and Asian people in the city and employ one or two in its administration. He also understood that new facilities would have to be developed if more violence was to be averted.

In setting up the Harehills and Chapeltown Liaison Committee, consisting of members of all the Black and Asian community organisations and council officers from every department, and in forming an Equal Opportunities Unit within the council, George Mudie had met James Aboaba. Mr Aboaba, originally from Nigeria, was one of the politically-minded, highly educated Africans that Arthur had become friends with in the early 1970s. We'll meet him again in Chapter 7 when he was among the people who organised the campaign for David Oluwale's killers to be convicted. James Aboaba was later instrumental in getting members of the Nigerian Community in Leeds involved in the carnival – they formed a Pan African drumming troupe for the carnivals of the 1990s. George Mudie involved James in setting up Technorth, lodged within the council's economic development unit directed by Anna Whyatt.

James Aboaba immediately contradicted the council's idea that this was to be a centre training young Black people for jobs as carpenters or builders. James, rightly looking to the future and wanting to change the mould of Black people's education and employment, said he wanted a centre that would offer training in the emerging new technology of computers. James became the extremely effective chair of the management committee of Technorth.

Anna Whyatt's team in the council's economic development unit got the city to buy the old tramshed on Harrogate Road, on the northern edge of Chapeltown, and had it converted into an education and training centre. Along with James, Veryl Harriott and Gary Dore were other Black members of the management committee. Dave Williams, formerly Head of Complementary Studies at Jacob Kramer College of Art in Leeds, and already developing his skills in computing, was appointed Director of Technorth. Having lived in Chapeltown and worked with us on *Chapeltown News*, Dave knew that Arthur would make an excellent job of the 'general studies and personal development' teaching role at Technorth. Kam Sangra, a British South Asian, Norma Morgan and Arthur were the only non-white staff in Technorth's early days.

James was a very powerful influence as chair of management committee. He had a senior position in the science labs of the main hospital in Leeds. "James was very passionate and sincere. He had refused promotion so he could stay in Leeds." He had become a friend of George Mudie but that didn't stop him ringing up George and saying he'd chain himself to the railings if the council persisted in some policy or other that was detrimental to Technorth. George would change track because he knew James would carry out his threat. A Black man chained to railings would not be 'good optics'.

The late Dave Williams came in for praise, too. "Dave was very good at the job of managing Technorth. He was so genuine. I would never have believed a radical Pan Africanist like me could find a white man from Wales who understood me. I'd never had any boss who supported my politics and gave me all the leeway I needed to do the job as I knew it had to be done." Dave arranged for Arthur to go on a short teacher training course and later Arthur went on a counselling course too.

Arthur walked all over Chapeltown and further afield looking for youngsters to get them into Technorth. He knocked on doors and spoke with parents, aunties and uncles. This is the kind of proactive approach, recruiting for a new type of education, that they had pioneered with the Saturday School. He understood that lots of the Black youth who had left school at 16 had been "pissed off by the racist system in the schools they'd been to, and they thought Technorth was just another place that would let them down." Arthur was one of the few people in the education and training system in Leeds who could understand and sympathise with their point of view. He recalled a couple of the other Black teachers who joined the staff finding it very hard to get on with these recalcitrant young men.

Arthur reminded me that he once invited me in to give them a talk about my experience of being falsely charged by the Leeds police with affray and inciting the 'riot' by Black youth in Chapeltown on Bonfire Night in 1975. (I have since reconfigured 'riot' as 'violent urban protest'.) Apparently I told the Technorth youngsters that I'd only been given bread and margarine for breakfast when we had been locked up in Armley Prison before the trial opened. I'd been badly shaken up by the experience of being in jail. He said this "real life" story made a big impact on these young people, several of whom had also had bad times with the Leeds police.

Gary Grant came to Technorth when he was 16. Arthur said he was a quiet young man. Arthur set the class an exercise: to write about their previous two years of their lives. Gary was the first to hand his in. Arthur was immediately impressed by the accurate grammar and fine writing style. Gary's story was worryingly familiar. He'd been arrested by the police for no good reason and taken to court. His father came with him. Gary described how this experience had made him very hostile to white people. He wrote that he only came to Technorth because he saw that Arthur was on the staff. He could see that Arthur believed in him. Gary went on to become a highly respected member of Leeds Polytechnic's IT department.

Arthur was broadening these young people's horizons and he was also helping with their personal development, producing CVs and practising interviews. Almost 40 years later, Neil Dore told me that he repeats a point to his own children that Arthur made to him while he was a Technorth student: "Remember, when you go for an interview for a job, you are interviewing them, too. Ask yourself: do I really want to work here?" Technorth gave Neil a lot of confidence, and that's just what youngsters don't always get in conventional education.

Arthur's aim was to get to know the students as individuals. "I used to ask them to write down what had happened over the last two years of their life." Another exercise Arthur produced was to get them to say where they are now and what they'd like to achieve in a few years' time – and then they had to write down the message they'd like to see on their gravestones. This is just

L-R: Mike Laxton, Kam Sangra, Veryl Harriott, Simon Horner, Dave Williams, Mike Standing and Norma Morgan. Photo © Leeds Library and Information Services at leodis.net. Courtesy Tom Williams

the kind of 'reflexivity' progressive educators aim for in their students.

Technorth's approach to the technical education and training was different, too. Led by Kalwant Rahid, in 1984 the students installed the lighting system at the new West Indian Centre just off Chapeltown Road. In another Technorth initiative that gave students relevant practical experience, Dave Williams set up a system whereby local people could bring in electronic devices (radios, video recorders, etc) from their homes that needed repair, and the students would develop the range of skills to get each item working again, and at the same time build Technorth's reputation as a community service, as well as a training centre.

Arthur's friend Brainard Braimah MBE would visit him at Technorth and Dave Williams immediately spotted his talent. Brainard, originally from Janga in northern Ghana, with a BSc and an MSc in mathematics, was just the person they needed to bring the youths up to speed in maths. But, just as Technorth pushed the boundaries of education and training, Mr Braimah realised that there was a need for younger people, still at school, to develop their understanding of computers.

Again, the management of Technorth was able to take up the challenge. Staff members Sim Sobers, Lloyd Bassue and Arthur decided to investigate if school-kids could use computers and find their way forward with this mysterious new technology. They recruited six young Black children from among their own families and friends, with Martin Williams and Lloyd Bassue running the teaching of a six week after-school course. They made very good progress. The children were featured in *Caribbean Times*, edited by Arif Ali, because this course was unique in the UK.

Having proved there was potential here, with Arthur's help, Mr Bramah approached a government-funded project in Leeds called Task Force, and persuaded them that community-based education fitted within their 'community development' remit.

Their £100,000 grant led to the formation of the Chapeltown and Harehills Assisted Learning Computer School (CHALCS) in 1986. (Arthur, a lifelong Labour Party supporter, had to say it was a Conservative government that, to his surprise, made the grant.)

While it was aimed at children of African-Caribbean-Asian descent, CHALCS was based in Technorth and was open to everyone. Being enterprising and cost-conscious, they persuaded UNISYS, the global computer company, to give them £100,000 worth of computer equipment – Arthur was impressed by how supportive the UNISYS regional manager was of CHALCS's vision. Again they utilised the goodwill in their community network: the computers were installed for free by the brother-in-law of Technorth's teacher Kam Sangra.

Brainard Braimah has published maths teaching books, and on the 'authorsden' website he has written this about CHALCS's impressive achievements:

The School provides additional learning for mainly ethnic minority students after school, at weekends and during holidays. Students can study maths, science, including electronics, IT, English and self-awareness, using both traditional methods and computers. 33 Volunteer tutors, many of them students, help with the teaching, and these now include some graduate students who studied at CHALCS in the early years. Students are encouraged to take RSA [Royal Society of the Arts] exams from the age of 12, which provides powerful motivation at a critical point in their careers. CHALCS currently caters for 400-500 young people at any one time, and has a substantial waiting list. Of its many achievements one of the most significant is that 40 Afro-Caribbean young people have gone to university, studying a range of subjects including science and technology. Before CHALCS many of these students would not have entered for GCSEs [the exams British school students take at the age of 16].

On this website Mr Braimah made another statement which would no doubt be echoed enthusiastically by Arthur France: 'I believe that education is a social equaliser and educational underachievement is a personal tragedy for young people and a great loss to society. I also believe that every child is capable of learning and that no child should be allowed to under-achieve regardless of gender, race, social class and social background'.

Arthur was chairperson of the management committee of CHALCS and Braimah was director. When Arthur retired from Technorth in 2000 he continued as chairperson, such was his commitment to its mission. He said that Brainard Braimah was very good at fund-raising, principally because the companies they asked for support believed in what they were doing. "We sent more kids to university for science-based courses than all the schools put together." CHALCS also started a science lab for seven year olds. When Professor Hartley from Leeds University came to visit, he couldn't believe what he saw. Most of the teachers were Black professionals, rather than trained teachers, but they were achieving wonders.

CHALCS's reputation grew and one day Prince Charles came to see what they were doing. "I escorted him around. He didn't want to leave. The royal family know more about you than you think, you know. Prince Charles asked me where I was from, originally. I said, 'Nevis-St Kitts'. He said, 'How is Mr Bradshaw?' I said, 'He's dead ten years ago' – the photo of us laughing got into the newspapers," said Arthur.

As Arthur told me this, his thoughts went back to his childhood. "The royal family is drilled down your throat in the Caribbean. I sang the national anthem all the time." He has no time for the disgraces of the British Empire, but there is a soft spot for its emblems. "Charles has a fantastic memory, you know. He was visiting Harewood House and I was invited to be there. He walked straight over to me – he remembered me from the time he was at CHALCS – and he greeted me like an old friend."

L-R Vinod France, Tattra France, Prince Charles, Arthur France, with Brainard Braimah standing behind Tattra at Technorth, Leeds.

Then Arthur talked about one or two individuals whose progress from CHALCS meant so much to him. "So many young people have been marginalised by the racism in the educational system, but it's amazing what you can do when you can get these youngsters off the street." He gave the example of Colin Brown, who was a warehouse labourer when, aged 24, he applied to Technorth. Arthur gave him an evening programme, after he had finished work, that lasted until 9pm. Then he got him onto an access course, and then Colin did a computer science degree. Doug Kemp, the head of Colin's department, told Arthur that people like Colin would normally fail such a demanding course. "I said Colin's got my boot up his arse so he can't fail," Arthur laughed. When Colin graduated there was a group photograph of students who had come up the hard way that included an Arab woman whose husband was not at all keen on her being in education. The *Yorkshire Post* titled their story 'The Magnificent Seven'.

Another exemplary student was Delroy Goodison. Delroy had been thrown out of school at 16 for being disruptive. He never took an exam. Even Technorth wanted to throw him out.

Arthur took a step that might not have gone down well in another type of institution. "I held him against a wall and said I'd kill him," and this time Arthur wasn't laughing. Perhaps he was channelling his father, the redoubtable Ebeneza France.

Delroy ended up with 'A' level Maths which led to a university degree in computer engineering. Then he got a job at Barnbow Royal Ordinance Factory in Cross Gates in East Leeds. They made tanks for the army, and were taken over by Vickers Defence Systems in 1986. He was the first Black man they had ever employed. "I told the students: 'You see, I come from the Caribbean. I'm here to drive hell out of you'. They were a bit afraid of me. But they got the results they needed." CHALCS was wound up in 2008, and Leeds is all the poorer for that.

The UCA Supplementary School, Chapeltown Black parents' militant protests against racism and under-resourcing in mainstream schools, and the Technorth/CHALCS initiatives have all played their part in raising the educational achievement levels of Black pupils in Leeds. Every one of these ventures is an aspect of Black people's struggle for educational attainment over the last 50 years in the UK. Arthur France has been at the centre of each of these important events.

It is hard to find figures that effectively trace the gradual improvement over this long period, but a 2017 research study by Feyisa Demie and Christabel McLean produced some revealing statistics on the progress in English schools between 2004 and 2014. Measured by the percentage of pupils who have achieved five A-C grades at GCSE (including English and Maths), the results show that Chinese- and Indian-heritage children are the highest achievers (about 75 per cent of both groups got five A-C grades in 2014) and that Bangladeshi-heritage children are the fastest improvers (34 per cent in 2004 and 60 per cent ten years later). Black Caribbean children's results improved significantly in this period (from 23 per cent to 47 per cent), but remain the lowest of all ethnic groups.

The fact that white children's results (56 per cent in 2014, the same as Black African children's results) are below those of children of Chinese, Indian and Bangladeshi heritage reminds us that social class is as significant a determinant as ethnicity in educational outcomes. While Black children are steadily doing better, it is lamentable that less than half of them were achieving five grades A-C in 2014. Arthur is leading the call upon another generation of activists to renew this key field of political struggle.

Arthur had combined his work at Technorth with his community work which always fed into his passion for educational achievement. In 1986, Dave Williams allowed Technorth to host a series of high-profile events under the banner of Caribbean Focus. "That's the good thing about Dave, he give me scope to do these extra things." Through this he met James Porter in his role as Director of the Commonwealth Institute. James and Arthur became close friends. You can see why from this extract from Mr Porter's obituary: 'James Porter's vocation was teaching. His mission was creating and strengthening ties between races and peoples across the globe. In the process he set out to bulldoze the barriers to interracial harmony' (*The Times*, 9.11.2012).

James Porter put Arthur in touch with the late Christopher Price, a former Labour Cabinet Minister who became Director of Leeds Polytechnic in 1986. Price, ever affable, invited Arthur for Sunday lunch to meet the Director of New York City College. "At the lunch in his house on Beckett Park I challenged Chris Price to take some of the kids from Technorth into the Polytechnic," Arthur said.

Mr Price put Dr Alan Maybury from the Poly's engineering department on the job and an access course was established. "Alan was very helpful: he was able to help break down the psychological barrier for Black youths when they were thinking about going into Higher Education." Perhaps later than they should have, Leeds Polytechnic/Metropolitan/Beckett University awarded Arthur an Honorary Doctorate in 2018. Leeds University made the same award in 2017.

When Arthur looks back on this he always remembers the people who had official roles in Leeds and were able to make the changes that were needed if Black people's lives were to be improved. "Anna Wyatt understood the ethos of Technorth" – probably because she listened closely to what Arthur, James Aboaba and Dave Williams had to say. "I have great respect for George Mudie," he added, "He was able to break down a lot of barriers in the council. I would phone him at 11 o'clock at night or 7.00 in the morning when the fowl on the roost. I'd say 'Meet me in Morrisons, just me and you, and we'll sort this out'." Morrisons was the supermarket close to the Leader of the Council's office in the Civic Hall. And that personal touch made all the difference. George and Arthur would walk the supermarket's aisles and make their deals.

Anna Whyatt's career took off and she left Leeds for London. George moved on from the council to be the MP for East Leeds. But Arthur of course stayed in the same house, serving the same

Arthur France receiving his honorary doctorate from Leeds University in 2018.
© Yorkshire post newspapers, courtesy of Arthur France

people, just as he always has. He said: "Last year [2019] I was in Leeds City Market when a white lady came up to me. She said 'Thank you very much. My two sons are doing well because of you'. That's why I do what I do. I give one hundred percent. What's the point otherwise?" Perhaps this might be the motto on Arthur France's gravestone.

References in this chapter

Brian W Alleyne, *Radicals Against Race: Black Activism and Cultural Politics*, Oxford: Berg, 2002, explains the political movements initiated by John La Rose and his comrades.

Beverley Bryan, Stella Dadzie and Suzanne Scafe, *Heart of the Race – Black Women's Lives in Britain*, London: Virago, 1985; second edition London: Verso, 2018.

Brainard Braimah and his work with CHALCS – see his entry here https://www.authorsden.com/braimah Accessed 28.2.20

Bernard Coard, *How the West Indian Child is made Educationally Subnormal in the British School System: The scandal of the Black Child in Schools in Britain*. Published for the Caribbean Education and Community Workers' Association by New Beacon Books Ltd, 1971. Coard's reputation suffered catastrophically after his conviction in 1986 for the murder of his fellow Grenadian revolutionary Maurice Bishop, but there is no doubt about the importance of his analysis of the failure of the British Education system.

Chapeltown News is available online at https://harehills111.wordpress.com/chapeltown-news/ (Most issues.)

James Currey, 'Ngugi, Leeds and the Establishment of African Literature', Leeds *African Studies Bulletin* 74 (December 2012), pp. 48-62. Available at https://lucas.leeds.ac.uk/article/ngugi-leeds-and-the-establishment-of-african-literature-james-currey/ Accessed1.3.2020. This article references Dave Williams, referred to in this chapter, when he was one of the radical students at Leeds University who interviewed Ngugi in 1966.

Feyisa Demie and Christabel McLean, *Black Caribbean Underachievement in Schools in England*, Lambeth Education and Learning, 2017, ISBN: 978-1-910428-18-4

Max Farrar, Christian Høgsbjerg, Louise Lavender, Mike McGrath, Sarah Perrigo and Tom Steele (2020): "'Paris Today, Leeds Tomorrow!' Remembering 1968 in Leeds', *Northern History* https://doi.org/10.1080/0078172X.2020.1747723. Accessed 17.12.2020.

Max Farrar, 'Racism, education and black self-organisation', *Critical Social Policy*, Winter 1992-3, Issue 36, pp. 53-72. Available at https://

/journals.sagepub.com/doi/abs/10.1177/026101839301203604 Accessed 1.3.2020.

Max Farrar, 'Rioting or Protesting? Losing it or Finding It?' *Parallax*, 2012, 18:2, pp. 72-91. Available at https://www.maxfarrar.org.uk/writing/culture-politics/rioting-or-protesting-losing-it-or-finding-it/ Accessed 1.3.2020.

Beryl Gilroy, *Black Teacher*, London: Faber & Faber, 2021. (First published by Cassel & Co., 1976.)

Gus John, *Taking a Stand: Gus John Speaks on education, race, social action and civil unrest, 1980-2005*, Manchester: Gus John Partnership, 2006. ISBN 0 9547842 1 6.

Lauri Johnson, 'The lives and identities of Black and South Asian Headteachers: Metaphors of leadership', *Educational Management and Leadership*, 2017, 45(5), pp. 842-8.

Odessa Stoute, *When Our Ship Comes In – Black Women Talk*, edited by Palorine Williams, Pontefract: Yorkshire Arts Circus, no date, c.1992. ISBN 0 947780 83 1. (Other Chapeltown women featured in this booklet are Fay Comrie, Agnes Hinds, Joyce Bernard, Elaine Davis, Katie Stewart, Georgina Webbe, Jean White, Carol Comrie.)

Paul Warmington, *Black British Intellectuals and Education – Multiculturalism's hidden history*, Abingdon and New York: Routledge, 2014.

Joe Williams, interviewed by Christian Høgsbjerg, 'The Leeds Black History Walk', *African Studies Bulletin*, No. 78, 2016-7. Available at https://lucas.leeds.ac.uk/article/the-leeds-black-history-walk-an-interview-with-joe-williams/#_ftnref3 Accessed 15.3.20. Joe's 'Heritage Corner' project is at https://heritagecornerleeds.wixsite.com/heritage-corner/1 Accessed 17.12.2020.

Chapter 5

WORKING FOR THE MAN

Th is chapter tells the story of Arthur France's many years of working for 'The Man'. Back in the day, The Man was the metaphor employed by radical Black Americans to describe not just the white men who dominated America and oppressed its Black citizens but the whole white, capitalist system. Caribbean people who became Rastafarians used 'Babylon' to mean pretty much the same thing. They called the system 'the shitsem'. One of the reasons I admire Black Power and the genuine Rastas is their ability to speak in metaphors far more powerful than you find in the leaden prose of conventional politics.

In the previous chapter there was a section on Arthur's work as a teacher at the Technorth Centre. It was included in the chapter about Arthur's own education, and his endless work in developing the educational opportunities of Black children and Black youth, despite the fact that in one sense, at Technorth he was actually working for The Man. His boss and the leaders of the city council who controlled Technorth were white and (mainly) male. But, as we have seen, Technorth had Black leadership too and in several ways it broke the mould The Man had set down. In this chapter we examine Arthur's working life in much more orthodox industries. Against the odds, Arthur seems to have persuaded even the more conservative Man that he had much to offer.

Arthur's work ethic is rooted in his family life in Mount Lily, Nevis (described in Chapter 2). As well as all those jobs he had to do on the farm, Arthur took note of how his father treated the people he employed. "With the five men he paid, he was strict but flexible." His father was there for him as he made his transition from school-boy to worker. As we saw in Chapter 2, Ebenezer got him an apprenticeship with Johnny Howell. Then he got a maintenance job at the last surviving sugar factory on St Kitts. This internal discipline and training set him up well for his working life in England and Germany.

First jobs in Leeds

Britain was begging for labour in the 1950s (explained in Chapter 3). Research by Stephanie Snow and Emma Jones showed that British Ministries of Health and Labour, along with the Colonial Office, started an active programme of recruitment of nurses from the Caribbean in 1949, and by 1965 there were between 3,000 and 5,000 Jamaican nurses in British hospitals. By 1972, an estimated 10,566 student nurses had been recruited from abroad. In 1963, Enoch Powell, Minister of Health in the Conservative government, recruited 18,000 trained doctors from India and Pakistan. (Ironic, given the vicious racism Powell launched in 1968 with his notorious 'rivers of blood' speech against the Black and Brown British citizens he called immigrants.)

Ron Ramdin recorded that London Transport already had 4,000 Black workers by 1958, a year after Arthur arrived in England. In 1956, Tom Baistow interviewed Jim Campbell, the General Secretary of the National Union of Railwaymen, the union that these workers had joined. Until recently, he said, the union had integrated its Black members well, but now:

We must be careful in the selection of West Indians in the railways. In small numbers they fit in, but it creates difficulties if too many come into the railways – they should be more evenly spread over industry generally. The men complain that in numbers they tend to form clubs, that they work at a slower tempo and in the case of tonnage handling, for instance, the gang's bonus suffers.

Racism in the trade unions was experienced in the early 1950s by Beryl Gilroy, a qualified teacher from Guyana, at first refused jobs in London's schools. Her autobiography revealed that her application to 'one of the leading unions' for a clerical job was rejected because of her skin colour. While this refusal stimulated a member of the Communist Party who worked for the union to come round to her digs to apologise, the damage was done.

A senior manager made this allegation to Tom Baistow: 'If you send any more [Black workers] the men will demand separate canteens and lavatory facilities'. Baistow noted that on the buses, also recruiting from the Caribbean, the Transport and General Workers Union had passed a conference motion saying that discrimination was 'un-Christian and contrary to trade union principles', while simultaneously demanding that the government introduced immigration controls.

Jack Jones, then the union regional secretary in the Midlands, but later the T&G's General Secretary, was more circumspect in his language, but his view – that an influx of 'any' workers in the Birmingham area would 'create problems' – was a coded expression of the work-based racism endemic in British industry. Ron Ramdin quoted a General Council statement to the 1958 Trades Union Congress that condemned 'every manifestation of racial prejudice and discrimination', and advocated understanding and 'joint efforts in local communities ... to further tolerance'.

But Ramdin showed that these progressive ideas weren't always taken up in local branches. He noted a strike in February 1955 in West Bromwich against the employment of an Indian trainee bus conductor and an overtime ban a few months later to enforce the local union's demand that there should be a quota of 5 per cent of 'coloured labour' on Wolverhampton's buses. Just at the time when the trade unions needed to take a stand for the rights of all workers, irrespective of colour, they manifestly failed.

The material injustices against immigrants in the UK are many and foul, but the sheer hypocrisy of those racists who blame Black people for 'stealing our jobs' – the very jobs Commonwealth citizens were asked to come to Britain to do – is one of Britain's psychic boils that still needs to be lanced. Far from stealing anyone's job, Arthur was immediately employed by British Railways in Leeds in the late summer of 1957, precisely because of the labour shortage in Leeds, as in every part of Britain.

His sister Elaine, already working as a secretary at Union Cold Storage in Hunslet, had told him who to go and see at the rail depot, and Arthur immediately became a 'relief railway porter'. Each morning he would report for duty and he would be sent to whichever place needed more hands that day. Normally he was in Huddersfield. "They were goods depots. We would move goods off the container and put them into one of the four lorries. I was the only Black person there. I would be lifting with several white guys – we were young and we were fit and strong, and we had fun."

Arthur found the management at the Railways to be quite friendly. "The boss would invite me into his office to have a chat – he seemed interested to talk to me and find out what sort of a person I was." He said they were not well paid, "But you were contented with what you got." He had £5 a week (about £120 in UK sterling in 2020) to pay the rent and pay for his food and entertainment. (As we saw in Chapter 3, entertainment was mainly going to The Forum Picture House on Chapeltown Road – currently an empty site opposite the current Roscoe Methodist Church.)

Arthur wanted to transfer into the engineering department of British Railways, but they wouldn't take him. There was no test – they just rejected him, and to this day he doesn't know why. The one big advantage of a labour shortage (so-called 'full employment') for the working man or woman is that they have lots of other avenues to pursue, and that's what Arthur did.

Some time around 1960, he got a job at Simpson & Cook, the builders. He saw they were putting up a new building on Dewsbury Road in south Leeds. Arthur put his carpentry skills to use in making shuttering for curing the concrete in the building's foundations. "I was willing to work at anything that came along. There was a Jamaican guy called Stanford already working there and he took an interest in me and showed me the ropes."

He found the work interesting, learning new building techniques that were quite different from those he'd encountered in Nevis, but the skills he'd learned at home were easily transferred to Leeds. Again, Arthur found the management and the other workers to be easy to get along with. He said that he and Stanford just put their heads down and got on with the work. "There was no trouble at all."

The job with Simpson and Cook came to an end so he moved on to another one, this time with the huge Kier construction company. Keir was building Skelton Grange Power Station in south Leeds. Skelton A had been built between 1947 and 1948, but Leeds needed more electricity than this power station could supply, so Skelton B was built between 1960 and 1962. This time Arthur had more responsibility. His job was to create the structure needed for the conveyor belt to transport the coal to the power station. "They gave me the drawings and told me to get building. I'll never forget this. It was quite a funny experience. They put me through the mill."

Typically, Arthur calls a funny experience what others might have made into quite a big issue. He could see that nearby there was a crew doing the same job as him, but with three joiners and three labourers, whereas he was alone with one labourer. "I think they wanted to test me out. And I came out quite good – I was producing the same amount with just one labourer!"

Yet again, his boss, a man named Tony Crossfield, took a liking to him. "He had a lot of confidence in me. He gave me a lot of technical stuff to do and a lot of responsibility. I liked that," Arthur said. He had an Irish friend called Pat who took him to work in his car each day. But this 'friend' pulled a dirty trick on him. The steel work was coming up wrongly installed in the concrete and Pat blamed Arthur for the mistake. But Tony Crossfield said it cannot be Arthur's fault – "Arthur's work is never wrong". Pat eventually admitted that he had got the measurements wrong and Arthur was in the clear. "Pat had messed me up. We were no longer friends."

I wanted to know why Arthur thought Pat had done this. I wondered if he would think that Pat was in some way racist, despite the lift to work. But Arthur said he didn't know – "Maybe he was jealous?" Sociological research around this time throws some light on this issue. A 1960 book called *Newcomers* by Ruth Glass and Harry Pollins concluded that white people were much more concerned about having a Black person living near them than they were about working alongside them. Research by K L Little just after the 1939-45 war ended concluded that around 60 per cent of middle class white English people 'specifically refused to take a coloured person into their homes'. We can conclude that many whites would work alongside Black people, but wouldn't take them into their private lives. Pat seemed friendly enough. He got along with him at work, even giving him a lift, but when things went wrong for him, Pat would try and dump the blame on Arthur. He was no real friend.

As we saw above, there was racism in the workplace, but some employers were more positive. Ron Ramdin quoted a manager reported in *Newcomers* saying: 'Well, definitely, there's some good working men amongst them ... and I've got some good working men now'. Ramdin cited a 1959 survey of 20 managers in Willesden, London, who all said there were no serious difficulties in employing Black workers. Arthur's boss Tony Crossfield must have thought the same. He said to Arthur: "I don't understand exactly what's happened [with Pat] but I know you know what you're f***ing doing!" The boss remaining supportive, despite the significant cost to the company of Pat's mistake, meant a lot to Arthur. But this incident was one of the reasons why he decided to move on, and he joined another huge construction company, Wimpey, in about 1966.

The post-war surge in house-building was still going on and, thanks to government subsidies, Wimpey were building multi-storey flats on a site between Leeds and its neighbour Bradford. (In the 1960s, half a million flats were built in London alone.) The job was to build the partitions and install the doors in each room in each flat. Because of his skills, Arthur was the highest paid person on the job and he was pleased to see his wage going up.

"I got along fine with most people. Some of them weren't very friendly but we had a laugh." He was particularly amused by an Irish guy who was doing some labouring for him. "He used to tell us the fun he'd had when he was a postman. In one house a dog bit his hand through the letter box." Everyone thought this misfortune was hilarious and they laughed even more when he said he'd made a claim for compensation for his injury and the

New housing in Ebor Gardens, Leeds, built by Wimpey, opened in July 1960

house owner counter-sued him for putting his hand through the door in the first place.

His memory is hazy on the dates, but he went back to Kier for a while because they searched him out for a job. Keir had the contract to build some new schools in Cookridge (in north Leeds). This period didn't go so well. "There was an engineer doing the laying out but he wasn't up to scratch. He didn't know what he was doing and I had to do his work for him." There was insufficient information in the drawings they were being given to do the job properly. A new team was brought in. Arthur saw that a man who had previously been under him was now in charge and being paid more. "I said f**k it. He can't do the job, but the boss has got promoted and sent to Bradford. But then he'd been sacked because he couldn't do the job without me."

This is where you see Arthur's resilience come into play. "You have to put up with a lot of crap sometimes – it's part and parcel of the system – but I wasn't disillusioned. I just would not allow it to get me down." He weighed up whether or not the problem was racism and his conclusion was that he got unfairly treated sometimes but it wasn't necessarily because he was Black – "Bosses are often unfair, to everyone. You get some racial shit sometimes but it wasn't a big thing."

Some Black people Arthur knew had some very bad experiences at work. Quite a few just accepted it and kept quiet. But some others didn't – "They got the bull by the horns and sorted their differences out, verbally and physically". Arthur gave the example of Mr Mills, who used to work nights in a factory. He was the type of man who co-operated with all the other workers and was always helping them out. He became such good friends with one of his white colleagues that this man would come to Mr Mills' house. "He'd even help himself in their kitchen, that's how good mates they were." There was an informal rule in the factory that if work was slack people would take turns to go off for a quick sleep. One night Mr Mills took his turn to have a quick sleep in a corner. For some reason, this so-called mate called the boss and showed him the sleeping man, to get him into trouble. Mr Mills (like Arthur's experience with Pat) had an odd kind of friend.

Arthur joined the building workers' union (UCATT, now Unite) and later he joined the union for building managers. Predictably, he was an activist for the workers' rights. He recalled an incident in Bradford. The boss in the warehouse was very rude and disrespectful to the workers. "We had a meeting to decide whether to strike. I had a lot to say about what we should do to the boss," Arthur laughed.

In Arthur's commitment to workers' rights there is a link back to the France family's commitment to Methodism. While John Wesley, Methodism's founder, was a stout support of his monarch and of loyalty to the state, EP Thompson has argued that early Methodism shaped 'a democratic spirit' among the people. Its preachers formed 'self-governing bodies' which fed directly into the emerging working class movement. Famously, Dorset's Tolpuddle Martyrs were led by a Methodist lay-preacher named George Loveless. 800,000 people signed a petition supporting Loveless and his five associates when they were sentenced to transportation in 1834 for forming a secret association of agricultural labourers – this massive protest resulted in the Tolpuddle workers being pardoned in 1836.

Arthur's fighting spirit thus has deep roots. But by no means all workers shared his radicalism. Some of his 'friends' among the workers at Kier reported what Arthur had said about their boss. The boss came back to Arthur with some threatening remarks. "I said to him you can do what you like, I don't need your f***ing job." Black guys at work such as Conway Walwyn and John Walters at Wimpey's were worried because he was so outspoken – they thought he might make things worse for them. "They wanted to keep their heads down, earn their wage and go home." Arthur on the other hand wanted much more. He urged everyone to get organised. "People don't realise the power of politics," he said. (That's the topic of the next chapter.)

There were times when racism against Arthur did come into play. "Sometimes I did have a hard time getting jobs because I was Black. Racism comes in so many different forms." For example, he got a knock-back from Leeds city council. When preparations were being made for building Leeds's inner ring road the city council's planning department needed a programme controller. This was a huge project, initially drawn up in 1955, but in 1963 there was a change of thinking: the ring road was to be an inner-city motorway, but the plans hadn't been substantially changed. They had already demolished 365 houses and 174 other structures to make way for this major development, in which the road was to go under the city. The first three stages of the project would start in 1963 and would be completed in the next decade (and stage seven was only finished in 2008).

Arthur applied for the job of programme controller and at the interview the council's planners showed him their drawings and asked him what he thought. "I'm Black Power, and I'm not begging for nothing. There were five of them around the table. I said your system is out-dated and I can update it for you." No one in power likes being told they are incompetent. White men are going to take it worse when their helpful informant is a Black man. "I knew they wouldn't employ me from the way they reacted."

At Wimpey he met quite a few other racist incidents. He was taking a course at the Polytechnic (see Chapter 4) and he asked for time off under Wimpey's in-service training scheme, but he was turned down. "And I wanted more technical jobs in the office but they wouldn't give them to me either, even though my tutor at the Poly gave me a positive recommendation."

He was invited for an interview by the British Air Corporation who had him in mind for the role of technical adviser in their division in Saudi Arabia. "I fell out with the interviewer when he made derogatory remarks about the Arabs. 'How dare you say that?' I said. 'You are getting a well paid job

off the back of the Arabs you are talking about. I bet you'll say
the same about me after this interview'." He walked out. As we
will see in the next chapter, Arthur's increasing political
awareness was already being expressed at work.

Working in Germany

By this time Arthur needed a change. His talents were no longer
being properly recognised and the racism he was experiencing
was beginning to get him down. The statistics on Black people's
employment in Britain in the 1970s indicate how heavily the dice
were loaded against people like Arthur. A 1976 study quoted by
Ron Ramdin showed that 42 per cent of Black male workers
were in semi- or unskilled jobs, compared with 18 per cent for
white workers. A more reassuring figure was that another 45
per cent of Black men were in skilled manual jobs, compared
with 42 per cent for white men. But a 1977 study showed that
there was 'considerable discrimination' in promotion prospects
for Black people. Shockingly, only 31 per cent of ethnic minority
men with degree level qualifications were in professional or
managerial jobs (whereas 79 per cent of degree level whites were
in such positions).

Nevertheless, in 1975 Arthur was contacted by the Guibo
construction company. It was headed by its chief architect,
George Henry. They wanted him to apply for a very important
role: to be their contract manager for their construction projects
in the Caribbean. He got the job, to be based in Guyana.

Politics and friendships were to intervene in Arthur's life
once more. Before the job started, he decided to go and see the
Trinidadian friends he had made in Leeds on his way to see his
family in Nevis. His pals in Trinidad were most upset that he was
considering a job in Guyana – surely he should be coming to work
in Trinidad instead? The people at Guibo were quite upset when
he turned them down. They had liked the fact he was so open-
minded and had a 'big picture' of the Caribbean – not hampered
by particular loyalties to any single island.

When he got back to England he found a letter from the German construction company Hochtief. (Today, this is one of the world's largest construction companies.) The project they wanted him for was building a nuclear reactor. Arthur has no idea who had recommended him to Hochtief – presumably one of their contacts at Wimpey or Kier.

He decided to take up their offer. "My good friends Calvin Beech and George Archibald were amazed. They said: 'You preaching Black Power and you going to work for a country renowned for its racism!'" Of course he remembered what he had learned at school about the way British prisoners-of-war had been treated and about the genocide of the Jews, but he thought "Why not give them a chance?" His friends took him to the station to see him off. When he arrived in Arnhem he heard what sounded just like the harsh voices he had heard in broadcasts from the war. "Oh no! Hitler is still alive!" was his first thought.

Straight away he went to College for night school classes in German. It wasn't easy, but "I thought if a man can spend ten years in jail I can stick this out." His boss, Manfred Bockhol from the Black Forest area "seemed to take a liking to me. My work discipline fitted very well with the Germans'." Herr Bockhol spoke a little English and younger workers could speak some English too.

Arthur's job as an engineer was to supervise the building of the foundational structures of the nuclear reactor. In contrast to his experience in England, "Bockhol promoted me – he had a lot of confidence in me." There was a dispute on one of the jobs with a Dutch man who was trying to discredit Arthur, but the boss said Arthur was the best man, and supported him.

Arthur was amused that his project manager at Hoctief was called Herr (Mr) Dryer. The joke 'hair dryer' always came to mind. Arthur was granted residential status in Germany but he had met Tattra, and their relationship was developing. "She had become one of our crowd, and we kept in touch by phone while

I was in Germany." His employer gave him a week off every 28 days, so he would return to Leeds, and Tattra would come to see him from her hospital in Grassington.

They decided to get married. "It's funny, people didn't expect me to settle down – 'Is it for real?' they said." His sister Hyacinth and other siblings wanted him to get a proper home, and all his friends were getting married. Instead of having an organ play for the wedding in Roscoe Methodist Church, the music came from Paradise Steel Band. For the reception, Bear brought his steel band over from Manchester.

When their daughter Mahalia was born Arthur realised that he did not want to settle in Germany. It was a well-paid job and he was able to claim his expenses to and from Germany on his tax return so he felt well off, for once. But the pull of Tattra, Mahalia and Leeds meant that he wasn't going to stay there.

"What I liked about the work in Germany was that they respected me for my ability – they weren't bothered by the colour of my skin. It was less racist than England." And he liked Mr Hair Dryer too. He thought Dryer was right when he said:

Arthur and Tattra outside Roscoe Methodist church,
21st August 1976. Photo courtesy Tattra France

"Arthur, you and me are the happiest of men – because we are both a little bit crazy."

Nevertheless, he left that job in 1982. He had had enough of the travelling back and forth. And the company was putting him under pressure to stay permanently in Germany – the pressure included three months paid leave in England to encourage him to settle in Germany. But they didn't get their way. As we saw in the previous chapter, back in England he quickly landed the teaching job at Technorth.

References in this chapter

Tom Baistow, 'What Does Brotherhood Mean to You?' (Part Four of an enquiry), *News Chronicle*, 11.10.1956. The *News Chronicle* supported the Liberal Party, but was merged with the *Daily Mail* in 1960.

Beryl Gilroy, *Black Teacher*, London: Faber & Faber, 2021. (First published by Cassel & Co., 1976.)

Clare Griffiths, 'From "Dorchester Labourers" to "Tolpuddle Martyrs": Celebrating Radicalism in the English Countryside', in Quentin Outram and Keith Laybourn (eds.), *Secular Martyrdom in Britain and Ireland*, Palgrave-Macmillan, 2018.

Ron Ramdin, *The Making of the Black Working Class in Britain*, Aldershot: Wildwood House Ltd, 1987

Stephanie Snow and Emma Jones, 'Immigration and the National Health Service: putting history to the forefront', *History and Policy*, 8.3.2001. Available at http://www.historyandpolicy.org/policy-papers/papers/immigration-and-the-national-health-service-putting-history-to-the-forefron Accessed 8.4.2020.

E P Thompson, *The Making of the English Working Class*, Harmondsworth: Pelican Books, 1968.

Chapter 6

A POLITICAL LIFE

E mancipation is Arthur France's watchword. This chapter is about his awakening to the necessity for political action, and he usually reserves Emancipation for his discourse on carnival, so that is the title of Chapter 8. But this chapter is also about emancipation, because 'freedom' is a fundamental goal of politics.

When you ring Arthur and ask him how he is, he'll normally say "Strugglin'". He will elaborate with "Too many people kicking my arse." But he'll soon turn to his favourite topic: how bad a job the world's leaders are doing, how many ordinary people are suffering, and what we need to do to make fundamental changes. Something on TV or in the newspaper will start him off. During the Black Lives Matter upsurges, he would switch from tears to outrage.

Politics, for Arthur, is a continual struggle for emancipation and social justice. That struggle is endless. Too many – Black people and white – have lost sight of its meaning and its purpose. Of course, racial justice is very close to his heart, but he is equally passionate about justice for all those, whatever their skin colour, who suffer. People of colour – to use the American term – endure the twin yokes of economic exploitation and racial oppression, but Arthur also has compassion for those white people who are held in their place by the structures of capitalism. If this chapter concentrates on Black struggle it is because Arthur follows a basic principle: you start your politics from your own experience, and then you broaden it outwards. His starting point, therefore, is racism and its consequences. This chapter sets out the context of racial oppression in St Kitts and Nevis and in England that helped make Arthur who he is.

St Kitts and Nevis

Arthur France's political awakening began at home, in Nevis and in St Kitts. One of the founders of radical politics and arts in Britain, the late John La Rose, who was born in Trinidad but lived most of his life in London, made the important point that the Black people who arrived in England in the post-1945 period brought their politics with them. The people who arrived in England from the Caribbean didn't invent their politics in the UK – they, and their parents, had struggled against white colonial rule for years and years back home: that's where they formed their political ideas and identities.

The Black people of St Kitts and Nevis had a proud history of political struggle against slavery and Imperial domination (as explained in the Appendix to this book). John La Rose summed up is views about that history in the evocative phrase: 'We did not come alive in Britain'. Like John La Rose and the other pioneers of radical Black British politics, Arthur brought with him to England his commitments to equality, human rights and justice that were formed in St Kitts and Nevis.

Arthur's father Ebenezer was a life-long member of the St Kitts and Nevis Labour Party. His brother, Joseph, was the backbone of that party, and for Arthur and his family politics were always very close to home. From childhood, Arthur was attached to his uncle – who was eventually knighted for his political and personal service to his country. "Sir Joseph had a special liking for me," and Sir Joseph went out of his way to talk to Arthur, ask him questions and, from the age of about 14 onwards, explain complex political matters to him.

All the big issues were on the agenda, and trade union rights for workers were top of the list. We saw in Chapter 5 that Arthur always joined his trade union in England and was outspoken on issues of fairness in the workplace. "Sir Joseph believed that the system itself was bad, setting landowners against workers." The really big landowners were white, but brown people also owned some land, and were not always well disposed to their workers, so workers' rights were clearly a class issue, with racial codes operating alongside.

One structural problem that put Arthur's back up was the banks on Nevis and St Kitts. They were owned by white people but staffed by some people of African descent and the bank managers were unwilling to lend money to most Black people. To build a house, for instance, a family needed cash on credit to buy the materials they needed. If their ambition was to start their own business and improve their family life, the loan they required would most likely be denied.

A particularly graphic example was when Arthur's boss John Howells (whom we met in Chapter 2) wanted to purchase Pinney's Estate when it came up for sale in the 1950s. (The historical significance of Pinney's coconut plantation is explained in the Appendix.) Part of this estate is where The Four Seasons Hotel now stands, close to Charlestown. The transformation of Pinney's into the Four Seasons tells us a great deal about how capitalism is transforming Nevis today.

The Four Seasons hotel chain majority shareholder today is the Microsoft billionaire Bill Gates. Gates and a fellow-billionaire (from Saudi Arabia) bought the hotel chain in 2007 for $3.8 billion, and they acquired the Four Seasons on Nevis in 2016. The design of its two-year make-over was inspired by the colonial architecture of the island and included doubling the length of its dock to meet the mooring needs of the super yachts owned by fellow multi-millionaires. The cost of the purchase and the re-design has not been disclosed. If the bank had been willing to lend the money to the Black businessman John Howells, with his thriving construction business, the recent history of Nevis might have been quite different. Sir Joseph explained this systematic unfairness to Arthur as the system's way of "Keeping down the little man."

Prudence France, Sir Joseph's daughter, spoke to me in 2017 with great pride about her father and his work. Born in 1907, he was the last child of Mary and Thomas France of Mount Lily, Nevis. Their four sons were Ebenezer (Arthur's dad), Nathan, Benjamin and Joseph. (They had one sister, too, from her mother's first marriage.) Prudence explained that Black people were able to obtain land on Nevis because of an exodus of white settlers hundreds of years ago. Three of the France boys became adept farmers, but Thomas was keen that Joseph did not follow suit. Thomas himself was something of a prodigy on the church organ, and all the children were taught to play.

At the age of 13, Joseph was sent to St Kitts by his father so that he could improve his education. He studied alongside white people at Mr Sprott's night school while working as a cleaner. He also got a job as a messenger in Matthew Sebastian's printing company. (Matthew's son, Sir Cuthbert Montraville Sebastian, was the Governor General of St Kitts and Nevis from 1996 to 2013. Sir Cuthbert progressed from pupil-teacher, to pharmacist, to obstetrician-gynaecologist, having trained at Dundee Royal Infirmary in Scotland.)

At Sebastian's company, Joseph progressed to being head printer. Having printed the *Union Messenger*, he became its editor, and then edited its successor, *The Labour Spokesman*. Both papers exposed the injustices of the plantation system and urged working people to fight for their rights. In her profile of this distinguished man, Prudence France wrote:

[Joseph] France never lost his focus – that of pulling people out of slums and poverty ... [He] always believed that education was required to elevate the living standards of his people ... [His] greatest satisfaction and rewards came from witnessing the working class – his people – take their place in the social strata, emerging from the throes of poverty to hold worthwhile positions in the land of their birth.

Ms France explained that Mathew Sebastian was a powerful advocate of the rights of working-class people and his print-shop was the place where the organisers held their meetings. In the 1930s it was illegal to form a trade union, so they established a Benevolent Society instead. Conditions for working people were deplorable and health care was non-existent. They had no real educational opportunities, because an earlier governor had decided that too much education would make Black people 'swell headed'. Schools were set up by a few churches, which made all the difference to some of the descendants of the African slaves. The St Kitts United Benevolent Society took up all these issues and organised demonstrations on the streets of Basseterre.

Washington Archibald has vividly described ordinary people's living conditions in a speech to school students in St Kitts. He told these well-turned out youngsters with their cell-phones turned off about the conditions that sparked 'The Buckley's Affair' protests in 1935:

Their ancestors lived in ghauts [ravines] like snails and hogs. When there was an abundance of rain, the rushing waters from the mountains used to take their animals and their trash houses to the sea. They lived in trash houses, made from the cane stalks which the estates also fed to their cattle. The floors were dirt, the furniture was make-shift. Everything was in one, the bedroom and the living room. Eating was outside, sitting on a stone. Bathing was in the open. Defecating was in the nearby canefield. No, this was not a primitive age of basic living. This kind of living was reserved especially for Black people. The white and brown people lived in conspicuous luxury. Their houses were huge, with upstairs and downstairs, kitchens and closets. They had cooks, butlers, maids, washer women, gardeners. Some of them had chauffeurs to drive their vehicles and run their errands.

Nigel Boland's research on the economic situation of Black workers in the Caribbean at this time has been summarised as follows: 'The inability of most households to meet the most basic of financial needs ensured that malnutrition and substandard living conditions created unbearable conditions'. These are the circumstances that fuel rebellion by the workers. Washington Archibald named Matthew Sebastian and James A Nathan as leaders of the Buckley's revolt, and praised a man named Thomas Manchester for breaking with the other 'brown people' who, Archibald wrote, normally sided with the whites in oppressing the Black workers.

From 1934 Sebastian and Nathan had been arguing for wage increases for the St Kitts sugar workers, finally calling a strike for 28th January 1935. They wanted 3 pennies per ton of cane harvested, 1 penny more than the manager, Mr E D B Dobridge was offering. This would bring the workers back to the purchasing power they had in 1932. (The 'Historic St Kitts' website entry for Buckley's strike says they demanded 1 shilling (12 pennies) a ton. Whatever the exact amount, their demand was refused.)

James Sutton, who was a teacher at Cayon School at the time, has provided a lively account of how this unfolded:

Most labourers in the countryside, although dissatisfied, were ready to start [the annual cane cutting]. But a group of labourers on Buckleys and West Farm Estates, near Basseterre, were not ready. They walked up to the manager of Buckleys Estate, Mr Dobridge, and demanded higher wages to cut the canes. When they were refused, they declared "We strike! An' we will see that every estate on St Kitts stop wok today!"

They then took up sticks, stones, machetes and any weapon they could lay their hands on, marched to the cane field at Buckleys and compelled those who were willing to work, to quit work and join them. Those who refused were beaten. So began the 1935 Riot in St Kitts ...

Someone in the school shouted "De Riot a come!" ... in a minute the school was empty. Teachers and pupils alike could not miss this once-in-a-lifetime event. There were the rioters – hundreds of them, all in working clothes, bare footed, with sticks, bills [metal blades for cutting cane] and other weapons in their hands shouting: "We strike for higher wages! Everbody mus' stap wok today!" Someone gave an occasional blow on a conch shell, between their shouts. But they all seemed fairly orderly as they made their way across Dunn's Cottage, heading for Brighton's Estate, where, according to later reports, there was a hostile confrontation between them and Mr George Yearwood, the manager.

When a crowd of about 500 people (another report says 'a large crowd') assembled outside his premises on the Buckley's Estate at 3pm on 29th January, Dobridge shot and wounded some of them. The Historic St Kitts website reports that:

Magistrate Bell went into Basseterre and returned with Rev. Williams of the Moravian Church, Thomas Manchester and Victor John of the Workers League and Clement Malone, a member of the Executive Council. The crowd listened to Manchester's plea for order and many left with him but a significant number stayed behind.

Between 6 and 7pm the Defence Force Reserve, led by Geoffrey Earl Boon, attempted to disperse the crown, and then killed three men (Joseph Samuel, James Archibald and John Allen) and wounded eight others. By 9.30pm 'all was quiet'. The leaders were subsequently put through the courts and sentenced to jail.

Margaret Stevens' research revealed the importance of educational work in the period leading up to the demonstrations at Buckley's Estate. But this work did not take place in the colonial schools. The International Trade Union Committee of Negro Workers (based in Harlem, New York) had circulated leaflets condemning the sugar workers' wage reductions, and the US Consul reported that 'communist propaganda' that had previously been ignored by St Kitts sugar workers was now being taken up. 'A gradual but distinct change in the attitude of the negro population toward the white man in Bridgetown' (in Barbados) was simultaneously noted by the American Consul as communist ideology was spread across the Caribbean. James Sutton's first-hand portrait reinforced the research mentioned above: Black Caribbean people 'were suffering from low wages, poor housing, malnutrition, insanitary conditions, poor education facilities, and limited higher education opportunities'. They weren't going to take it anymore.

Margaret Stevens reported that the US Consul drew special attention to the work of the St Kitts-Nevis Labor Defense Committee based in Harlem, publicised in the *Negro Worker* newspaper. Its September 1935 issue lambasted the St Kitts' Chief Justice Sir James Rac's claim that the killing of Samuel, Archibald and Allen at Buckley's Estate was justified – Rac had said they had to be shot, otherwise the plantation owners' property might have been destroyed. 'Shoot first and find out later' was the St Kitts' government's policy, said the *Negro Worker*. The Consul claimed these radical ideas were 'straws in the wind', but Black people's protests during this period were very real, more like a hurricane than a breeze blowing through the straw. As Margaret Stevens put it: 'Seemingly by osmosis, the wave of rebellion on the islands spread from St Kitts into St Vincent', resulting in communism being banned on that island.

These and disturbances in other parts of the Caribbean (referred to in the Appendix) led to an enquiry into conditions in the British Caribbean islands where disturbances had taken place, led by Walter Guinness (his aristocratic title was Baron Moyne). The enquiry started in Jamaica in November 1938. The Report by the West India Commission (known as the Moyne Report) urged immediate health and education initiatives and subsidies to the sugar manufacturers to stave off the impending collapse of the economy.

Kelvin Singh has pointed out that the Report was scorned by Black radicals and activists because it did not address the underlying structural problems of the colonial economy, nor the lack of freedom, nor did it advocate comprehensive social reform. But Washington Archibald has argued that the Moyne Report led to the legalisation of trade unions and political parties – Black people were then able to vote in elections for their own leaders. Reform, not revolution, after all, is all that a government report is going to suggest.

These recommendations were so unpalatable to most whites that only a summary of the Moyne Report was published in 1940; the full report did not appear until 1945. K L Little reported Moyne's words for the Royal Empire Society's meeting in London in 1941: 'If we are fighting for liberty we cannot set bounds to the advance of other races. We must avoid any reproach that, when we blame Hitler for his poisonous doctrine of the Herrenvolk [Master Race], we have a similar doctrine lurking in our own hearts'. While Hitler's Aryan supremacist ideas were largely quelled in the post-war period, 'bounds' clearly did remain on the advance of people with black and brown skins.

Black workers' struggles for better wages and liberty did not end with the Moyne Report. Hansard, the British Parliament's record of its proceedings, has an entry in 1948, in which Mr Mayhew, the Minister of State for the Colonies, answered a question from John Rankin, the Labour and Co-

Operative MP for Glasgow Tradeston, about a recent strike by sugar workers in St Kitts. Mr Mayhew said it had ended on 9th April 1948 with an agreement to go into arbitration. Rankin's next comment indicates not only that sugar was still providing huge profits for some, but also that the miserable wages offered to the workers impelled their militancy:

Will my Honourable Friend keep in mind that industrial conditions there [in St Kitts] have been greatly inflamed by the fact that last year 1,000 million dollars of profit were made from sugar and cotton while estate workers were getting a wage of £41 5s a year [£1,500 in 2020's British money], and that if these conditions were altered, we should not need more police to keep the peace?

The Minister would say no more than to offer him a copy of the forthcoming Commission of Enquiry into the strike. That was hardly likely to stifle the Black workers' sense of grievance.

In the 1940s, political action on St Kitts-Nevis was led by Robert Llewellyn Bradshaw. Bradshaw, son of a domestic servant and a blacksmith, was a 16-year-old apprentice at the St Kitts sugar factory in 1932, and he became a clerk for the St Kitts and Nevis Trades and Labour Union in 1940 after participating in the 1935 strike. In 1944 he became president of the union. (There's more on Bradshaw in the Appendix.)

Arthur saw as a young man how effective the union could be – it was powerful "Because everyone joined up." It organised a 13 week strike in the mid-1950s against the owners of the St Kitts sugar factory and the remaining sugar plantations. Arthur's close friend Calvin Beech was among those organising that strike. After that strike the owners responded by replacing the oxen and their drivers with tractors to reduce the workforce and dissuade the remainder from striking again. Arthur could see the point: tractors can't strike. The bosses would do whatever it took to keep the workers down.

All this militancy was highly influential on Arthur. He could see how hard the men in the fields worked and how badly they were treated; all this made more difficult by the fact that the work was seasonal, so they couldn't earn a full year's wage to support their families properly. On St Kitts the land was mainly owned by whites, but on Nevis there were many Black landowners too, so there was less protest there, but the underlying inequalities remained visible.

Arthur remembered his father's kindness to the less fortunate on Nevis, but, on the question about what to do to remedy the situation, Arthur was more strongly influenced by uncle Joseph, who took the radical view that systematic change was needed, not just kindness. Arthur's values and his radical politics were shaped in Nevis and St Kitts, and he brought this knowledge with him to England (just as John La Rose and the other Caribbean-born comrades had done).

England: the Bad Mother's children go 'n****r-hunting'

Within a year of Arthur's arrival in England, two portentous events took place. Peter Fryer has described them as 'race riots'. In Nottingham in 1958, there were about 2,500 West Indians and 600 Asians, out of a population of 310,000. Thus, 1 per cent of its population was 'coloured', to use the antiquated term of that era. From 1956 onwards there had been a steady increase in the attacks by whites on this small number of Caribbean people and South Asians who were beginning to settle in the city.

On 23rd August 1958, Black and white people fought each other in the St Ann's area, north of Nottingham city centre. The local press reported a Black miner being mobbed and told get back to his own country; there were claims that 'coloured people' should be banned from the pubs and subjected to a curfew. Both the local Labour and Conservative MPs called for a ban on further immigration and a law permitting deportation. This evidence of racism within the Labour Party, the party that

Thousands of racist whites attacked Notting Hill's
Caribbean citizens in the summer of 1956

claimed to stand for the rights of working people everywhere,
was significant.

The arrival of 35 national press hounds sensationalising the
fights on 23rd August led to thousands of racist whites invading
St Ann's on 30th August shouting 'Let's get the blacks' and 'Let's
lynch them'. ('blacks' was the term of abuse at that time;
'coloured' was the term used by people trying to be polite.) But
Black people wisely stayed home – so a journalist staged a mock
battle, resulting in 24 arrests. A few days later the homes of some
West Indians had their windows shattered and one man was
stabbed in the back. At this point the local Labour Party branch
said that Black people were being scapegoated, indicating that
some in the Labour Party were more progressive than their MP.

There were similar events in London, but even more serious.
There had been a petrol bomb attack on a Black family's house
in Camden Town in 1954, and by 1958 racist attacks, stimulated
by Nazi propaganda, 'were a commonplace of black life in
London', as Peter Fryer put it. In July, five white youths wrecked
a Caribbean café in Shepherd's Bush. On 17th August a white
crowd smashed the windows of a Black people's rooming house
in Shepherd's Bush. A few days later, six West Indians were
badly injured as white youths went 'nigger-hunting', actually
using the chilling phrase of America's Ku Klux Klan. Nine white
youths were later sentenced to four years in jail by a Judge who
said that everyone, regardless of their colour, had the right 'to
walk through our streets with their heads erect and free from

fear'. A modicum of justice was seen to be done. Much more would be needed.

By the end of August, brawls were taking place all over north Kensington (often referred to as Notting Hill), petrol bombs were thrown into Black people's homes, and a Jamaican was shot in the leg. An African student was given shelter in a greengrocer's shop from a mob shouting 'Lynch him'. There was sensationalist reporting, and occasional more sympathetic background reports, such as one in the *Manchester Guardian* which included this quote: 'A black man's treated worse than a dog in this country. They watch you wherever you go. You daren't go out in the evening – it's a prison, this country'. Others said they were on the verge of going home.

Edward Pilkington described Majbritt Morrison's encounter with white youths on 30th August 1958. 'Nigger-lover! Kill her!' they jeered as they jostled her on her way home. Majbritt was a Swedish woman married to Raymond Robinson, a Jamaican. Colin Grant quoted Colin Jordan, neo-Nazi leader of the White Defence League, active during these riots, showing the peculiar sexual/social fear underlying this layer of white racism: 'There are many immediate evils of the coloured invasion ... But in our opinion the most important is the long-term one of mass inter-breeding ... that must ultimately lead to a mulatto Britain ... that must mean the downfall of civilisation in this country'. Colin Jordan led a succession of Nazi organisations in Britain, one of which was called the White Nationalist Party, right up to his death in Yorkshire in 2009. (His standing in fascist circles fell somewhat when he was arrested in 1975 for stealing three pairs of women's knickers from Tesco in Leamington Spa.)

Hostility to miscegenation was the root of Enoch Powell's antagonism to 'New Commonwealth' migration. In addition, Aryan supremacist ideas still lurked in Britain, despite Hitler's defeat and the exposure of his extermination of an estimated six million Jewish people. The result has been periods of murderous violence against Black people in Britain. In her autobiography, quoted by John Williams, Majbritt wrote that her house was petrol-bombed shortly after she was called a 'nigger-lover'. That's a measure of the ferocity of this fear that Black and white people might love each other. While the crowd went on the rampage, the police escorted West Indians out of Notting Dale, averting further trouble that night.

About 100 whites, armed with sticks, iron bars and knives, gathered the following night. 300 more joined them, but local Black people stayed indoors, so the whites turned on the police, whom they accused of protecting the Black people. Serious rioting broke out on 1st September. The NLP, a Nazi organisation, circulated a leaflet that said 'Your country is steadily being taken over by a triumphant alien'. Its leader repeated Colin Jordan's fear: 'We will be a nation of half-castes', anticipating Enoch Powell's infamous 'rivers of blood' speech ten years later.

Another leaflet, from the British Union Movement, a Nazi organisation led by Sir Oswald Mosely, who had been interned during the war, said 'Take Action now, Protect your jobs. Stop coloured immigration. Houses for white people – not coloured immigrants'. One of its leaders whipped up a crowd of 700 people, from all over London, saying Notting Hill had been turned into a brothel, and the mob rushed off shouting 'Kill the niggers'. They made random attacks and wrecked buildings, as described by Fryer. For the next two days and nights, Black people stayed at home.

But, as Edward Pilkington has described, the West Indians were not going to let this go on much longer. On the third day of the attacks, Caribbean people met at the Calypso Club in the centre of Notting Hill. Baron Baker, Frances Ezzrecco, Frank Critchlow, a defendant in 1971 at the famous Mangrove Trial, and Michael de Freitas (more on him later) were among those who met to plan their response. De Freitas wrote in his autobiography that he said this at the meeting: 'We don't want committees and representatives. What we need is to get a few pieces of iron and a bit of organisation so that tonight when they come in here we can defend ourselves'.

That night, 300 West Indians crammed themselves into two houses, armed with sticks, knives, meat cleavers and Molotov cocktails. Baron Baker told Pilkington: 'We were absolutely terrified' as the white crowds gathered in the street outside. 'But we had decided to go down fighting ... When they started screaming "Let's burn the niggers out", that's when we hit'. Other local West Indians then joined the counter-attack.

When a tall Black woman ran out of her burning house with an axe in her hand shouting 'I'll murder you for this', the whites turned and ran. More Jamaicans arrived from Brixton and the police realised that a 'full-blooded racial war' was imminent; they sent reinforcements and the riot was quelled. Eight West Indians were charged with affray. The following night, as whites circulated shouting 'We want a nigger', 49 of them were arrested.

The shock for Black people caused by these tumultuous attacks was enormous. 4,500 West Indians packed their bags and went home in 1959 (usually only about 150 left the UK each year). But Baron Baker stayed. He told Pilkington: 'I was determined to stay to the bitter or sweet end. For me it would have been a terrible blow, having come here [from Jamaica] to fight in the war, to have the natives kick us out. We were all prepared to challenge it, which we did'. He said, however, that his image of Britain as the Mother Country 'vanished overnight'.

It's surprising how little scholarship there is on this extraordinarily important turning point in post-1945 Black British history. Kennetta Hammond Perry is an exception. In an excellent analysis of this period, she included the international press responses to these white riots. While some Americans gloated that this racist violence showed that the Brits had no right to claim the high ground when discussing racism and segregation in the USA, in the Caribbean and South Asia there was heated discussion about what this meant for their idealisation of the 'Mother Country'. As Perry pointed out 'the mystique of British anti-racism' and the 'ostensibly racially progressive virtues of British liberalism' had been punctured. She quoted the Jamaican Premier Norman Manley as saying, in September 1958: 'I am satisfied that the great majority of the English people are not against West Indians, only a narrow section of the community. No doubt this is agitated by the 'Keep Britain White' Fascist movement.' He was right about the fascists, but Black British people did not feel that the 'great majority' were on their side.

There was one good outcome from these terrifying days. Frank Critchlow said it brought all the West Indians from the different islands together – 'We had all suffered the riots, and we had a lot in common to talk about'. Baron Baker set up the United African-Asian League. Amy Dashwood Garvey (Marcus Garvey's widow) set up The Association for the Advancement of Coloured People. Frances Ezzrecco set up the Coloured People's Progressive Association, with de Freitas as Vice-President – it had 500 members at the end of the year. Claudia Jones, recently deported from the United States because of her radical political activities, had founded the *West Indian Gazette* in 1958. With a circulation of 15,000, she was able to promote these organisations' activities.

A different kind of response came from stars in the world of music. The Grammy award-winning singer Cleo Laine, born in 1927 in Middlesex, England, to a Jamaican father and white mother, told Rick Blackman in 2017 that, in 1958, Britain was far from the multicultural society we know today. She continued:

After the events in Notting Hill that summer we felt we had to respond to the violence and racism that had caused the riots. The best way we knew was through music. My late husband John Dankworth [a celebrated jazz saxophonist] and I were proud of the part we played in SCIF and our attempt to make England a more tolerant society.

SCIF stood for 'Stars Campaign for Interracial Friendship' and it included huge names in British entertainment of that time, such as Lawrence Olivier, Tommy Steele, Tony Hancock, Hephzibah Menuhin, Eamonn Andrews, Lonnie Donnegan and Alma Cogan. The British-Guyanese writer E R Braithwaite was also member (his novel *To Sir, With Love* was published in 1959 and the film, starring Sidney Poitier, came out in 1967). Claudia Jones was highly instrumental in linking SCIF to the emerging radical organisations of Black Londoners listed above.

SCIF's first gig was in the Skiffle Cellar in Soho, with Long John Baldry, a 'very tall white kid who sounded like an old delta bluesman', according to SCIF founder, Fred Dallas. They established the 'Harmony Club' in Notting Hill's Blenheim Crescent – Trinidadian Edric Connor, father of Geraldine Connor who appears in Chapter 8 of this book, was one of the stars at the first event in the club in January 1959. With its positive message of racial harmony and social integration and a bevy of stars, SCIF attracted a great deal of media attention, but the Harmony Club only lasted for six weeks, folding when two of the founders had a serious disagreement. The blues musician Alexis Korner went on to organise SCIF events in other parts of London, but its work fell off in 1960. Historian Eric Hobsbawm later commented that SCIF's 'strength lay in [getting] stories into the press and programmes on to television, and [it] produced newsworthy ideas such as the televised interracial children's Christmas party of 1958'.

Much greater coverage went to lurid details of the riots. Most Black people, recently arrived and still finding their feet, were terrorised. That was the exact purpose of those whites who beat, stabbed, wrecked and bombed the new migrants, aided and abetted by Nazi proponents of White Power. Their shouts were heard by some white people throughout the nation; for Black people there was a deafening roar. Those 300 West Indians who gathered in Notting Hill in 1958 to fight back, set in motion a process of radical, progressive resistance that Arthur France would soon amplify with his enormous energy and charisma.

Cricket is more than a game

It was the shock of conditions in England that drove Arthur to develop his interest in politics. It started with cricket. The West Indies had toured England in 1957 and Arthur told me: "I couldn't believe how they were treated off the pitch". He must have heard reports from his friends in Leeds, since the tour ended before Arthur had arrived. He was told that the crowds and commentators admired the West Indies on the pitch – but, during their Test Match at Headingley, Leeds hotels would not provide accommodation for the team. "They had to go to Harrogate instead." (Harrogate is about 17 miles away from the Headingley stadium.) If that's true, it's odd to find on the web a photo of the signatures of all 19 members of the touring team on the headed notepaper of Leeds's premier hotel, The Queens.

Whatever the facts about the hotel accommodation of the touring West Indian cricketers, it's indisputable that there was racism within cricket. The captain of the West Indies team was a white man, John Goddard. The refusal of the (white) management of West Indian cricket to appoint a Black captain had already been the subject of major disturbances in the MCC tour of the Caribbean in 1953 (and huge protests were repeated in the 1960 tour). These 'explosions', as the Trinidadian Marxist scholar and activist CLR James called them, 'were not in any way directed at the British players ... they were very popular'. Bottles rained onto the pitch because the Black crowds 'felt that for years conscious and indefensible efforts had been made to maintain the exclusion from the West Indies captaincy of men black in skin'.

James went on to give an example of more subtle racial politics in the 1957 tour. At their match in Hastings (against Leg Ames' 11, 31st August to 3rd September), Frank Worrell, the great Bajan batsman and seam bowler, was allowed to captain the team. Worrell had told their Jamaican fast bowler, Roy Gilchrist, that it was bad form to bowl bumpers in 'festival cricket' (as this match was described). Gilchrist, a year later, was expelled from the tour of India by the white captain for refusing to obey his instruction not to bowl bouncers. But, in Hastings, under a Black captain, Gilchrist, 'a notably tempestuous member of a tempestuous breed, fast bowlers ... allowed himself to be driven for five fours in one over' without retaliating with a bouncer.

James explained the class and 'race' dynamics operating here. Frank Worrell was middle-class, a Senator, with an economics degree from Manchester University, and Roy Gilchrist, the 21st child of a rural family, was, in James's description, a 'plebeian'. James explained that, despite the class difference Worrell was able to influence Gilchrist because he, like Gilchrist, was Black. Cricket is not merely a game of bat and ball. For CLR James it is crammed with political and social meaning (explained brilliantly in his book *Beyond a Boundary*).

Arthur France's interest in the politics of cricket developed further when he heard on the grapevine that during the 1957 tour Frank Worrell had told his colleague Everton Weekes (later Sir Everton De Courcy Weekes) who had been born in a wooden shack in Pickwick Gap, Barbados, that "He should kick John Goddard's ass." "You wouldn't think Worrell was a Bajan, he so radical," Arthur said. Arthur was further outraged to hear that, during the MCC's 1959-60 tour of the West Indies, Goddard would tour the islands in the company of the English team, rather than his own.

The improved experience for the West Indies team when they toured England in 1963 was understood by Arthur in terms of the politics, as well as the majesty of the game of cricket. By now, the authorities had learned their lesson: Frank Worrell was captain and Goddard was absent. "The 1963 tour was something else. Cricket was virtually dead in England. The West Indies brought it back to life and the English really appreciated us."

L-R Frank Worrell, Everton Weekes and Clyde Walcott, 1957

At an early match of the tour, Yorkshire played the West
Indies in Middlesbrough, on the 15th to 17th May. The year 1963
was one of the coldest on record for the UK and it was still very
cold in May. (Arthur said it actually snowed during the game.)
The match did not go well. "The Yorkshire team gave us a
thrashing by 111 runs." The *Daily Mirror* said that the West
Indies team (after a very successful tour of Australia) was over-
rated. But, Arthur remembered, "Freddie Truman [Yorkshire
and England's best fast bowler] say don't speak too soon – [the
West Indians are] wearing their overcoats. When sun come out
it will be different."

And sure enough, the tables were soon turned. The West
Indies won three and drew one match – England won only once.
The West Indies delighted the English crowds (they played 31
matches, altogether, covering the whole country) and the *Daily
Mirror* moved cricket to the front page with the headline: "Bring
Them Back". Arthur was rightly proud of this achievement in
reviving the popularity of the sport of cricket in England. But
it was more than a game: this tour showed the world how
important the West Indies, with their well-educated Black
captain and star Black players like Kanhai, Hall and Sobers, had

become. (I remember watching those test matches on TV while revising for my 'O' levels and marvelling at the skills of these Caribbean players.) The success resulted in the rules for tours being changed so that the West Indies could return in 1966, much earlier than the previous rules had allowed. Again, the West Indies, with Gary Sobers as captain, triumphed – winning three, drawing one and losing one – and again the by now larger numbers of West Indians in Britain had a huge surge of pride.

It is not idle to speculate that, if political, civic, cultural and religious leaders in Britain had fully recognised the popularity of these phenomenal Caribbean cricketers across the country – even among the notoriously ethnocentric Yorkshire crowds – they could have used this affection to strongly oppose the undercurrent of white nationalism that had reared its ugly head in Nottingham and Notting Hill. Progressive leadership could, and should, have led the charge for multicultural cohesion and conviviality.

The United Caribbean Association

If cricket energised and politicised Arthur, it was the real, material conditions of life in Leeds that propelled him into action. "In England, Black people were not treated well. We had to do something about it." It wasn't just the people of Arthur's age and above who could see this. Benjamin Zephaniah has described his experience in the early 1960s as a child in Birmingham, where his was the only Black family in the street. From the age of five or six, he wrote, 'I tuned my ear to the language of the people around me, I started to realise that some people were hostile; they used words to express their dislike of us ... I was only small but I sensed in my heart that no one around us was going to defend us'. A bit later, out with a couple of friends, 'If someone gave us racial abuse, we didn't go home and tell our parents, we'd get stuck in and have a fight'.

As Benjamin was learning to fight, Arthur France and his close friends initiated the Leeds United Caribbean Association

(UCA) on the last Sunday in November, 1964, with a plan to make radical change in Black people's lives. Along with Arthur, George Archibald was a prime mover. George had served in the British army until around 1962, and he was he was a joiner by trade. Both Arthur and George had been in the same union, UCATT (the Union of Construction, Allied Trades and Technicians).

Later in the 1960s George was one of the members of the Workers' Education Association class with Dr Christoper Duke that produced the book *Colour and Rehousing,* referred to in Chapter 3. "We could see that the council and its housing policy wasn't right. They had an office up in Headingley, miles away from where we lived in Chapeltown. Mr Harris was in charge. He said Black people couldn't get council houses anywhere else in Leeds – they had to live in rooms in Chapeltown." George and Arthur would talk about this and other injustices, and they decided that there had to be a response.

They called a meeting and 27 people crammed themselves in Arthur's bed-sit at 15 Grange Avenue in Chapeltown. They had invited Cedric Clarke from Nevis, and Stanford and Colly from Jamaica. "I was the youngest one there, but George let me do most of the talking. I said we needed an organisation to speak for us and we had to unite all the Caribbean people in Leeds." George was elected Chairperson, Cedric was the Secretary and Arthur was the Treasurer. Cedric did not turn up at the next meeting. Despite George and Arthur keeping their radical politics fairly quiet, it is likely that Cedric, who was later to become a well-respected Labour Party Councillor in Leeds, felt that the UCA wasn't going to do him any good.

George and Arthur's plans for unity among the various islanders in Leeds had been inspired by the West Indies Federation that was established in 1958. The Federation included Antigua, Barbuda, Barbados, Dominica, Grenada, Jamaica, St Kitts and Nevis, St Vincent and the Grenadines, Trinidad and Tobago, Anguilla, Montserrat, the Cayman

Islands, and the Turks and Caicos Islands. British Honduras and British Guiana held observer status. Arthur explained that Guyana (as it later called itself) was not allowed to join because its leader, Cheddi Jagan (1918-1997), founder of the People's Progressive Party, was a Marxist-Leninist.

Nevertheless, the West Indies Federation held the possibility of providing a large economic bloc with significant political power. Where the British had practised 'divide and rule', it looked like the English-speaking Caribbean, with its population of between three and four million, could offer the lesson that 'unity is strength'. Although it disintegrated in 1962, Arthur was not deterred. "We called our organisation The United Caribbean Association (UCA) because we wanted to continue in the Federation's spirit of unity." When Forbes Burnham, who became the Prime Minister of Guyana, visited Leeds he put his arm around Arthur and told him how happy he was to see that his UCA blazer was sporting the Federation's coat of arms. "We had the best blazers, made by Rawcliffe's, with a proper wire coat of arms, to show how proud we were of the Federation's aims," Arthur explained. He added with a grin that the blazers would make them look the smartest at the UCA dances.

Before the UCA emerged there was the African, Caribbean and Asian Organisation, established by Mrs Eulalie Procope, Mrs Elaine France-Archibald and Mrs Gertude Paul. (Arthur said that none of the South Asians who had settled in Leeds joined.) They organised large dances which Arthur liked to attend, and he didn't want to challenge them, but he was convinced that the West Indians in Leeds had to do much more than socialise.

On the other hand, the UCA needed to raise funds and Arthur's competitive spirit kicked in. "We had to chop the ground from under Mrs Procope an' them." So, while Mrs Procope and Mrs Paul would hold their dances at the impressive Astoria Ballroom on Roundhay Road, the UCA went up several notches and booked the magnificent Leeds Town Hall in the heart of the city. As usual, Arthur used his charm. "We hit it off with the manager by talking cricket." But the booking cost them £72 and they had to pay 30 days in advance. This was a lot of money: the average wage for a manual worker in 1964 was just under £18 per week. For a white collar employee it was £23. "But we scraped our savings together and paid up."

Then came the crucial issue of the music. "Mrs P. hired Prentice's Invaders Steel Band and we had to do better than that." So they invited the Huddersfield-based Trinidad Steel Band, led by Raymond Joseph. On the night they'd booked the Town Hall, Raymond's band was scheduled to play in Harrogate. But Raymond said he really wanted to play for the Leeds West Indians and Mr Lockhead, his agent, agreed to switch the booking.

"We charged 7 shillings single, and 10 shillings a couple, and everyone dressed up in their finest." Raymond played the whole night, for free. "The Trinidad Steel Band was so good that even Prentice had to come to the dance to hear them." With the whole UCA crew behind the dance it was an enormous success, "And we put Mrs P. out of business." Eventually she and Mrs Paul joined the UCA. Arthur said all this with a laugh, but as usual there was a serious side: this was already about the leadership and direction of Caribbean politics in Leeds. The UCA had an inner core. Arthur France, George Archibald, Calvin Beech (all from St Kitts-Nevis), Vernon Baptiste (Trinidad), Tony Lewis (Jamaica) and Salim (Grenada) formulated its policies at UCA House, No 3 Cowper Street, in the heart of Chapeltown.

Calvin Beech had arrived in Leeds from St Kitts in 1965, aged 19. He had a major influence on Arthur's development. In our interview in Basseterre in 2017, Calvin told me he'd been politicised long before he got to England. His great-grandfather was a white man named Rawlins, who, when it was apparent he had had a child with a Black woman, was shipped back to his original home in Scotland. As compensation, Rawlins gave his grandmother some land and animals, and she took the name

Rawlins, too. (You can find more about the Reverend Henry Rawlins and Governor Stedman Rawlins in the Appendix to this book, detailing the history of Nevis and St Kitts.)

Calvin's grandfather was Mr Francis. He was a blacksmith in St Paul's Village near the northern point of St Kitts – "Which meant he had no chance to realise his dream to be a teacher." Instead he went to Basseterre and became a sailor on a schooner bringing oil drums from Trinidad into St Kitts. His grand-dad was also a lay preacher in the Methodist Church.

Calvin's father worked on the docks as a stevedore, but like so many far-sighted people of these islands, he saw the value of education and he sent Calvin and his brother to the grammar school. "Why do that? That schooling is not for our people," his contemporaries said to his father. "That's how they thought," said Calvin, with a weary sigh. Calvin's father was "steeped in the Labour Movement, like Uncle Joseph," and Calvin took on the progressive ideas of his father and Joseph France. Joseph had been a lodger with Calvin's great aunt, and her daughter had been secretary to Matthew Sebastian when he was leader of what was then called The Workers' League. "Uncle Joe got his first job with the League through lodging with my great aunt."

Calvin, like Arthur, had noticed as a young man that Black people could not get a loan to buy land. As Calvin put it, "School never taught people enough to run a business. And the banks preferred to lend to the English." The Portuguese, who historically had been slave overseers and were "one rung lower than the English," could get small loans to run the shops. It annoyed Calvin that "Black people were conditioned to 'know your place' and always defer to the whites."

Arthur paid tribute to the impact Calvin had on him and the UCA. "Calvin brought us new strength. He was more radical and political than I was, and I learned something else really important: when you start something, you see it through." He also taught Arthur that you cannot compromise on your principles. He gave me as an example the parties the UCA had organised in the premises at the top of International House on North Street (close to the city centre).

Since the UCA had displaced the African, Caribbean and Asian organisation's role in creating dances, Mrs Paul asked if she could work with Arthur, George and Calvin in organising the International House parties. She brought Kenneth da Costa (known as Mannabee) with her. Calvin rejected her overtures, because their political differences were already clear to him. Arthur agreed: "They had no agenda apart from keeping a dance." Calvin was equally clear about their differences with another Chapeltown-based group called The West Indian Afro Brotherhood – "They were more militant than us, but they didn't carry much weight."

The UCA developed further when Maureen and Paul Baker joined. Maureen (1932-2012) was Irish and Paul (1937-1998) was the son of Lithuanian immigrants to Leeds, who had escaped the anti-Jewish pogroms. Speaking of Arthur, Calvin said that he was always primarily focused on the rights of (and wrongs against) Black people, but he was never "anti-white." Proving this point, despite some other white people being rebuffed, the UCA had two white members. Maureen, a powerful and fierce orator, would occasionally be heard to say, in full flight against The Man at a public event, "We Black people think that ..." Only white people like me would turn a hair at this bizarre phrasing.

Arthur described Maureen, approvingly, as "very radical." She was a member of the Liberal Party, whose leaders were among the pioneers in legislation outlawing discrimination in Britain and she was – perhaps drawing on her Irish identity and experience of the deep prejudice against Irish people in Britain – vigorously opposed to racism of any kind. Maureen Baker was the Secretary of the Leeds branch of the national Campaign Against Racial Discrimination (CARD) and of the Congress of Racial Equality (CORE), and she never ceased to struggle for the rights of all people of colour up to her death in 2012.

Arthur France and Maureen Baker, August 2003. © Max Farrar

Tom Steele, one of the radical white students at Leeds University Arthur might well have bumped into, has an undated press cutting from an anti-racist intervention at the Fforde Grene pub, on Roundhay Road. Maureen Baker had carefully staged this assault on racism in this pub, on the edge of Chapeltown and Harehills and already popular with the Black and Brown people of these neighbourhoods, as part of her work for CORE. Tom wrote this account for me in 2017:

> The thing about the Fforde Grene protest was that we'd been rounded up by Maureen Baker during the summer vacation because sometime previously the landlord had banned 'coloured' people from the bar because a couple of Sikhs had had a fight. Maureen told us to get a drink in the bar and wait till she arrived with about ten or so members of CORE, mostly Sikhs and Caribbeans, I think. [The press report says that Maureen was there 'with 18 coloured friends'.]

But the landlord had installed a bunch of National Front [NF] geezers to keep watch. When I went in to sit down at a table in the bar with a couple of Jewish ex-soldiers from AJEX [the Association of Jewish Ex-Servicemen, the Jewish self-defence organisation] there were two heavy NF guys at the end of the bar who took a dim view of our presence. We got drinks and started chatting under the doleful gaze of the NF – I don't remember there being many others in the bar. Then after what seemed several years, Maureen and her guys filed in and started ordering drinks. The NF got off their bar seats but when they could see they were outnumbered they sat down again. It was chaos. The Sikhs were being refused drinks and the NF were getting agitated and there was lots of shouting.

All a bit scary, but then Jeff Brownhutt, the AJEX guy I was sitting with, went over and ordered drinks which he then handed out to the Sikhs! It was very tense but the NF stayed put though not without taking a long hard look at us. The landlord then panicked and closed the bar and ordered everyone out. I don't know where the NF went but Maureen had arranged for the press to be there and suddenly we were being interviewed and photographed. It was a great piece of work as the bar remained closed for a couple of days and then Tetley's [the brewer that owned the pub] sacked the manager.

She [Maureen] was great like that. I remember another occasion when there were riots in Burley. I got rounded up and with a couple of others and was driven down to Burley in an old Land Rover with a load of pick axe handles in the back! Fortunately the cops had arrived and we weren't required to use them. I still get a bit sweaty thinking about it.

We know from other sources that this second protest took place in the summer of 1969. It's more than likely that the Caribbean people were UCA members, and that Paul Baker was the intermediary with AJEX. This Jewish self-defence organisation had been set up because of the violence meted out to Jews in Leeds over many years by a succession of Nazi groups in the city. In the press report, however, Jeff Brownhutt is described as the 'race relations secretary of the Sinai Synagogue' in north Leeds. AJEX was a very private affair.

Tom Steele referred to Maureen organising self-defence in the July 1969 riots in Burley, a neighbourhood on the west of the city centre, near Leeds University. This violence was yet another example of how intense racism was in Leeds in this period. Here's a summary I wrote in another publication (about David Oluwale, discussed in the next chapter):

Racists attacked Asians in Leeds shortly after David Oluwale died [in April 1969]. A small white gang set upon Bhupinder Singh and Dian Singh Ball and other Asians in the Burley area of Leeds, just north of the city centre, on 27th July 1969. One of them, Kenneth Horsfall, was killed. A few days later, somewhere between 800 and 1,000 white men and women surged into Hyde Park Road, attacking Asian-owned shops and setting fire to a car believed to be owned by a Pakistani. Humphry and John reported: 'Nazi salutes were given and cries of "sieg heil" as scuffles between the police and the crowd broke out. Four policemen were hurt making twenty-three arrests'.

This was the context in which Maureen Baker persuaded the UCA to hold its first demonstration. "We caused havoc, we blocked Chapeltown Road shouting slogans and holding our placards against police brutality," Arthur said. They had invited the local press, and the *Yorkshire Evening Post* reporter turned up; the media presence "forced the police to back off and let us demonstrate." Arthur can't remember the date, but it sounds like this was in the last year or two of the 1960s. His political development in the Black Power Movement over the next few years is described in the next chapter.

References in this chapter

Washington Archibald, 'I Am Appalled', *St Kitts & Nevis Observer*, 22.2.2008. Available at https://www.thestkittsnevisobserver.com/i-am-appalled/ Accessed 17.3.2020.

Washington Archibald, 'Buckley's Shame', *StKN List*, n.d. Available at http://sknlist.com/Washie/20120714b.html Accessed 17.3.2020.

Rick Blackman, *Forty Miles of Bad Road – The Stars Campaign for Interracial Friendship and the Notting Hill Riots*, London: Redwords/ Bookmarks, 2017. ISBN 978 1910 885 536.

Burley Road 'race riots' quote is from Max Farrar, 'Remembering David Oluwale', in *African Studies Bulletin*, Leeds University Centre for African Studies, No. 78, 2016-7. At https://lucas.leeds.ac.uk/article/ remembering-david-oluwale-max-farrar/#_ftn5 More on the David Oluwale Memorial Association can be found at www.rememberoluwale. org Accessed 22.12.2020.

Caribbean workers' protests and strikes: *The Report by the West India Commission* (known as Moyne Report) in Wikipedia here https://en.wikipedia.org/ wiki/Report_of_West_India_Royal_Commission_(Moyne_Report) Accessed 17.3.2020. This entry refers to: O Nigel Bolland, *On the March: Labour Rebellions in the British Caribbean,* Kingston: Ian Randle Publishers, 1995, and Kelvin Singh, *Race and Class Struggles in a Colonial State*, Calgary: University of Calgary Press, 1994.

Prudence France, 'A Humble Leader – Sir Joseph Nathaniel France', *St Kitts and Nevis Visitor*, Vol. 2, 1997-8.

On CARD, mentioning Maureen Baker, see Benjamin W Heinemann, *The Politics of the Powerless – A Study of the Campaign Against Racial Discrimination*, London: Institute of Race Relations and Oxford University Press, 1972, and Rosalind Eleanor Wild, *Black was the Colour of our Fight,* PhD Thesis, University of Sheffield, 2008. Available at http://etheses.whiterose.ac.uk/3640/ Accessed 23.3.2020.

Peter Fryer, *Staying Power – The History of Black People in Britain*, London: Pluto Press, 1984.

Colin Grant, *Homecoming – Voices of the Windrush Generation*, London: Jonathan Cape, 2019.

Kennetta Hammond Perry, *London Is The Place For Me: Black Britons, Citizenship, and the Politics of Race*, New York: Oxford University Press, 2015. This important book provides an in-depth analysis of racism and citizenship in the UK in the 1950s and 60s.

Derek Humphry and Gus John, *Because They're Black*, Harmondsworth: Pelican Books, 1972, p. 151.

CLR James, 'Cricket in West Indian Culture', *Index on Censorship*, Vol. 4, 2000. Available at https://journals.sagepub.com/doi/pdf/10.1080/03064220008536783 Accessed 18.3.2020.

John La Rose's comment 'We did not come alive in Britain' is included in Roxy Harris, 'Openings, Absences and Omissions: aspects of the treatment of "race", culture and ethnicity in British cultural studies', *Cultural Studies*, 10 (2), May 1996.

K L Little, *Negroes in Britain – A Study of Racial Relations in English Society*, London: Kegan Paul, Trench, Trubner & Co., 1947.

Edward Pilkington, *Beyond the Mother Country – West Indians and the Notting Hill White Riots*, London: IB Tauris, 1988.

Margaret Stevens, *Red International and Black Caribbean – Communists in New York City, Mexico and the West Indies, 1919-1939*, London: Pluto Press, 2017.

John L. Williams, *Michael X – A Life in Black and White*, London: Century, 2008.

On the 1948 sugar workers strike, see Hansard, Vol. 450, 28.4.1948. Available here https://hansard.parliament.uk/Commons/1948-04-28/debates/6057eb4f-a52b-411b-b3a6-a7006aa64fab/SugarWorkersStrike Accessed 18.3.2020.

Wikipedia and cricket specialist sites provided background on the West Indies cricket tours.

Benjamin Zephaniah, *The Life and Rhymes of Benjamin Zephaniah – An Autobiography*, London, Simon and Shuster, 2018.

Chapter 7

BLACK POWER

A rthur remembered the late 1960s and early 1970s as one where he and other leaders of the United Caribbean Association (UCA) in Leeds were making connections with like-minded groups all over England. "We linked up with groups in Leicester, Manchester, Birmingham and London and we formed an umbrella group to keep us all in contact." It was in 1968 when he first met Darcus Howe, a relative of the Trinidadian Marxist intellectual and activist CLR James. Howe came to be one of the most prominent Black revolutionaries in the UK. Black radicals in this period were numerous and diverse in national origins and in ideology. "Black Power" was a term, adopted from the USA, that loosely united all those who were deeply critical of the white establishment and all its agents, particularly the police; politicians in all the main parties were also held in contempt. They wanted wholesale, structural change. Many (but not all) of the advocates of Black Power were revolutionaries of one stripe or another.

Black Power in England

An early manifestation of Black Power in London had appeared in 1965 when Michael de Freitas (1933-1975, originally from Trinidad) and Roy Sawh (who landed in Britain from Guyana in 1958) formed the Racial Adjustment Action Society (RAAS) in Notting Hill, London. They adopted this title to make themselves laugh at the credulity of the English each time the word 'raas' appeared in the press. De Freitas had for some years moved easily among the Notting Hill hippies and underworld hustlers when he became aware of the extraordinary work in the USA of Malcolm X. Malcolm X, born in 1925, came to prominence as a follower of the Black American Wallace Fard Muhammad, founder of the Nation of Islam. Malcolm became a real threat to the USA when he saw through Fard's teachings and adopted the more universalist, and non-racial, Sunni teachings of Islam, combining this with a version of socialism. He was assassinated by the American government's FBI agents in 1965.

Malcolm X's visits to England in December 1964 and February 1965 prompted Michael de Freitas to form RAAS. Following Malcolm's visit he changed his name to Michael X. Roy Sawh soon realised Michael had a good eye for the media but no substantive politics and he quickly split from Michael X. Later, Michael de Freitas, after intensive telephone conversations with the Nation of Islam leader Elijah Muhammed, changed his name to Michael Abdul Malik, thus destroying his limited credibility. (De Freitas was convicted of murder in Trinidad in 1972, and executed in 1975.)

The next step in the development of Black Power in Britain was initiated by Obi Egbuna (1938-2014), who, in 1967, formed the United Coloured People's Association (UCPA). Egbuna was the chair and Roy Sawh his deputy. Ajoy Ghose, of Indian origin, was another of its leaders. Egbuna was born in Nigeria and had arrived in England in 1961 after studying at universities in the USA. He immersed himself in the arts, particularly theatre, attending events organised by the Caribbean Artists Movement (CAM), established by Trinidad-born John La Rose and others.

The UCPA seems to have allowed sympathetic white people to join. Egbuna told *The Times* that he had recruited 778 members within seven weeks but it's likely that he was practising the dubious arts of PR spin. Tony Soares has a UCPA membership list for 1967: it includes 27 people. Five had South Asian names, some were originally from Africa, and most were from the Caribbean. This exemplifies the notion, common among radicals in the UK until the late-1980s, that black was a 'political' colour, embracing all those whose skins were not white. Egbuna, like Sawh, a powerful orator at Hyde Park's Speakers Corner in London, got a suspended sentence in December 1968 for publishing a pamphlet deemed to incite violence; this had its no doubt intended effect of intimidating him into political silence.

Following the speech delivered by the African-American Stokely Carmichael (1941-1998), co-author of the book *Black Power*, at the Dialectics of Liberation Conference in London in July 1967, Egbuna expelled the UCPA's white members. (Did it really have white members, or was this another publicity stunt?) By September, he and Sawh had fallen out and Sawh founded the Universal Coloured People and Arab Association. In November 1967 Egbuna resigned from his post as chairman of the UCPA and formed the British Black Panther Movement (BBPM).

The BBP Movement, drawing from the USA's Black Panther Party, expounded both Black consciousness and Marxism, while maintaining a focus on the arts. John La Rose, in his report to the Caribbean Artists Movement's AGM in August 1968, said: 'The effect of Stokely Carmichael's presence ... last year was a catalyst in a way nothing before had been'. CLR James also welcomed Carmichael's contribution, but cautiously expressed his differences.

James could see that Carmichael's trajectory was to dismiss the Western Enlightenment tradition, and he seemed to be aligning with Marcus Garvey's call to go 'Back to Africa', whereas James took a more universalist position, drawing on radical philosophers and revolutionary movements of all colours. In particular, James argued that the white working class was capable of playing a progressive role in the struggle for equality and justice, a view that Egbuna and Carmichael had rejected. Carmichael was briefly involved with the USA Black Panther

Party, but he left the Panthers because of their alliances with white radicals. He was targeted for assassination by the FBI's COINTELPRO programme and left the USA in the early 1970s, living the rest of his life in Ghana, as a leading member of the All-African People's Revolutionary Party.

These differences within Black Power ideology and practice in the UK became bewildering for anyone outside the tight circles of its militants, and Arthur, Calvin, George and the UCA more or less avoided the factionalism. They stuck with the UCA as their progressive organisation, never joining any of the Black Power factional groups. In London, Egbuna's demise put Althea Lecointe, a Trinidadian postgraduate student, in charge of the Black Panther Movement (BPM) in 1969. Barbara Beese and Darcus Howe, formerly leaders of the Black Eagles, and Linton Kwesi Johnson and Farrukh Dhondy, joined the BPM around this time. (Beese, the late Darcus Howe, Johnson and Dhondy have made lifelong contributions to the arts and radical politics.)

The London Black Panthers were ideologically demanding and tightly organised. L K Johnson told Rosalind Wild that he had to prove himself as a member of its youth league before he could join. Tony Soares, who joined in 1970, said they had about 50 members in total. The Metropolitan Police thought they had 800. While most of the members were men, the BPM, with Althea Lecointe and Barbara Beese as powerful advocates for the rights of women, regarded sexism as just as damaging as racism. Another member of the London Black Panthers, Beverley Bryan, took a full part in their supplementary school activity and she made an important additional point in a 2021 interview: 'The Panthers weren't just about the politics, but also young people interacting. We found purpose in the work we were doing, but we also found pleasure'.

They were also unusual in regarding work in the arts and culture as highly important. They had no time at all for the 'cultural nationalists' in the UK or the USA. (In America, where the nationalists were much more prominent, they were later lampooned by Mario van Peebles as they strutted their sexist stuff in their African outfits in the 1995 movie *Panther*.) The London Panthers' leadership, however, turned towards an orthodox version of Marxism, closer to Trotskyism, and in June 1973 they changed their name to the Black Workers Movement. Meanwhile, Darcus Howe, Leila Hassan, Linton Kwesi Johnson and Farrukh Dhondy took over the editorship of the magazine *Race Today* and formed the Race Today Collective.

The UCPA had reconstituted itself in 1970 as The Black Unity and Freedom Party (BUFP), professing Chinese-style Marxism-Leninism. Harry Goulbourne was a member (soon losing his enthusiasm for their theocratic Marxism, Harry moved on to become an important academic), and A Sivanandan (famous for his writing and research at the Institute of Race Relations) was a supporter. The BUFP dissolved some time in the 1990s. Another splinter from the Panthers formed itself into the Black Liberation Front (BLF) in 1971, somehow combining a Chinese branch of Marxism-Leninism with elements of cultural nationalism. Their ideology has been described as 'black nationalist'.

Beverley Bryan, Stella Dadzie and Suzanne Scafe's important book about Black women in Britain, first published in 1985, has explained that sexism was rife within their movement. One of their interviewees said: 'The men certainly didn't understand anything about women's oppression. In fact, they didn't have the faintest clue about it. Nearly every one of them was a die-hard sexist ... No attempt was made to seriously take up women's issues, they just weren't considered immediately pressing'. They formed the Black Women's Group in Brixton, London, in 1973, and made links with other Black women's organisations in other British cities, and with the national Organisation of Women of African and Asian Descent. Another interviewee said 'It took us a long time before we worked out a Black women's perspective which took account of race, class, sex *and* sexuality'. And that is what they did.

Cities outside London had their adherents to some or all of these groupings. Ron Phillips, author of the first substantial writing on the 1969 killing of David Oluwale in Leeds, led the UCPA in Manchester until he was expelled in May 1970. Apparently there was yet another group, calling itself the Black People's Action Collective, which, Colin Prescod told Rosalind Wild, had branches in Birmingham, Nottingham, Leeds and London. But there was no public sign of them in Leeds.

Tony Soares told Wild that the underground organisation called the Fasimbas had 500 members, and merged with the BLF in 1972. (They did have members in Leeds.) Those numbers should be taken with caution; Wild asserts that none of the Black Power groups had more than 300 members. Each of these had publications of one sort or another. This was a time when radical, Black ideological ferment and organisation was high and, despite the sectarian differences between the organisations, hundreds of Black people would attend demonstrations, often with white leftist supporters (like me) around their edges.

Black Power in Leeds

Rosalind Wild's extensive research into this complex milieu mentions a United Caribbean Association in Cardiff, but she has no record of the UCA in Leeds – perhaps because Leeds did not formally align with any of the Black Power groupings. But Arthur laughed with delight at his memory of being a steward at Roscoe Methodist church in this period, sporting his Afro haircut, a black beret and a Black Power badge. He had the regalia, and in many respects supported the ideology, but he avoided the internecine strife of the Black Power movement.

This didn't stop the wife of one of his childhood friends from Nevis telling her husband that she must never speak to that Black Power man, Arthur France, ever again. "My friend had to cross the road to keep his distance every time he saw me," much to Arthur's amusement then, and now. Calvin Beech remembered that he and Arthur "Often got blamed by other Black people for teaching Black Power."

While Arthur's politics have never been over-burdened with the ideological trappings of the groups described above, he was willingly engaged in some of their activities. After his 1968 meeting with Darcus Howe and Barbara Beese he made links with the London Black Panthers. "We'd go to London to have meetings with them, but we decided not to join – we wanted to stick with the UCA and develop that." Calvin recalled the UCA responding to a tip-off from a Jewish organisation of the plan by a Nazi organisation to hold an event at the junction of Spencer Place and Roundhay Road in the heart of Chapeltown. "We got a demonstration together and we broke up the meeting, throwing stones. It was the first time I saw the police take our side: they just sat in their cars watching us chase them away."

Leeds was not immune to Black Power's sectarian differences. Arthur and Calvin both recalled the West Indian Afro Brotherhood being set up by Veryl Harriott and her husband George. Susan Pitter, in her book *Eulogy*, records the Harriotts' fellow Jamaicans Trevor Winter and Gloria and Ferdy Cruise as among the founders. It included some people younger than themselves, such as Errol Caesar (who became Imruh Bakari), Violet Hendrikson and Annette Francis (Liburd), so it wasn't composed only of people of Jamaican heritage.

Arthur said he didn't know why they felt the need to set up this new organisation. Calvin Beech remembered inviting Darcus Howe, Althea Lecointe and Bernard Coard (whose pioneering work on the education of Black children was discussed in Chapter 5) to a demonstration the UCA called in Leeds in early 1971. Arthur remembered: "We tried to draft the Brotherhood into our march through Chapeltown with the London Black Panthers but the Brotherhood wouldn't join in." It ended up at the Jubilee Hall at the South end of Chapeltown Road. (I was inspired by the rousing speeches as I stood at the back of the hall, having seen the demo pass my flat on Spencer Place.)

Arthur said that Calvin used to make fun of Errol, who often wore a long mackintosh, likening him to the American TV detective Colombo (played by Peter Falk), and he said that Errol disliked him and Calvin: "He cut us out completely." Whatever the personal issues, when I occasionally saw their newsletter, I could see that the Brotherhood used a militant rhetoric like the one I read in the Black Liberation Front's newspaper *Grassroots*.

Perhaps Lecointe, Howe, Beese and the other Panthers weren't sufficiently African-centred for the Brotherhood. Arthur had no time for them: "The Brotherhood was serious but it never did anything. They just blew hot air." The Barbados Overseas Association had been formed by this time and Arthur invited them to join the demonstration with the Panthers. "They too refused to join us – because they weren't as radical as we were."

The UCA, led by Arthur, Calvin and George, was a figurehead in the national network of Black organisations that was created in this period. The London chairperson was Loxley Comrie (from Jamaica). Arthur recalled that they organised a demonstration against the Jamaica Labour Party's leader Sir William Bustamante (1884-1977), the independent nation's first Prime Minister, when he visited London. Bustamante was furious and threatened to arrest any of the demonstrators if they visited Jamaica. Arthur also pointed out that Trinidad's Prime Minister, Dr Eric Williams, used to teach Stokely Carmichael, but when he became a prominent activist for Black Power, Williams banned him from entering Trinidad, even though he was born there. "We were very much against some of the Caribbean leaders," was Arthur's understated way of explaining their politics.

Black Parents' Power in Education

Soon after he reached Leeds, Calvin Beech had joined the UCA. He thought they spent too much time organising dances and too little time agitating for change. Calvin began to ask why Black children were doing so badly in school. "In St Kitts and Nevis, some Black kids did well at school and some didn't – but in Leeds, all of them were being marked as failures. That couldn't be right," Calvin told me.

The city authorities were in denial about this issue. In an interview in 1969, Mr J H Taylor, Leeds City Council's Chief Education Officer, told Dave Durman: 'I can assure you there is no discrimination in Leeds schools'. Insofar as there were problems, the 'immigrants' have caused them and the establishment has responded effectively: 'If immigration in Leeds has brought problems, I think we've met them adequately'.

Durman ended his report by displaying the racist assumptions of the day. Speculating on the possibility of racial violence in 1975, he wrote (for his Leeds University student readers): 'The coloured immigrant – and he is usually West Indian – violent by nature, by instinct suspicious, resenting authority and injustice, will be the leader of such unrest'. When a young university-educated journalist can dole out those offensive stereotypes, we get a hint of the state of ignorance of the rest of the white population in the 1960s and 70s. But he was right that Black people would lead the fight against racism. He chose 1975 as a wild guess, but it turned out to be a good one, as we will see.

Calvin said he started "indoctrinating" Arthur and George to raise their game, politically. He recalled bringing Harry Stapleton into the fold, and a white guy, a pharmacist, whose name he couldn't recall, who was a good pianist and was "very receptive", allowing them to have meetings in his house. Arthur remembered a white guy from Leeds University who came to an early UCA meeting. But George was rude to him and he never came back. "George had a quiet voice but he was deadly, very sarcastic." There was a white Jewish barrister who was very helpful to the UCA when anyone got arrested. "But we didn't trust nobody who was white, so we told them to go, because we wanted to do things our way, on our own."

One of the UCA's most important achievements was setting up the Saturday Supplementary School (described in Chapter 4). Calvin remembered: "We went to London to buy relevant materials from the two Black shops [Bogle L'Ouverture and New Beacon Books] and we attended lectures by the followers of CLR James." (Some of the members of the London Black Panthers were Jamesians; as mentioned above, led by Darcus Howe, they took over *Race Today* magazine in 1973-4.) The UCA understood that education and cultural expression should be inextricably linked. "We had a dance group led by a Jamaican-Chinese lady called Jennifer Mandy. A Cuban lady who was a dancer joined it a bit later, and we had an arts group." Calvin recalled that they took the children to London to look at African artefacts in the museums. "We taught them African and Caribbean history; we taught them to believe in themselves."

Their school work improved and their aspirations were raised. One of the younger members of the UCA, Vince Wilkinson, realised that he had the ability and motivation to do well at university, so he applied. Reminiscent of attitudes he'd encountered in Nevis, Calvin said that Vince's parents couldn't understand why he would want to make this unusual step. "But George Archibald persuaded them," and Vince duly succeeded. "In the Caribbean, teachers would know their pupils' parents and keep their parents informed. So they trusted them and left all educational matters in the teachers' hands." They expected English teachers to be equally disciplined and well-educated. "We found out it wasn't so. The teachers in Chapeltown schools turned out to be so lazy."

In our interview, Calvin didn't say these teachers were racist, but as we saw in Chapter 4, some undoubtedly were. "When I go back to Leeds, I meet some of the men and women who were pupils at the Saturday School. It's always good to see how well they did." The UCA were behind the Chapeltown Parents' Action Group's militant struggle to improve the education at the city council's Middle School in Cowper Street (described in Chapter 3). Calvin and Arthur played a central role in that historic example of powerful community organisation.

Calvin recalled another kind of controversy when the UCA organised a demonstration against prostitution in Chapeltown in April 1975. Chapeltown had long been portrayed in negative terms by the Leeds newspapers. Bruce Smith's front page story in the *Yorkshire Evening Post* of 31st January 1974 was headlined 'Spotlight on Leeds Mecca of Vice', with a photo of Hamilton Place, including interviews with people living nearby, in the heart of Chapeltown. Mr Alphonse Klamec was quoted as saying that there are 'Sometimes as many as 50 young lasses and they're always busy'.

The UCA strongly opposed these defamatory portraits of the neighbourhood, and knew that Klamec was wildly exaggerating the numbers, but, at that time, 'working girls' and prowling cars were often seen on Spencer Place, and the UCA had been alarmed by reports that Black girls were being solicited on their way home from school. The UCA demo marched up Chapeltown Road past the Lamport Club (also known as the Colony Club)

'Prostitution out of Chapeltown' demonstration, April 1975. © Max Farrar

where, Calvin recalled, "Some of the girls mooned at us out of the windows."

They marched into Chapel Allerton, about a mile north, and picketed the police station, because "We believed the police were deliberately creating a prostitution zone in Chapeltown." It was a fact that the police tolerated the street girls, fining them occasionally and letting them get back to work soon after. The pimps were rarely troubled and, in those days, there was little or no attention to the blues parties located in several basements in Chapeltown. The establishment connived with the 'mecca of vice' picture of Chapeltown.

At the meeting in Chapeltown Community Centre after the demonstration there were speeches, including one from Leila Hassan, of the Race Today Collective. (Leila is now Leila Hassan Howe.) Calvin recalled, "The pimps came to the meeting and threatened us with violence – we told them to get lost and get a proper job." One of the UCA's worries was that the police would put pressure on the pimps to pass them information on what the UCA was doing. But the UCA leaders were fearless and would not bow to the police or the pimps.

Divisions among the radical leaders in Chapeltown resurfaced in 1977. After the Bonfire Night Trial in the summer of 1976 (see below), the original group that had published *Chapeltown News* handed the paper over to new editors. Some of them had been in Brotherhood and had been teachers in the Saturday School. They accused the people who had set up UCA House of 'trying to monopolise community property in the sole interest of [the United Caribbean Association]'. They described the 'dictatorial individuals' running the UCA as 'a group of blacks with a totally colonialistic mentality, lacking in political ideology and therefore ill equipped to aid the struggle' (*Chapeltown News* No. 41, February 1977). As we have seen, Arthur had no time at all for this group. Since he was now working in Germany, and Calvin Beech was about to move to Canada, there was some fire, but little action over the next few years.

The Hounding of David Oluwale

In Chapter 4 we saw how Arthur was inspired by the Pan African week at Leeds University in 1974; he was instrumental in ensuring that Darcus Howe and Farrukh Dhondy, key members of the Race Today Collective, spoke at that illustrious gathering. He did interact with the radical white students at the University and the Polytechnic as well, but the Black students' organisation always maintained its separate identity. Back in November 1971, some of the white students organised a march from their union building to join with the picket called by Arthur and others outside the Leeds Crown Court. Nigerian-born James Aboaba (introduced in Chapter 4) was one of those organisers: he was enraged about the killing of David Oluwale, a Nigerian who had arrived in Leeds in 1949, and the picket was to tell Leeds that Black people were carefully watching the trial of two Leeds policemen accused of causing David's death.

Louise Lavender, a founder of the Leeds Women's Liberation Movement, was among those who picketed the court in solidarity with Arthur, James and the other politically-conscious people of African descent in Leeds. It's very likely that people in the Leeds University Union anarchist and socialist groups would have been there too. David Bryan told me in 2020 that he vividly remembered as a teenager in Brixton coming to Leeds with other Black militants, including the London Black Panthers, to join the picket outside the Crown Court, which in those days was inside the majestic Leeds Town Hall, opened by Queen Victoria in 1858.

The picket was to draw attention to the trial of Inspector Ellerker and Sergeant Kitching, two Leeds policemen accused of the manslaughter, and actual and grievous bodily harm of David Oluwale in April 1969. Arthur remembered sitting in court hearing the testimony of some brave police officers who dared to give evidence against Ellerker and Kitching. "The stories they told made me want to cry. One time, Kitching kicked David so hard while he was lying on the floor in the police station that he was raised off the ground."

David Oluwale was one of the West African pioneers in Leeds. He spent a month in Leeds Prison in 1949 for the crime of not paying his fare on a cargo ship from Lagos to Hull, in East Yorkshire. He was a stowaway, but he was also a British citizen, so the punishment was light. For the next four years he did the jobs reconstructing post-war Leeds that white people were already refusing to do, such as humping carcasses in the abattoir, and hod-carrying bricks on building sites, and he spent his wages in the usual way – having a drink and going out dancing.

In 1953, at the King Edward Hotel, near the market in the centre of Leeds, there was a dispute in which the group of Africans were accused of not paying their bill. David, who, his friends recalled, would not back down when falsely accused or subjected to racial abuse, was arrested and sent to prison. David's friend Gabriel Adams told me that when he and the other West Africans living in Leeds went out for a drink in the evening they would always make sure they were in a large group, because they were likely to encounter young white men who would abuse them and try to start a fight.

David Emare, born near Benin City in Nigeria in 1914, arrived in Manchester in 1940. He described the violent racism he and his friends encountered to Emmanuel Nwene-Osuh:

> In the 1950s and 60s, the Teddy Boys like to move about with bicycle chain and beat up Black men. So we had to group up to defend ourselves or to fight them ... When the White men called us Nigger or Sambo, we would fight them. Then, when Police came, he said 'white man is right and we blacks are wrong.' They never gave us any right and they defend their own kind and always stick together.

Gabriel Adams told me that when he and David and their friends were confronted by young white men like these, their normal response was to walk away – except for David. In the King Edward Hotel in 1953, he was probably accused of lying about paying the bill. Like David Emare, David Oluwale objected strongly to racism. When the police were called to the King Edward Hotel, the situation must have been similar to Mr Emare's: the Africans were assumed to be at fault. David Oluwale was arrested and, according to his friends, hit on the head with a truncheon. Sentenced to Armley Jail in Leeds, the prison doctor said he was mentally ill – and David spent most of the next 14 years in a psychiatric hospital on the outskirts of Leeds.

When he was out of hospital, with no welfare support, his friends said he seemed very ill indeed. It might be that it was an ethnocentric diagnosis that put him in hospital in the first place; the treatment he received (the drug Largactil and electro-convulsive therapy) certainly ruined his life. For the last two years of his life the abuse got worse. The police officers in the dock singled him out for degrading and violent treatment.

David was last seen being pursued by two men in police uniform very close to the River Aire in the centre of Leeds. The judge refused to allow the jury to hear this evidence of manslaughter because, he said, neither Ellerker nor Kitching could be identified by the witness. But they were convicted of assaulting him, and they received short prison sentences. Arthur France was one of the first people to join the campaign for a proper public memorial in Leeds to David Oluwale when it began at Leeds Metropolitan University in 2008 at the suggestion of Caryl Phillips, who had just published his book *Foreigners*, with a chapter on David Oluwale.

In November 1971 the killing of David Oluwale prompted Maureen Baker (by then an officer of the UK Immigrants Advisory Service for Yorkshire and the North East, based in Leeds) to meet with Mr Haywood, the Deputy Chief Constable. Around the same time, the Liberal peer Donald Wade, in an understated report for the Yorkshire Committee for Community Relations, noted that there was 'growing tension between the police force and coloured communities in Leeds'.

Lord Wade reported that Mrs Baker and Mr Haywood arranged carefully-prepared discussions in an 'informal atmosphere' between 'coloured participants of West Indian origin or descent' ranging from grandmothers to teenagers, with selected Leeds police officers. Wade stated that by the end of the programme of meetings, the majority accepted that 'many of the complaints [against the police] were based on rumour and not on reality'. The programme, which came to be called the 'Leeds Scheme' for training police officers – it was recommended by the Home Office for replication across the UK – continued for several years.

Arthur and his comrades, however, were not reassured. For them, the Oluwale tragedy was a terrible sign of how dangerous Leeds had become for Black people. "When we met with the police, I told them straight: 'You've killed Oluwale. Don't think you're going to kill another Black man in this city.'" Arthur's daughter Mahalia proposed that there should be a memorial garden in his name when she became a member of the David Oluwale Memorial Association (DOMA) charity in 2014. When the public campaign to remove statues to British slave-owners erupted in 2020, calling for a post-colonial analysis of British history, DOMA was proud to announce that the British-Nigerian artist Yinka Shonibare CBE, RA would make a sculpture for the memorial garden in honour of David Oluwale, to be opened in conjunction with the Leeds 2023 cultural festival.

In the early 1970s, this ominous period in Leeds's racial history was noted by South Asian organisations, too. Representatives of the Indian Workers' Association and the Muslim Council both referred to David Oluwale's life and death when they spoke to the House of Commons Select Committee on Race Relations which visited Leeds in 1972. They spoke of 'racial prejudice' in the city and referred to 'the ordinary man's suspicion about the partiality of the police'.

Joyce Bernard spoke of the difficulties young people in Chapeltown had with the police at this time in a booklet published in the early 1990s. Her son was ten and he was out playing with his brother on their new Chopper-style bikes when they came home in tears – the police had stopped them and accused them of stealing the bikes. Mrs Bernard was so worried in December 1975 when her 17 year-old son was out at a house party, and didn't come home at the agreed time, that she and another son went out to search for him in the early hours of the morning. When she found him she was so upset she beat him with her shoe. She told him: 'If you stay on the street until this time and the police see you and arrest you, they going to beat you ... Because of what I have read in the papers and hear from other children they are going to harass you, so don't give them a chance to do that'.

Police harassment of Black youths was a subject very close to heart of the UCA. Calvin Beech had been surprised that the police didn't weigh in to arrest them when they stoned the Nazis gathering on Spencer Place – there was already a history of police officers stopping and searching Black males as they went about their daily business, and of using brutal force whenever it pleased them. Ellerker and Kitching were not just two rotten apples; the whole barrel was rotten. In 1975 that barrel was seriously shaken by Chapeltown's rebellious Black youth.

The police versus the youth and the Bonfire Night Trial

The warning signs that Black youths born in Leeds were not as settled as they would have been if they lived in a fair and equal society appeared at least as early as 1969. Maureen Baker, who at this point was the organiser for the Leeds branch of the Congress of Racial Equality, was quoted by Dave Durman:

It's the kids aged 15 on the streets today, born in this country, whom I'm worried about. Listening to their fathers say – "I didn't get this job, cos I'm coloured." These kids have no family responsibilities, no allegiance to [the Commonwealth] or anywhere. To them it's just the place

where grandma lived. They are the people who will refuse
to be discriminated against.

Not only, as Mrs Baker suggested, would they push back against
racial prejudice, they would object increasingly strongly to police
harassment.

Mrs Gertrude Paul was by no means as militant as Arthur,
Calvin and George, but she did put her name to this statement
by the UCA to the 1971-2 House of Commons committee of
enquiry into 'police-immigrant relations':

> Harassment, intimidation and wrongful arrest go on all the
> time in Chapeltown; Black teenagers returning from Youth
> Centres to their homes in groups are jostled by the police,
> and when the youths protest, police reinforcements with
> dogs are always ready just round corners ... Police boot and
> fist youths into compelling them to give wrong statements,
> but the right one that the police requires ... We believe that
> policemen have every Black person under suspicion of
> some sort and for that reason every Black immigrant here
> in Leeds mistrusts the police, because we think that their
> attitudes are to start trouble, not prevent it.

This was a strong complaint, and it was not particular to Leeds.
Benjamin Zephaniah wrote of his experience at this time in
Birmingham, noting that there were white racist youths who
were frightened of the tough Black youths who controlled the
streets in Handsworth and Aston, and that there were white
youngsters, male and female, who enjoyed sharing their 'cool
music, cool smokes and cool style'. But the racist youths were
not the main problem. 'No, the racism I was seeing at this time
came firstly from the police – who were relentlessly stopping and
searching us, even right outside the school gates.' When he
became a Rastafarian, 'The police were arresting us all the time'.
One policeman said to him: 'Most of us are hardworking racists,

with the power of arrest'. Another showed him dreadlocks pinned to the wall of a police station. 'They were like scalps', Zephaniah wrote, and it 'scared the hell out of me'.

Mrs Baker's 'Leeds Scheme' was in place and if change was occurring in the police force, it wasn't filtering through to Chapeltown. Black youths were not going to put up with ill-treatment by the police any longer. Glenville Sheriffe, also known as Shaft, described the situation of Black youth in 1976 to *Race Today*, the magazine edited by Darcus Howe:

> I find the police involved in a lot of my life. Put it this way, living in Leeds feels as if you're in jail. If you put one foot wrong, accidentally or whatever, it's like your sentence. You fear to do anything ... I try to be like a ghost [to the police]. Every time we play the sound [his Sound System was called Screaming Target] I expect them to be there.

In an interview with Counter Information Services (CIS), Shaft made a wider point: 'The older people have adapted, they've been forced to live the only way they can live. The younger people now, we're not accepting that way, we can't accept that way'. Danny Cohen, who produced Screaming Target with Shaft, elaborated on this in his interview with CIS:

> Most of our parents have never been in trouble with police because they're afraid, them work and them go to them house an then watch television and that's it and them got to work. Not we, young people today, them daring.

By 'daring' Cohen meant they would take the offensive to the police, which is exactly what they did on 5th November 1975. During a Bonfire Night gathering on Spencer Place they stoned police cars driving through Chapeltown. This was the first example of post-war violent urban protest by Black youth in Britain. (In August the following year, Black youths' anger erupted again at the Notting Hill carnival, gaining enormous media attention.)

On Bonfire Night 1975, about 300 youths in Chapeltown were engaged in running battles with the police who arrived in force after their first car was attacked. Two police officers were very seriously injured as their vehicle hit a tree, and an abandoned police car was overturned. That night Glenville Sheriffe and Tony Pyke, both aged 17 and identifying as Rastafarians, and myself, were arrested. Later, nine others, including Danny Cohen, also a follower of Haile Selassie, were arrested. The Bonfire Night Twelve appeared in Leeds Crown Court in June 1976. I was charged with incitement to riot and most of us were charged with affray as well. Long jail sentences were in store.

Calvin Beech was involved in organising a team of Black lawyers for eleven of the defendants, building on the expertise developed by Darcus Howe and others at the Mangrove Nine trial in London in 1971, and elaborated upon in the pages of *Race Today* magazine. Calvin remembered that the Crown Court officials were reluctant to let the community into the court to observe the trial – "But we beat down their doors".

The Black defence team, led by the redoubtable Rudy Narayan (1938-1998), who had settled in England in 1953 from Guyana, got almost all the youths acquitted after forcefully arguing that the police had beaten false confessions out of them. My (white) barrister also persuaded the jury that the police were giving false evidence about me. The all-white jury included six young men who themselves had been fitted-up and ill-treated by Leeds police officers, so they found the defence argument completely plausible. They persuaded the rest of the jury to find us 'not guilty'.

Arthur France explained some of the background to these traumatic events. "There had always been a problem with the police, and the older West Indian parents just didn't understand the youths." Arthur, Calvin and others did want to protect them

"But we weren't going to protect them blind. The youngsters had to realise that they have to work within a certain system, within parameters."

He recalled an earlier incident when he and George Archibald were driving down Roundhay Road, around midnight, some time in 1973. They turned into Gathorne Terrace (which runs parallel to Spencer Place in the centre of Chapeltown) and saw a police van parked up, watching youngsters who were standing around on the street. "We knew the police would hassle them, so we said to youngsters, 'You have a right to be there' and we told the police they must leave them alone."

The following morning the same youths were on Chapeltown Road and they saw George. George told them that they had to understand that the dice were loaded against them and that must behave sensibly. They wouldn't listen and they turned their backs on George. Later that night Arthur saw them again out on the streets. "I told them 'You have to stick together and go home'." As he was driving off he saw a police van coming up after them, so he blocked the van off with his car and told the police to leave them alone. In the circumstances, this was risky behaviour and it demonstrates how brave Arthur was, and how far he would go to support the youth and keep the peace.

But by the morning they had arrested some of these same youths. "The *Yorkshire Post* had a ridiculous story saying they had broken an old lady's gate and the woman was in tears." The police separated the youths into different cells and intimidated them. "West Indian parents always believe the police and they wouldn't support the children, so we got a solicitor from Zermansky and Co. to represent them." They hadn't done much wrong but the police put them on a charge of riotous assembly.

Calvin and Arthur spoke to the lawyer who said 'It's a serious offence'. Arthur remembered Calvin being angry and instructing the lawyer to tell police they won't get away with it. Zermansky's office on Chapeltown Road was staffed by Howard Cohen, who was well connected locally and he knew a lot about police malpractice. (Apart from everything else, Mr Cohen would read each issue of *Chapeltown News* before it went to press and advise us if we'd written anything libellous.) So he would have put the case very firmly to the police. Arthur said: "We were proactive and the police knew who we were, and that we meant what we said, and they dropped the riotous assembly charge."

Some time later, on 5th November 1974, an altercation took place just off Spencer Place. "The youths always had a bonfire on Rossington Grove. Me and Calvin and George used to be there some times. Just normal Bonfire Night stuff." But for some reason the Fire Brigade arrived in 1974 and started putting the bonfire out. The youths threw stones at their vehicle. "I had to fight with some youths to quiet them down." In the hot debate that followed, one youth said he was so angry because he was frequently rejected when he applied for jobs.

The facts about discrimination in employment have been set out in Chapter 4, so we know this young man had good reason to be angry. Danny Cohen, unemployed, put the job situation slightly differently to *Race Today*:

> I've not had a really steady job for the last year and a half ... The jobs they offer I don't want them, they are indecent. I used to work as a labourer on a building site and it was hard. I had to lift wood and other heavy things, in the cold as well.

The older generation would tell them they were having it easy; they had worked at much more 'indecent' jobs, under much worse conditions. This generational divide was understood by Arthur, but he would not support the youths' violent reaction to the exploitation and oppression they experienced. In the dispute in Rossington Grove in 1974, one young girl said to her friends as Arthur remonstrated with them: "Listen to him because he is the only one who come to defend us." No doubt some of the youths were listening to Arthur, Calvin and George, and their parents, but, as Arthur put it: "Next year it all got out of hand."

After the Bonfire Night riot, Darcus Howe, Leila Hassan, and the *Race Today Collective* unequivocally supported the 1975 Bonfire Night youths. What the media called a 'riot', one of their key members, the reggae poet Linton Kwesi Johnson, called an 'insurrection'. They understood the youths' anger and interpreted their response as a legitimate political reaction. In Chapeltown, in contrast, there was shock and incomprehension from almost everyone.

Arthur was spending a lot of his time in Germany. He knew that pretty well all Black parents condemned the youths' violence. Nevertheless, "We got lawyers – Rudy Narayan and them, including a woman barrister." Arthur did think the youths had gone too far, but he knew that they had legitimate grievances, and he knew that the police were quite capable of illegally using force to extract false confessions.

Narayan and some of his team were also well aware of police malpractice and they subjected Leeds police officers to ferocious interrogations in court. The police had never experienced anything like this before.

Whereas the Judge in the trial of Inspector Ellerker and Sergeant Kitching in 1971 had been favourably disposed to the police, by 1976 at least some in the judiciary, influenced by the revelations in the Oluwale trial, knew that there were serious problems inside the police force, and the Judge didn't impede the Black barristers' cross examination. One police officer almost fainted under the Narayan barrage, and the trial stopped while he had a glass of water and was allowed to sit down. "I became good friends with Rudy after that trial. He was fantastic in these court room battles," Arthur told me.

Caryl Phillips, born in St Kitts, has reflected on his experience as a young man growing up in Leeds in this period:

Like all non-white children in the Britain during this time I tiptoed somewhat cautiously through life, knowing full well that Britain's ambivalence towards me and my parents' generation could cause a stranger, a friend or even a teacher to turn on me when I might least expect it.

The key issue for me and my generation – the second generation, if you will – growing up in the Britain of the late 1960s and 1970s was identity. We spoke with the same accent as the other kids, we watched the same television programmes, we went to the same schools, we did the same exams. Surely we were British. Well, of course, we were and eventually we insisted that we were even in the face of a nation which continued to invest a racially constructed sense of itself. We endured discrimination in schools, in jobs, in housing, the same discrimination that was earlier visited on our parents. However, our response was different from that of our parents, who often held their tongues in order that they might protect their children ... [It was clear to us] that a British future involved not only kicking back when kicked, but continuing to kick until a few doors opened and things changed.

This second generation was also witnessing the radical politics that some members of the first generation, including Howe, Hassan and Johnson, had generated, and they were inspired by it.

Building a centre for West Indians in Leeds

Arthur recalled the first effort to create a community centre for Chapeltown. *Chapeltown News* reported in November 1972 that an Urban Aid grant of £20,000 (about £185,000 in 2020 money) had been received from the government in 1970 for a community centre. Nothing had happened, despite repeated applications from the United Caribbean Association and Chapeltown Community Association for a centre that would serve the neighbourhood. In April 1973, *Chapeltown News* reported that the Psalms of David Synagogue in Reginald Terrace had been purchased by the council for this purpose. A year later, it had a front page story announcing the names of the people elected at a public meeting on 11th March 1974 to its management committee. Arthur remembered how this community control came about: "Me and George and Hughbon Condor had derailed the meeting at Cowper St School when the council was hand-picking the management committee. We said these people cannot be the management – they don't live here. The Council guy afterwards said he was too scared to challenge us."

The new committee had 17 members, representing a wide and multi-cultural set of local organisations: Roscoe Church, Studley Grange Children's Association, Chapeltown News, the Sikh Temple, the West Indian Afro Brotherhood, the Chapeltown Community Association, Barbados Overseas Association, the Chapeltown Women's Group, St Clement's Church, the United Caribbean Association, the West Indian Dominoes Team, the Community Relations Council, the Indian Workers' Association, the Jamaica Alliance, and the Communist Party.

The report pointed out that it wasn't clear what the committee's powers would be, nor how many council people would be involved in the management. It flagged up a problem that would be one reason why this centre never really took off: 'a licence for drinking and dancing would only be granted on exceptional occasions'. Mr John's statement was greeted with much applause: "We want a free rein in running this centre, but it seems our freedom is being severely restricted."

In 1982 a purpose-built centre for all the Caribbean people in Leeds was opened. Mrs Gertrude Paul was its first Chairperson. This was a major achievement, and it represented about fifteen years of effort. Arthur explained: "From the late-

1960s we were trying to get a United Caribbean Centre, but the council didn't want us to have one. They feared Calvin, George and myself – we were driving with a strong political slant and a strong focus on Black culture, and they were very worried about that." Nevertheless, the UCA persisted, but "At that point we didn't have much knowledge of how the political system in the city worked." They got a lot of help from Errol James and Councillor Dougie Gabb.

Errol James had arrived in England from Jamaica in 1944 to become a Leading Aircraftsman in the Royal Air Force. He'd given up a place in Teacher Training College to risk his life for 'the mother country'. He settled in Leeds at the end of the war and was a founder of the Leeds Caribbean Cricket Club in the late 1940s. He became a senior member of the Leeds Community Relations Council and was awarded the MBE. So he knew his way around the institutions of Leeds. "He was closer to the establishment than us, but he wanted the West Indians to have their own Centre." Assisted by Cllr Gabb, they all went to visit a Working Man's Club in Halton Moor to see how that kind of social centre worked.

"We didn't need any funds from the council – we had a brewery lined up that was going to sponsor the whole thing." They contracted with a company called Club Transformation to build the UCA Centre for them, on the site on Chapeltown Road where Roscoe Methodist Church is now standing. They had the drawings and planning approval for the club all in place. There would be a cellar downstairs for the youths. Arthur remembered his friend from the university, Tony Lewis, who went back to Jamaica to be a dentist, bringing his friends down to the site: "Tony was jumping up and down singing 'Here we gonna be' – Tony was so full of life."

Suddenly, planning permission was rescinded. "It was a farce. They said the Catholic Church had an option to build on the land." They didn't know it at the time, but the church's option had run out of time. "But we still banging at the door to build our own centre." They asked about vacant land at the south end of Chapeltown Road near the Ramgarhia Centre. "That was blocked." Then they enquired about spare land at the south end Scott Hall Road. "They were blocking us because we were promoting Black Power." The Council people said to Arthur "If we give it to the UCA, then the Jamaicans will want land and the Bajans will too". As we have seen in Chapter 4, by the end of the 1970s, the UCA did manage to buy a property in Hall Lane in Chapeltown.

The Leeds West Indian Centre did eventually get built. But, after permission was granted, subsequent planning for this centre took place while Arthur was working in Germany. The Barbados Overseas Association put in an application for a centre of their own, but their big-hearted chairperson, the late Ralph Maynard, said if the Barbados application would jeopardise the West Indian Centre application he would withdraw theirs, which he did.

The process of building the West Indian Centre was led by Calvin Beech, Mrs Paul and Errol James. "Calvin drove it, mainly. He is a trained engineer and he understood the building structures like I did." But Calvin left Leeds to settle in Toronto,

Arthur France outside Leeds West Indian Centre, 24.3.2021 © Max Farrar

"and they wouldn't invite me to meetings after Calvin had left."
Arthur felt that Errol and Mrs Paul were taken advantage
of – "I looked at the drawings and pointed out certain things that
were wrong with the building." But it was too late. They had
some retention money which the company forfeited after Arthur
pointed out to them the mistakes they had made. Nevertheless,
the building was there and it has been improved upon and is
used to this day, steered until recently by Ian Charles MBE,
filled to capacity for events associated with the carnival.

Soon after the violent urban protest that swept the country
in 1981, with two nights of upheaval in Chapeltown and
Harehills, the leader of the council, George Mudie (whom we met
in Chapter 4) set up the Chapeltown and Harehills Liaison
Committee. Arthur took an interest in the Liaison Committee
when he got back from Germany, but, for him, it was being
wrecked by the militant youngsters, who wanted much more
control, and much more resources, than he believed they could
realistically expect.

By this time it was Arthur's view that you can't make real
progress without the support of the Labour council: "You've got
to be realistic." The Liaison Committee did actually deliver quite
significant improvements, both in infrastructure and in opening
doors for Black people into council jobs, including (ironically,
given the point quoted above about everyone wanting their own
land) separate centres for the Jamaicans and the Bajans, as well
as all the South Asian groups.

In 2009, Arthur summarised his political life to Rob Dale,
for the BBC website:

I was probably more of a Malcolm X character back in the
day, very out-spoken in my beliefs. Any time I am told I
can't do something, it just energises me to try harder. But
I am a realist, I don't enjoy arguing, I enjoy discussions.
I'm an optimist and believe a resolution can always be
made – it's through these tactics that real change comes

about and this has been crucial to helping the community of Chapeltown. Many now say I'm more in line with Martin Luther King – that radical side of me has calmed a little, but the drive still remains.

His drive remains, but Arthur is disappointed at the decline in Black struggle. "When I came back to Leeds in the early 1980s people say we're doing well. But I said we're going backwards." By that Arthur meant the Black people were losing their unity and their independence. For Arthur, "Black politics in Leeds went down hill in the 1980s and 90s."

There have been real changes since then. Lord Simon Woolley is a Black man adopted by white parents who developed a passion for social change. He founded Operation Black Vote in 1996 to increase Black and Asian people's representation in mainstream politics. Four MPs with backgrounds in the New Commonwealth had been elected in 1987, and each of them championed Black people's rights and supported the struggle against racism. (These pioneers were Diane Abbott, Paul Boateng, Bernie Grant and Keith Vaz, all members of the Labour Party.)

When Arthur met Mohammed Ali, at the Park Lane Hotel, London, 24.4.1984. © Hansib Publications. Courtesy Arthur France

By 2021 there were 65 Members of Parliament with origins in Africa, the Caribbean and Asia. Twenty two of them were Conservatives, demonstrating that class interests can trump 'race' identification. Some of them had been mentored by Lord Woolley (he took his seat in the House of Lords in 2019). Arthur would agree with Lord Woolley that this increase in representation is a mixed blessing.

Woolley told Alex Mistlin in 2021 that he was 'dismayed by the rise of prominent Black and Asian politicians who "seek to deny the levels of systemic racism that exist today"'. He was referring to senior members of the Conservative government's Cabinet. That government appointed the Jamaican-heritage academic, Dr Tony Sewell to produce an official report in 2021 which Lord Woolley described as a "historic denial of the scale of race inequality in Britain". We can take this as sign that multiculturalism has come of age – why should all Black people share the same politics? – but it's a deep blow for Arthur's Black Power generation to witness this denial of history and structure.

On the other hand, while it's true that militant, on-the-streets Black struggle disappeared in Leeds the 1990s, powerful demonstrations have taken place repeatedly across the UK when British police have killed Black people in custody. For example, Janet Alder has campaigned tirelessly on behalf of her brother Christopher who died in custody in Hull in 1998. Benjamin Zephaniah – British born to Bajan and Jamaican parents – has written about the death of his cousin Mikey Powell at the hands of the police in 2003. Zephaniah wasn't surprised – he already knew about the deaths of David Oluwale (1969), Colin Roach (1983) and Joy Gardner (1993). His brother Tippah Napthali has been a prime mover in the national campaign protesting about Mikey's and other deaths in custody ever since.

Zephaniah's autobiography was published in 2018, and he knows that the situation for Black people in Britain still leaves much to be desired. Born in 1958, he wrote that some things had got better, but with:

We had come a long way and it would have been wrong
to say [in a 2015 TV programme he made with the BBC]
that things were the same as they'd been when I was a
boy ... but that's not to say that things were great. The new
racists had learned to be a lot subtler than they used to
be ... their brand of racism was more insidious, more
sophisticated, more institutional ... The racists had grown
up; they'd put on suits and ties and formed political
parties.

But protest had not stopped. Caryl Phillips, also born in 1958
(in St Kitts) often re-visits Leeds, where he grew up, and he
noted a big change in the city in 2005:

Leeds was the city that took us in, back in 1958. My
parents and I were assimilated into cobbled streets,
introduced to dark, gloomy buildings, and situated around
the corner from pubs that still operated a colour bar. But
whatever the difficulties, this was our home. Today's
newly-constructed city centre, with its young multi-racial
population, speaks eloquently to a kind of self-belief that
the city has not known since its mid-nineteenth-century
heyday.

Sure enough, confident enough: demonstrations – with large
numbers of Black and white people in solidarity – reappeared
in Leeds (and all over the UK) with the Black Lives Matter
protests in the second decade of the 2000s. Arthur's daughters
Asha and Mahalia were instrumental in the BLM
demonstrations organised in Leeds in 2020.

Some things have got better. The globally acclaimed singer
and song-writer Corinne Bailey Rae was born in Leeds in 1979.
Her father is from St Kitts. Described in one interview as 'an
old-school leftie', she loves Leeds because, she said in an
interview in 2016, it is an integrated city that celebrates

diversity, so people of all different backgrounds can co-exist. Importantly, in Leeds, it's 'not such a big deal' that her mother is white. 'I feel like Leeds has nurtured me.'

It's not sufficiently understood that the steady progress of Leeds – where there is now much conviviality and a good degree of cohesion – owes immeasurably to the struggles that Arthur France and his brothers and sisters led in the 1960s, 70s and 80s. The youths who engaged in violent urban protest in the 1970s and 1980s gave added urgency to those campaigns, and the establishment was forced to respond. That was what laid the foundations for the 'self-belief' of the 'multi-racial' city that is so obvious to Phillips when he's back in Leeds.

But those were hard times and the establishment's response included hard policing. Calvin Beech left for Canada in 1978 partly because he was under surveillance from the police, with his phone being bugged. His militancy was needed to keep momentum up in Leeds. Arthur doesn't mean to disrespect anyone but he felt that some of the younger ones were too extreme. "George [Archibald], Calvin [Beech] and myself were very strong, very close together, networking all the time – we were the driving force and when we dispersed the whole thing collapsed. I felt very sad. We had made so much progress."

"From then on, my energy went into carnival." That's the topic for the next chapter.

References in this chapter

Brian Alleyne, *Radicals against Race,* Oxford: Berg, 2002, explains the political achievements of John La Rose and his comrades in Britain from the 1960s to the 1990s.

Joyce Bernard, *When Our Ship Comes In – Black Women Talk,* edited by Palorine Williams, Pontefract: Yorkshire Arts Circus, no date, c.1992. ISBN 0 947780 83 1. (Other Chapeltown women featured in this booklet are Fay Comrie, Agnes Hinds, Odessa Stoute, Elaine Davis, Katie Stewart, Georgina Webbe, Jean White, Carol Comrie.)

Black Power in Britain material is mainly derived from Anne Marie Angelo, 'The Black Panthers in London 1967 – 1972', *Radical History*

Review, 2009 (103); Robin Bunce and Paul Field, 'Obi B Egbuna, CLR James and the Birth of Black Power in Britain', *Twentieth Century British History*, 2010; Robin Bunce and Paul Field, *Renegade – The Life and Time of Darcus Howe*, London: Bloomsbury Academic, 2017; CLR James, 'Black Power', in *CLR James – Spheres of Existence , Selected Writings,* London: Allison & Busby, 1980; Rosalind Eleanor Wild, *Black was the Colour of our Fight,* PhD Thesis, University of Sheffield, 2008. Available at http://etheses.whiterose.ac.uk/3640/ Accessed 23.3.2020; and John L Williams, *Michael X*, London: Century, 2008.

Beverley Bryan was interviewed by Tobi Thomas, 'A Lot of People had their Lives shattered by the Police', *The Guardian*, 28.01.2021. https://www.theguardian.com/society/2021/jan/28/beverley-bryan-the-british-black-panther-who-inspired-a-generation-of-women Accessed 06.02.2021.

Beverley Bryan, Stella Dadzie and Suzanne Scafe, *Heart of the Race – Black Women's Lives in Britain*, London: Virago, 1985; second edition London: Verso, 2018.

On the 1975 Bonfire Night events, see: 'Remember, Remember the 5th of November - The Bonfire Night Case', *Race Today,* September 1976, p. 181; and Max Farrar, 'Rioting or Protesting? Losing it of Finding It?' *Parallax*, 18:2, pp. 72-91, 2012. Available at https://www.maxfarrar.org.uk/writing/culture-politics/rioting-or-protesting-losing-it-or-finding-it/ Accessed 22.12.2020.

Rob Dale, 'Gallic Flair – Arthur France is one of Chapeltown's favourite sons, due to the enormous contribution he's made to his community'. BBC (Leeds) 05.06.2019. Available at http://www.bbc.co.uk/leeds/content/articles/2009/06/05/people_arthur_france_feature.shtml Accessed 4.4.2020.

Dave Durman, 'Leeds Immigrants', *Union News*, (Leeds University Student Newspaper) 31.91.1969. I'm grateful to the local historian Danny Fryer for supplying this article.

Max Farrar, *The Struggle for 'Community' in a British Multi-ethnic, Inner-city area,* Lampeter & New York: Edwin Mellen, 2002. This book discusses the UCA Saturday School, the Cowper Street School strike, the representation of Chapeltown in the media, the 1975 bonfire night events, the Harehills and Chapeltown Liaison Committee, and the succession of political movements in Chapeltown from the 1970s to the 1990s.

Prudence France, 'A Humble Leader – Sir Joseph Nathaniel France', *St Kitts and Nevis Visitor*, Vol. 2, 1997-8.

On CARD, see Benjamin W Heineman, The *Politics of the Powerless – A Study of the Campaign Against Racial Discrimination*, London: Institute of Race Relations and Oxford University Press, 1972; and Rosalind Eleanor Wild, *Black was the Colour of our Fight,* PhD Thesis, University of Sheffield, 2008. Available at http://etheses.whiterose.ac.uk/3640/ Accessed 23.3.2020.

Colin Grant, *Homecoming – Voices of the Windrush Generation*, London: Jonathan Cape, 2019.

House of Commons Select Committee on Race and Immigration 1971-2 *Report on Police-Immigrant Relations*, HC 471-1, HMSO, London, England.

Alex Mistlin, 'Nothing was going to stop me changing the world', *Guardian G2*, 15.7.2021. Available at https://www.theguardian.com/society/2021/jul/15/black-faces-in-high-places-how-simon-woolley-revolutionised-british-politics Accessed 18.7.2021.

Rudy Narayan, *Black Community on Trial*, introduction by Cecil Gutzmore, London: Blackbird Books, 1976. ISBN 0 901813 02 8.

Emmanuel Nwene-Osuh, *The Long Journey of Pa David Emare*, SheffieldL New Begin Publications, 2012.

On David Oluwale, see: Caryl Phillips, *Foreigners – Three English Lives*, London: Harvill Secker, 2007; and Kester Aspden, *The Hounding of David Oluwale*, London: Vintage, 2008. A summary of most published work on David Oluwale, including poems by Linton Kwesi Johnson, is included in Max Farrar, 'David Oluwale: making his memory and debating his martyrdom', in Quentin Outram and Keith Laybourn (eds) *Secular Martyrdom in Britain and Ireland – From Peterloo to the Present*, London: Palgrave, 2018. Available at https://www.maxfarrar.org.uk/writing/david-oluwale-was-he-a-secular-martyr/ Accessed 26.3.2020. More on the David Oluwale Memorial Association can be found at www.rememberoluwale.org

Caryl Phillips, 'The Pioneers: Fifty Years of Caribbean Migration to Britain', in Caryl Phillips, *A New World Order*, London: Secker & Warburg, 2001, is the source of the 'second generation' quote.

Caryl Phillips, 'Northern Soul', in Caryl Phillips, *Colour Me English*, London: Harvill Secker, 2011, is the source of the 'self-belief' quote.

Susan Pitter (edited for the Jamaica Society of Leeds), *Eulogy*, 2020, purchasable from https://coloursmayvary.com. Accessed 20.8.2020.

Corinne Bailey Rae, 'Why I Love Leeds', in *Yorkshire Life*, 13.06.2016, Available at https://www.yorkshirelife.co.uk/people/celebrity-interviews/corinne-bailey-rae-why-i-love-leeds-1-4569102 Accessed 17.10.2020.

Donald Wade, *Yorkshire Survey – A report on community relations in Yorkshire*, Leeds: Yorkshire Committee for Community Relations, 1971.

Benjamin Zephaniah, *The Life and Rhymes of Benjamin Zephaniah – An Autobiography*, London: Simon and Shuster, 2018.

Chapter 8

EMANCIPATION: MAKING CARNIVAL

These days, Arthur is best known in the city of Leeds for founding the Carnival, and for keeping it going through thick and thin for over 50 years. It took the city far too long to fully acknowledge the extent of this achievement, but it finally came to its senses, and Arthur received The Leeds Award on 3rd February 2015. (He is in very good company. The award list includes the top poet Tony Harrison, top cyclist Beryl Burton, top piano person Dame Fanny Waterman, top writer Alan Bennett, top soccer stars Leeds United (1967-74), and top of them all, Nelson Mandela.)

This book demonstrates that there's much more to Arthur than Carnival, but Carnival is his pride and joy. And this chapter shows that Carnival is a summary of Arthur himself. Carnival embodies his absolute commitment to the emancipation of all the people, (particularly members of the African Diaspora); it expresses his creativity; it shows his commitment to the well-being of the city of Leeds as a whole; and it flows with his good-humour and multi-cultural conviviality. Arthur is a Carnival man through and through and he is one of its principal leaders.

Arthur France made a key-note speech at the international conference on the Caribbean Carnival held at Leeds Beckett University (UK) in 2017 as part of the celebrations for 50 years of the Leeds West Indian Carnival. He said he was passionate about being an African. He believed that a person's race comes before their nationality. He argued that the great African continent is what drives Carnival. He said that this conference, gathering Carnival people from all over the world, was celebrating our forefathers and their emancipation, as well as the legacy of the Carnival in Leeds. He pointed out that the panel included some of the original committee members, emphasising that "You need a team for Carnival, just as a general needs an army." He added, wryly, that there has been mutiny on the bounty – Carnival is not plain sailing. "But we are a people full of compassion and love." Acknowledging the not always favourable context for Black people celebrating the arts of Carnival, he said: "We are not too worried about receiving love, but we demand some respect." (These are my notes of his speech.).

Delivered with his smile and his passion, this is the thinking that has driven the Leeds West Indian Carnival since 1967. As always, it all starts in Nevis.

Carnival in Nevis

As a child in Nevis, Arthur had witnessed the special form of Carnival that was created in the Caribbean soon after the abolition of slavery. It drew from the European Carnivals that appeared in the 13th century. They allowed for festivity before the abstinence imposed in Lent by the Catholic Church, so Carnival would take place in February or March (as it does today in Trinidad and Tobago). M A Katritzky has provided an example of early Carnival festivities, as described in a Shrovetide play in 1605:

What, are there masques? Hear you me, Jessica:
Lock up my doors, and when you hear the drum
And the vile squealing of the wry-neck'd fife,
Clamber not you up to the casements then,
Nor thrust your head into the public street
To gaze on Christian fools with varnish'd faces.

Arthur France performing on the road at Leeds West Indian Carnival in 2015. © Guy Farrar

So, from the start of Carnival, there is masking and dancing to the sound of the drum and the fife that Arthur witnessed as a child in Nevis. Right away, there are Christians who are highly critical of other Christians for making a fool of their religion by playing in the Carnival. What makes the Caribbean type of Carnival so important is its addition of new masks, costumes and rhythms drawn by the emancipated Africans from their own expressive cultural heritage. However hard they tried, the colonial masters had failed to suppress the enslaved people before and after formal abolition from appropriating the European Carnival and shaping it for their own purposes.

Michael La Rose, son of British-Trinidadian John La Rose, has continued his father's analysis of the cultural significance of the Caribbean form of Carnival. Michael has linked the Egungun, Gelede and Owi masquerades in different regions of

Nigeria, and the Djale masks in the Ivory Coast, to Carnival troupes in the Caribbean. Errol Hill has described the semi-military, semi-mountebank John Canoe character in the 19th century as 'another figure representing New World Africanism', combining this with the 'celebration of acquired elements from English mumming, Morris dancing, and French Carnival parades'. Hill referred also to the Moko Jumbie figure, known throughout West Africa, parading on stilts, sometimes fifteen feet high, with a fabricated head concealing the actor – Moko Jumbie has visited Leeds on several occasions.

Michael La Rose has also noted the infusion of South Asian culture into the Trinidad Carnival, carried by the indentured labour brought by the British from 19th century India, exemplified in the Hosay festivals in Trinidad. That history was carried into the Leeds Carnival when Sheila Howarth was crowned Queen in 1989 in a costume titled 'Pot of Gold at the End of the Rainbow', designed and made by Kam Sangra and his family.

Kam, a colleague of Arthur's at Technorth (see Chapter 5) is of South Asian heritage, and quickly understood the importance of Carnival. Sheila remembered that moment as Queen of Carnival in her interview with Colin Grant: 'Everyone was cheering me from being this ordinary woman. And I'd never seen so many Black people before. You weren't as alone as you thought you were ... for once I was important ... You are that costume, you kind of morph into what it is'.

Arthur is steeped in Carnival from his childhood. "I'd loved Carnival from seeing it in Nevis when I was a child. My parents liked it, but they wouldn't take part. I always wanted to." On Nevis, the Carnival revelries went on for eight days – troupes would parade all over the island. "They would be on the streets and they'd visit your yard."

In St Kitts, it was called 'Sports', Calvin Beech told me. James Sutton's autobiography provides this description of the Sports he knew as a child in St Kitts in the 1930s:

It was the rehearsal for 'Sports' (masquerade bands) in preparation for Christmas that was the most popular for young and old. The rehearsals brought out the big drum, and the string bands, and drew crowds not only from Greenhill and Cayon, but also from such distant places as Ottley's and Lodge villages to dance and 'wok up' behind the drums. It was these rehearsals, too, that gave us, the younger ones, the opportunity to be out later than usual at night, to meet our friends, and engage in youthful frolic, returning home well after 10 pm without incurring the wrath of our parents. Some of the participating bands were 'David and Goliath', based on the Bible story; 'Giant Despair', taken from Bunyan's 'Pilgrim's Progress' and others included 'Mummies', 'The Bull', 'Plait-the-Ribbon', 'Nagur Business', 'School Children', 'Clowns', 'Red Indians', called Masquerades, and others too numerous to mention.

'Sport' comes from the French word 'desport', meaning leisure, and its first noted use in English in 1300 is for 'anything humans find amusing or entertaining'. It's probable that the name 'Sports' and the practice of Carnival in St Kitts-Nevis at Christmas derives from the traditional festivities that the white masters and servants held in mid-winter in the mid-1600s, soon after they settled. Karen Fog Olwig has explained that Christmas folk theatre ('mumming' – could this be what Sutton meant by Mummies?) and 'mystery plays' had been established outside the ale-houses that appeared in England in the Sixteenth century. In Nevis, white masters and servants mixed during the Christmas period enjoying the food, drink and pageantry they had known in England. Here was one of those moments of convivial pleasure that provided temporary balm for the daily violence of enslaved labour.

This apparently offended the devout, and a 1659 law on Nevis banned 'loud talking, the singing of songs or any gaming' on Sundays. By 1675 it seemed that another law was needed to

stop 'the unchristian like association of white people with
negroes', with corporal punishment meted out to anyone found
'drinking, playing or conversing with negroes'; in 1697 another
law was passed providing for public whipping of any whites
found 'with any negroes at play' or supplying them with 'light,
liquor of otherwise'. It obviously took some violence to try and
stop white people and Black people enjoying themselves together
in Nevis.

All these fun and games were apparently taking place on
Sundays and at holiday times (such as Whitsun Tide, Plough
Monday, Harvest Festival, May Day), with Christmas providing
an extended period of revelry. Olwig noted that:

> Some of the drinking and sporting also involved the upper
> level of the hierarchy in the sense that masters usually
> donated food and drink for celebrations which occurred
> in connection with festivals. On Nevis it had apparently
> become a tradition for masters to give out special rations
> of fish or meat at Christmas and other festivals.

It's easy to imagine this English habit in Nevis of 'sporting' at
Christmas – involving drinking, gaming, mumming (enacting
folk stories) and performing scenes from the Bible in the mystery
plays – being transformed into Carnival at Christmas: it proved
impossible to stop the Africans from joining in, injecting their
drums and flutes and their masks into the festivities.

A report published in 1707 described African dancers in
Nevis with 'great activity and strength of the Body', who had
'Rattles ty'd to their legs and wrists and in their hands'. They
were 'keeping time with one who makes a Sound answering it
on the mouth of an empty Gourd or Jar with his Hand'. Dancers
often had horse hairs tied to their bottoms, giving them 'a very
extraordinary appearance'. 'Sports' in Nevis and St Kitts is a
term that would seem to capture the Carnivalesque spirit
perfectly well.

In Novelette Morton-Henry's history of carnival in St Kitts and Nevis, the modern form of carnival on the island starts in 1957, thanks to the energetic work of Basil Henderson, but earlier manifestations of the carnival arts are referred to:

> String band and big drum music usually accompanied the folk performances. The instruments which were played to create the lilting, rhythmic music were guitars, quartos, the fife, triangle, 'baha' which is a long piece of metal pipe that is blown, and the 'shack-shack', a tin can containing beads. In the case of big drum music, a huge drum along with a kettle drum beating out pulsating rhythms and a fife were played.
>
> During the late 1940s, the iron band was introduced and was mainly made up of car rims and drums, creatively played to create music for street jamming. It was during this period as well that a number of community bands, consisting of trumpets, saxophones, drums, and double-bass guitars, thrived. Bands such as Esperanza, Music Makers, Rhythm Kings, Brown Queen and the Silver Rhythm Orchestra were some of the established ones which featured at dances and concerts.

Ian Charles, originally from Trinidad, is another pillar of the Leeds Carnival, central to its organisation for almost as long as Arthur. Ian told me in an interview in 1988 about joining a Sailor Band when he was about 16, having moved from Arima to Port of Spain to go to College. His ambition as a child was to join a band of robbers: "They would catch you in a corner and pull out their guns – you couldn't get away until you paid them something."

Arthur's favourite was David and Goliath, with fabulous costumes, music, and a dramatic performance of the Biblical story. The giant was played by Gerry Ward, who was already six feet tall – "He was born to do that part" – with George Byas playing the kettle drum, Ebeneeza Queerly on the fife, and there was a bass player called Bolton. Other masqueraders in Nevis would read and perform more parts from John Bunyan's *Pilgrim's Progress.*

Speaking to Colin Grant, Arthur put it like this: 'The first Carnival masquerade I ever saw as a little boy in the Caribbean was David and Goliath, based on the Bible story, and that captured me. It was magic. I can see it in front of me now. All that colour and drama is in complete contrast to what we find in the Motherland'. "I didn't understand the politics of David and Goliath, at the time, of course, but I do now," Arthur told me. As we have seen, Arthur's family was steeped in Christianity, so a Bible story was bound to appeal; unconsciously, the story of the little man defeating the big man, by using his intelligence and smart technology, would shape Arthur's life.

James Sutton has described this masquerade as follows:

> The dialogue of the 'Giant Despair' or 'David and Goliath' band was handed down from one generation to another; sometimes from a father who played from year to year, to his son who might carry on after his father died. So the players spoke their parts in local dialect, adding their own lines when they wished to make the dialogue more humorous and amusing.

Sutton went on to link this performative pleasure to the special meals of Christmas, reminding us that, however poor were the Black people of St Kitts and Nevis, their access to fertile land and their skills as small farmers meant they could put on fine festive meals:

> The provision lands were filled with food planted expressly for the Christmas feast. The pigeon-pea trees would be blooming, the sorrel plants would put out their beautiful light-pink bell-shaped flowers, which soon gave

way to bright red pods of sorrel, the traditional Christmas drink in St Kitts and most of the West Indies ... The Christmas pig, long chosen for fattening to produce the Christmas pork, was now reaching its peak condition.

Then and now, there are Caribbean Christians who condemn Carnival, regarding it as excessive and sinful, perhaps because it drew people's attention from their proper devotions at Christmas and Easter. Arthur's parents didn't disapprove but they only watched. Arthur did drama at school, appearing in plays, but he was not allowed to play mas. He made up for lost time in Leeds. He had experienced the sheer joy, excess, creativity and conviviality of Carnival in Nevis, and he was going to make sure it warmed Leeds up, too.

Starting the first Caribbean Carnival in Europe

As we saw in the previous chapter Arthur had co-founded the United Caribbean Association in 1964 and in 1966 he thought he would suggest to the UCA that it should make a Carnival in Leeds for its growing population of West Indians. Sometimes Arthur says his motive was to provide a cure for the homesickness that so many people were feeling. But when he talks politics, Arthur says he thought up the idea of making a Carnival to show the white people of Leeds that Caribbean people weren't limited to political protest – he wanted to show that Caribbean people are artistic and playful and joyful, too.

One of the great things about Carnival is that people can make of it what they like. For Arthur, its roots are in the emancipation of the slaves in the West Indies, and he is emphatic that it must stay true to its roots. The Queen and troupe costumes he makes every year invariably express the power and beauty of his African heritage. "A lot of people in Carnival still don't understand that Carnival is a mix of masquerading and the politics of emancipation." Making mas is an intensely creative art, where new ideas, new materials, new techniques are highly prized. Arthur has always made Queen and troupe costumes. And he's always inserted his radical, intellectual energy into the art, so he can tell stories that will promote the never-ending struggle for freedom.

There are Carnival artists worldwide who aren't interested in the politics, but Leeds Carnival attracts lots of people who, in one form or another, do see that Carnival is more than just a few days of fun, food, dancing and drinking. It's that too, of course, but it carries a wider message, celebrating African history and advocating a new world of justice, equality, the breaking of all chains, historical and contemporary. It's the 'freedom for all people' message that drew me in as a young white postgraduate student and political activist in Chapeltown in the early 1970s.

Arthur's first effort to get the UCA to back the Carnival project fell flat. He'd done some preparation. He had spoken to people in the city council to see how they would respond to a street parade in Carnival costume. Perhaps because they were familiar with the idea of the English Carnival parade – some parts of Leeds had May Fairs and the annual Leeds Lord Mayor's parade expressed elements of the Carnival tradition – or perhaps because they thought that a Caribbean Carnival would be a useful addition to the city, the city leaders said they'd welcome Arthur's Carnival.

He had persuaded some of the UCA leaders that it was something they should do. But, at the meeting, "Most people thought I was mad. They said it couldn't happen here." Arthur is not easily deterred. He took it back to a second meeting. "They said, OK, and a few said they would join an organising committee, but they were very half-hearted." He set his committee members some tasks, and none of them delivered, "So I sacked them all. I formed a new group and the same thing happened. Nothing."

While all this was going on he went to see his sister Elaine at her house in Grange Avenue. One of her friends came into the

Arthur France (right) with his Windrush masquerade troupe at the Leeds West Indian Carnival, August 1998. © Max Farrar

room and everyone kept quiet while she said: "There's this crazy Black man from Nevis who want a Carnival. He want to make us look like fool for the white people. But I hope the rain comes down and drown them." No one mentioned that this crazy man was in the room with them. Every time he tells this story Arthur lets out his huge laugh.

In 1966 a Carnival fête was staged at Kitson College of Further Education in Leeds City Centre. Tony Lewis (from Jamaica) and Frankie Davis (from Trinidad) put on an event headlined by the British Soul Band Jimmy James and the Vagabonds. Marlene Samlalsingh, also from Trinidad, created a troupe of Red Indians to perform on stage. Arthur was there – he wasn't one of the organisers – but he was inspired.

By 1967, he'd got the right people together to make the Carnival happen in Leeds. They included George Archibald, Calvin Beech, Ervin and Veronica Samlalsingh, Rose McAlister, Vanta Pule, Willie Robinson, Anson Shepherd, Ken Thomas and Wally Thompson. Vanta Pule had been a major player in the St Kitts' Carnival. Some of the others were from Trinidad so they had experience of the largest and best organised Carnival in the Caribbean islands and were very keen to make one in Leeds.

All of these were reliable partners, but Arthur paid special tribute to Willie Robinson, originally from Trinidad, who backed him from the start. Willie insisted on eliminating anyone who just wanted to talk and wasn't going to do the hard work that he knew was needed. In our book celebrating 50 years of Leeds Carnival, Willie wrote:

> We had the task of staging Carnival without any finance. We appealed to the business community in Leeds. None was forthcoming. By our own fundraising and the generosity of many individuals from the community, the first of what is now an annual event and the forerunner of Westindian Carnivals in most of the major cities of England, became a reality. What started as a fun event, quickly became a vehicle of co-operation between Westindian organisations from Huddersfield, Birmingham, Manchester, etc.

Reuben McTair was born in Trinidad and lived in Huddersfield, but he was linked into the Leeds Carnival right from the start. Remembering that first event, he told Colin Grant:

> I'll be honest, right up to the night before, no, even on the morning, I thought it was going to be a disaster. I had thought it impossible to achieve. But Arthur had something. I tell you, Black people are hell to move. Mr Arthur France must have had something. Must have had plenty. Still has today. Secretly, a lot of folk – and I mean Black folk – had come, I'm ashamed to say, had come to jeer. But the day there was a lot of Doubting Thomases converted. Brother, they had come to jeer but they stayed to cheer.

Carnival pioneers: L-R: Calvin Beech, Arthur France, Rashida Robinson, Ian Charles, Willie Robinson at the 50th anniversary Carnival, 2017. © Max Farrar

Reuben McTair added this analysis of the meaning of Carnival:

> What you have to remember is what Caribbean people were thinking. I'm not in Leeds. I'm in Chapelton [Jamaica], I'm in Basseterre, Castries, Port of Spain, Kingston. And before that I was in Accra, Lagos, Monrovia, Akan. My people are Yoruba, Ibo, Ashanti. I know my roots. And that is why ... that is exactly why we need Carnival. Carnival connect up all the dots. Yes! So we don't forget our roots.

Arthur and Reuben think alike. Arthur would probably add that, for the Trinis, there are roots in South Asian religious festivals, too. At the Leeds Carnival, with its utterly inclusive ethos, you can sometimes see bands of white masqueraders channelling modern English forms of Carnival, like the marching bands throwing their sticks in the air and catching them.

Rashida Robinson, born in Trinidad, talking to Colin Grant, pointed to another cultural reference in Carnival, and spoke eloquently of how Carnival transforms you:

The first costume I wore was Native American Indians with feathers and a beautiful headpiece. Putting a costume on was like dressing up as a little doll, it was something new ... It's me in a different light, something I enjoy; and it's no fairytale, it's reality now ... When you were in Trinidad you saw all these young people in a costume, never had the opportunity to do it although you wanted to. But now I can do it for real.

Angela Wenham was born in Barbados and grew up in Leeds. She remembered the first Carnival like this (to Colin Grant): 'To see a group of West Indians jamming on the road, it were fantastic, it was really good fun. You dance all the way, you lead the party, you just jam. And to see all these faces looking at you in shock – the Carnival is actually going ahead – and no policeman arresting, because that was one worry, it was fantastic'.

Hughbon Condor was born in St Kitts and arrived in Leeds in the 1960s as a schoolboy. He was drawn into Carnival costume-making as a young man in the early 1970s by Arthur France. At the 2017 Carnival conference at Leeds Beckett University, Hughbon, now Leeds's premiere costume designer with an international profile, made a very important point about Carnival: it is the only time when Black people can actually control the streets of Leeds, without any problems. Arthur's vision of making a political point without making trouble was coming to life.

1967: The first costumes

Arthur remembered those early days of Leeds Carnival as though they had happened last week. "None of us had actually made a Queen costume before. We'd seen them, that's all." Cleve Watkins from Trinidad had experience of making Queen costumes, and he gave a lot of assistance. Vanta Pule had made troupes back home, but not Queens. Nevertheless, in 1967 she made 'Fantasia Britannia' (inspired by the image on the British penny coin in those days). Willie Robinson made 'Cleopatra's Fan', Wally Thompson made 'Gondola', Betty Bertie made 'The Snow Queen', Melda Adams made 'The Hawaiian Dancer', Veronica and Ervin Samlalsingh made 'The Sun Goddess'. (Vicky Cielto performed that costume at the first Queen Show.) "It was an amazing effort by everyone." They all co-operated to make the 'Cheyanne Indians' troupe. (Ian Charles was their Chief.)

Carnival is, above all, a family affair, so a special troupe for children was made by Veronica Samlalsingh and Anson Shepherd. Mrs Pyke and her husband made a 'Sailors' troupe. "And Mrs Pyke painted on a moustache, which made everyone laugh." Sydney Brown produced some very authentic Mexicans with their broad hats. "Sydney slung a guitar over his shoulder, so we call him Que Paso."

Ian Charles was a survey engineer building the M62 motorway and most weeks he worked away from his home. When he got back he couldn't get into his house: it had been turned into a mas camp with every room full of people making costumes and the doors almost blocked shut. He just laughed at the chaos in his house: it's the Carnival spirit.

"The Gondola costume was a big problem – it was very technical. Without Cleve we wouldn't have been able to produce it." Carnival might be a family affair, but it can put stress on relationships. Cleve was an expert wire-bender. He was on the way with his girlfriend to the Hyde Park Picture House, near the university, when Arthur asked him to help. He came over to the mas camp straight away. "It was amazing to see how he used the wire to create the shape of the gondola." He stayed there for the next two weeks, completely neglecting his girlfriend. We don't know what the girlfriend had to say, but there is a whole category of people out there called Carnival Widows. Arthur's wife Tattra is probably Queen of the Carnival Widows.

Arthur France with his daughter Mahalia at the 1977 Leeds
West Indian Carnival. Photo courtesy Arthur France

"We had some fun making the Indians' costumes. You
couldn't buy costume feathers in those days like you can now.
So we had to improvise." First stop was the Polish man who sold
chickens on Chapeltown Road. (That shop became Harrison
Bundey and Co, the solicitors, for many years, until Harrison
closed it in 2018.) But he wet his chickens before he plucked
them and they didn't want those feathers.

In Otley, about ten miles north of Leeds, Arthur and Willie
found someone who would sell them live chickens. They bought
several and took them to Leeds in the back of their car. Then
they took orders from anyone who wanted a fresh chicken for
their Sunday lunch. Ian Charles's girlfriend said she wanted one
but it had to be a male. Not only could Cleve bend wire, he could
kill and pluck chickens, so he went to work. "Once they were

Ian Charles MBE and Arthur France MBE in the carnival
marquee, 1995. © Max Farrar

plucked, no one knew a cock from a hen. Ian's girlfriend found
herself with a chicken full of eggs." No matter, they had plenty
of feathers for the Indians' headpieces.

Carnival makes you laugh and it makes you expand your
horizons. Mrs Gordon made the Indians' costumes and Mrs
Morton made their headdresses. Mrs Morton had a dilemma.
She was an active member of her church and the majority of her
congregation strongly disapproved of Carnival mayhem. But
Mrs Morton loved making the costumes and didn't condemn her
friends who wanted to play mas in England. Her solution was
only to attend the house where the costumes were being made
at the dead of night. "She thought she would be thrown out of
her church if anyone saw her helping with the Carnival. They
thought it was the devil's work. We used to have a good laugh
about this at one o'clock in the morning."

The first Queen Show

The Carnival committee had booked the Jubilee Hall at the south end of Chapeltown Road for the first Queen and Calypso show. (This historic building, the Leeds Jewish Institute, was built in the 1930s by the Eastern European refugees who, from the 1920s, settled in Chapeltown. In the 1970s, it was the Leeds Trades Unions Club, and is now the Leeds Media Centre.)

"We were young and radical, and no one was taking us seriously, so we knew this had to be a big event." They knew there was a Black man presenting the news on Tyne and Tees TV, so they rang the studio and asked to speak to Clyde Alleyne. Clyde came from Trinidad so he knew how important Carnival was and he jumped at the offer to be the Master of Ceremonies at the first Leeds Queen Show.

"Seeing Clyde Alleyne on stage lifted my heart up. His presence and his voice brought silence to that huge hall. It was the icing on the cake." The Queens performed the five costumes described above to the collection of steel pan music they had on vinyl records. "There was a lot of drama behind stage. Mrs Morton was sewing in secret. Leo Lewis (Mixie) and Willet (the Calypsonians) were a big help. Getting the Queen costumes assembled and in front of the audience made for lots of problems."

The biggest problem was getting the giant Gondola from Ian's house in Headingley over to Chapeltown. Just in time, Mr Gaskin used his sand-delivery lorry to transport it to the Jubilee Hall. There's a lot of 'just in time' in Carnival, and there are lots and lots of people who've had a last minute call from Arthur to complete some impossible task. Despite all the obstacles, that first show was a huge success, and most of the doubters were quelled. Somehow, the Queen Show is always on the road, year after year, and it's always magnificent.

At that first Queen Show Artie Davis (aka Lord Silkie) sang his first calypso. "We called him Lord Silkie because he wore a fancy silk shirt." The name stuck and most people know him today simply as Silkie. For many years his crew, fuelled by whatever beverage manufacturer he could find to sponsor them, were the highlight of the Carnival parade: Tetley's Bittermen (and women) and, later, The Cockspur Crew were the bacchanalian spirit of Carnival. You don't have to be a Bajan to say that Cockspur is the best rum. Tetley's was Leeds's famous brewery. Its former headquarters is now a restaurant and contemporary art and education centre, which staged a memorable exhibition in 2017, organised by Susan Pitter, that celebrated 50 years of the Leeds West Indian Carnival.

Silkie's first calypso was played at that exhibition. In 2017, Silkie once again performed that calypso live, resulting in him being crowned Calypso Monarch, not for the first time. Titled 'St Kitts my Borning Land', the lyrics are:

St Kitts is my borning land, I say, I say
England is my home in every way, every way
No matter what people may say
In Englan' I goin' to stay
St Kitts is my borning lan' I say

We came here to get work and education, education
And now they're trying to keep us down, keep us down
One day we will be in power
But we must all unite together
Yes, that will be Black Power

Chorus:
St Kitts is my borning lan', I say, I say
Englan' is my home in every way, every way
No matter what people may say
In Englan' I bound to stay
St Kitts is my borning lan' I say

Give three cheers for Arthur France and Co., and Co.
For bringing Carnival to Great Britain, Great Britain

Arthur France with a carnival queen at Leeds West
Indian Carnival, August 1975. © Max Farrar

He has done his very best to make it a big success
Carnival is here, let's do the rest

[Chorus repeated with 'West Indies is our borning land']

Lord Silkie speaks:
    Yes, unity we want.
    All the Caribbean islands.
    You know, we have to stick together.
    Look what happening in the world today.
    We have to form a union in the Caribbean.
    Yes, I'm a Caribbean man.

(This song is now available on YouTube. In the 1967 version, the
words were 'England is my home in every way, every way/No

matter what Enoch Powell may say'.) If Arthur France is the embodiment of Carnival, calypso is its lyrical, satirical expression. Silkie's words succinctly express social and political themes present for all of that pioneering generation: two homes, one in the sun, one in a cold country where, whatever white people may say, they are bound to stay, where they have a right to work and to education. Note the stress on education.

Then there is the explicit commitment to full empowerment of all Black people in the UK. The song includes thanks to Arthur and a commitment to the ongoing success of Carnival in Great Britain – here is the sociability and creativity that characterises Carnival. It concludes with the plea, often expressed by Arthur, for unity among all the peoples of Caribbean; implicit is the notion that unity brings strength in the face of the world's problems.

George Hendrickson is another Leeds man who brings his talent to Carnival. He told me in 1990 that when he stopped "jumping up" in Carnival, he joined a string band. Nevis still has a band like this, but they are rare in England today. "The band had flute – which is the lead instrument – banjo, guitar, cuatro [a small, four-stringed guitar], boho [a long, pipe-like wind instrument], guiro [a bit like a steel-grater] and a triangle. Our band used to play during the Queen Show, in between the Queens coming on. We played by ear – no sheets: if I play a chord, they all respond." He was a big fan of calypso, too, recalling with pleasure when the Mighty Chalkdust's 1981 jibe at Trinidad's President Karl Hudson Philips, 'Ah Fraid Karl', destroyed his credibility.

The first Carnival parade

Arthur described the first Leeds West Indian Carnival parade, held on the August Bank Holiday Monday. His cousin Curtland Carter was making a steel band, and so was he. "We were two mad enthusiasts for steel pan music – we made 'The Gay Carnival Steel Band' with Dabbo as the leader." Later, this morphed into the Boscoe Steel Band, with Roy Buchanan, Rex, Curtland, Dabbo, Tuddy, Vince, Clark, Desmond and others. They brought the St Christopher Steel Band from Birmingham, and one from Nottingham, one from Manchester, and the Invaders, from Leeds, with Prentice as Captain, also performed.

Then, as now, everyone assembled in Potternewton Park in the heart of Chapeltown. Each band consisted of small pans that could be strung around each musician's neck, so he could walk and play. Small platforms were made on the grass for the larger bass drums. The Queens and troupes arrived in full costume and the public gathered all around admiring the spectacle.

Potternewton Park is one of Chapeltown's many splendours. It encapsulates the class history of the neighbourhood. Originally landscaped from 1817 onwards by its owner, the aptly-named Mr Brown, it has a flat expanse in the centre with steep slopes on either side, making a perfect amphitheatre for an outdoor spectacle like Carnival. (It now hosts the Leeds Black Music Festival as well, on Carnival Sunday in August.) Chapeltown has been stamped by the English aristocracy. James Brown was a Mini-Lord, a subsidiary to Earl Cowper, who, along with the Earl of Mexborough owned the land that is now Chapeltown, until the middle of the 19th century. Cowper and Mexborough sold their land but left their names, and the names of their sons, all over Chapeltown's streets. The far-sighted Leeds city council purchased the 30-acre park and mansion in 1900 and it has been an asset to the city ever since. Mr Brown did not have the status to leave his name on Chapeltown, but his home (once an adult education centre, then a Sikh Temple) remains in what was once his very own park; the sons and daughters of Empire put them both to much better use than he did.

Twenty-one years later, in an interview we did, Arthur remembered the feeling he had as he walked down to Potternewton Park where one of the steel bands were already playing. "I could hear the St Christopher Steel Band in the air and as I came round the corner I could see them playing ... I couldn't believe it. It was a dream come true. I saw this old lady walking in front of me and she put her hands in the air and said 'Lord it's been 15 years since I heard this'. People are thrilled to see this culture in Britain. It brings them together." Carnival soothes racism's wound.

With Inspector Exley of the Leeds Police in overall charge, the 1967 parade left the park and processed down Chapeltown Road and entered the Headrow in the city centre via Regent Street, finishing at the Town Hall, where the Last Lap Dance was held until 2am, with two steel bands playing for the whole night, competing for the 'best band' title.

Arthur payed tribute to Inspector Roy Exley, an unsung hero of Leeds Carnival, in an interview I did with them both in 1992. He went to Arthur's bed-sitting room at 15 Grange Avenue and Arthur's people-skills kicked in again. "I tell you what, we didn't know what we were getting into there," Inspector Exley told me. "I didn't know what to expect – the only Carnivals I'd heard of were in Rio." Arthur's enthusiasm took him along: "It was clear that this was going to be something, this Carnival." He could see that there was a traffic control headache ahead, but he immediately gave his permission for the street parade. It might have helped that Roy had only just transferred to Leeds from Barnsley, so he had no prior assumptions about the Caribbean people of Leeds. "The only black people I'd ever seen were the men coming up from the coal pit."

Inspector Exley's comments, after witnessing Carnival for 25 years, show that by the early 1990s some white people in Leeds were beginning to appreciate what Carnival achieves:

It's a binding of the community together – you get young people and old people working together ... [At the first Carnival] everyone carried on with the liveliness, the spirit, it was 'over the top' if you like, people were intoxicated, but not with drink. The English don't let themselves go like that with their summer fairs and trades ... Leeds is a cosmopolitan place and the Carnival helps bind all the communities together. It was a good way of Black people meeting the police but not in a confrontational situation.

He was proud to have been part of the team that launched Carnival, and he set a pattern that has never faltered: the police officers at the Carnival have always had good relationships with the masqueraders and the public (sometimes 100,000 people) who throng the streets and the park.

It's this impressive spectacle that attracts so many visitors, as the quality of the costumes has improved year upon year, and expert designers bring their Queens and Kings from as far away as Luton. Nowadays, the park has a stage and an arena, and the grassland is covered with stalls selling food, drink and merchandise. There are tents for the sound systems, and a small fairground for the children, so Carnival provides something for

Arthur France and Inspector Roy Exley at Leeds West Indian Centre, 1992. © Max Farrar

everyone who wants to enjoy Carnival's cosmopolitan, convivial creativity.

In that first year, however, much depended on people like Inspector Exley and the manager of the Town Hall (whom we met in Chapter 6). He was very happy to let out the Town Hall for the Last Lap dance. Ever mindful of the budget, the Carnival committee had arranged to buy drinks at wholesale prices, and John Hawley was put in charge of the bar. (John, from St Kitts, became an active trade unionist who ended up as a legal advice worker, specialising in employment issues, at the Harehills and Chapeltown Law Centre in the 1980s.) They made quite a bit on the bar, subsiding their costs.

By the early 1970s, Arthur had a committed committee that included people who had supported the first Carnivals and whom he could see had the creative talent and personal character needed to steer the good ship Carnival. Women have been absolutely central to the making and delivering of the Leeds Carnival, but in my 1974 photo of some of the Carnival committee members, there is only one woman, Kathleen Brown. She is the sister of Martin Brown, born in St Kitts, father of Spice Girl Mel B. Perhaps Melanie Brown's enthusiasm for the performing arts was carried from Aunty Kathleen's engagement with Carnival? (When, at the invitation of Dawn Cameron, Melanie Brown opened the Leeds Media Centre – adjacent to the Mandela Centre, the Leeds West Indian Centre and the Carnival HQ – Melanie's and Martin's delight at the presentation of the photo of the 1974 committee that includes Kathleen, was immense.)

Supporting the development of Carnival in London

The message that Leeds had held a successful West Indian Carnival got back to London via several channels. Lord Montagu (1926-2015), also known as Edward Douglas-Scott-Montagu, Third Baron of Beaulieu, was the owner of a stately home in Beaulieu, Hampshire, where he created the National Motor

Museum. Arthur recalled that Lord Montagu had suggested that there should be a Caribbean Carnival in the Midlands, and somehow he heard that there was going to be a Carnival in Leeds, so he came to have a look.

He was impressed by what he saw. He asked Arthur if George Lascelles (1923-2011), the Earl of Harewood, one of his pals with a stately home and a 'Capability Brown'-designed estate between Leeds and Harrogate, had given some funding to the Carnival. Arthur said he hadn't been asked. Lord Montagu said the Lascelles family had made its fortune from slavery, so they would probably want to assist Leeds Caribbean people in any way they could, and he promised to ask his friend to help out. Shortly afterwards, the Lascelles family did support Carnival, and have done so ever since, publicly acknowledging the nefarious source of their wealth and helping to explain colonial history.

Lord Montagu told the Carnival people he knew in Notting Hill, London, about the spectacle in Leeds. Junior Telford, a

Carnival committee members outside Cowper street school, L-R: Vince Wilkinson, Hughbon Condor, Hebrew Rawlings, Arthur France, Kathleen Brown, George Archibald, 1974. © Max Farrar

Trinidadian pioneer of steel pan music in London had been invited to judge the pan competition at the Last Lap dance at Leeds Town Hall, and he reported back to the group of West Indians that had performed in the 1965 street festival in Notting Hill.

The street festival in Notting Hill had been initiated by Rhaune Laslett, of Russian and Native American heritage, because she wanted to bring different cultures together to create warmth and happiness in that multi-ethnic part of London. Russ Henderson, a founder of the Caribbean style of Carnival in London that emerged from Mrs Laslett's multicultural festival, explained her significance to Colin Grant:

> There's a woman called Mrs Laslett, I used to live in the Grove, you see, and she used to do community work and put on things for the kids, you know, fêtes. And she, knowing that I had this steel band, which was a real novelty then, and saying, 'Could I come and play for the kids in a street Carnival?'
>
> So they put up some buntings and they block off the street, you see. They had a donkey ride ... [and] a clown. So after half an hour playing this and, I found it was getting boring. So I turned to the boys in the band, all of us were used to Carnival back home like we was taking a march. So I went to the chap with the donkey and I say, 'Look, follow us, because we taking a march and we making a block out of the streets' ... The crowds just started gathering the streets, you know. This was a novelty to them – 1965 – a steel band on the road ... The police were just helping us with the traffic ... There was no route, really – if you saw a bus coming, you just went another way. Rhaune Laslett was a good woman. I'd hate to think people left her out of the history because of her colour. I never went on the streets for anyone before I did it for her.

Clyde Alleyne and Allan Charles (Ian Charles's cousin, who worked at the Trinidad and Tobago Embassy), who also had first-hand experience of this momentous development in Leeds, took the Leeds message back to England's capital city. So an Irish lady who ran the Back-a-yard club and youth project in Notting Hill invited Leeds Carnival to perform at a special event in Notting Hill on a Sunday in September in 1967.

Two coach loads containing the core of the Leeds Carnival duly arrived in London. It poured with rain for the whole time. Ian Charles told me in an interview 21 years later that the rain didn't stop them. They couldn't play pan because of the deluge, "We just played iron," beating car hubs with metal bars. "I remember that iron so clearly, it reminded me of home." Arthur remembered dancing with bare feet and getting terrible cramp. No one ever pretends that making a Carnival is perpetual joy.

By 1969, the Notting Hill Carnival included an Afro-Cuban band, the London Irish Girl Pipers, Russ Henderson's West Indian three man band, the Asian Music Circle, the Gordon Bulgarians, a Turkish-Cypriot Band, the British Tzchekoslovak Friendship Band, a New Orleans Marching Band, the Concord Multi-racial group, and the Trinidad Folk singers. But it wasn't until the early 1970s that the Notting Hill Carnival took on its special flavour of Trinidad. Thus the Leeds West Indian Carnival, founded in 1967 by Arthur France, has the distinction of being the first specifically Caribbean-style street Carnival in Europe, created and led by Black people.

Developing Steel Pan education

Leeds Carnival has made a point of ensuring that steel pan orchestras are central to its Queen and King shows and (until recently) the street parade. In a book on the steel pan movement in Britain by the late Geraldine Connor, creator of the global hit stage show 'Carnival Messiah', Arthur spoke of his decision in 1984 to create the New Word Steel Orchestra in Leeds:

After waiting to see if the [Leeds city council] Music Service, or any other establishment would come up with a School of Steel Pan, by which I mean a 'proper Symphony Steel Orchestra', I decided to take the bull by the horns, get my own money and seek out a very dear friend, Raymond Joseph – one of the best Steel Pan player/arrangers and tutors around.

Sat at home with his wife and four children, I went over to his house and in his living room managed to persuade him to come out and let his light shine for us. I decided to buy a set of second-hand Steel Pans from Ebony Steel Band in London. Raymond and I travelled to London to purchase the Steel Pans from Pepe Francis, manager of, and Earl Lewis, captain of Ebony Steel Band.

At this time Gloria Fredericks was living in Francis Street [in Leeds] and as she had a huge cellar, she gave us our first place to practice in. We started in February 1984 and I wanted to prove what could be achieved, so, in the same year, at the end of November we came out of the cellar and staged the first Steel Orchestra concert at the Leeds West-Indian Centre.

In attendance were Colin Brackley Jones, the then Head of Music for Leeds Education, along with Roy Walmsley, the Deputy Head of the Leeds College of Music. There were also a few councillors in attendance representing Leeds City Council. It was interesting to see how shocked and amazed they were at the sight of the youngsters, led by Raymond Joseph, commanding such a performance. News of New World's achievements grew quickly, as did our skill, repertoire and reputation.

In 1986, Dudley Nesbitt was invited to Britain to arrange the Panorama tune for North Stars Steel Band, who were based in Huddersfield [about 20 miles from Leeds], (and also happened to include his cousins), for the London Panorama competition. While visiting Leeds,

Dudley fell in love with what New World were doing.

He used to regularly tune our Pans for us, and it was in doing this he realised that our second-hand pans would no longer do for such an Orchestra. On returning to Trinidad he vowed that he would locate a Pan tuner who would travel to Britain to tune our Pans for us. Dudley kept his promise and the New World Steel Orchestra's instruments and sound were transformed. We now had the instruments that we deserved. From then on it was all uphill.

1986, the year of Caribbean Focus across the UK, was pivotal for the development of Pan in Britain. Arthur was the chair of the Leeds Caribbean Focus committee, which showcased (amongst other activities) two of the world's most acclaimed steel bands, Catelli All Stars (with 55 playing members) and Casablanca (with 60) at a ground-breaking performance in the magnificent St Aidan's Church on Roundhay Road. In Geraldine Connor's book, Arthur continued:

The following year, in 1987, we were invited to London to perform at the Lancaster Hotel for the celebrations marking the election of the first four Black Members of Parliament. Whilst touring Carnivals worldwide, we also became the only steel band to win three Championship competitions in that one year! Then, in 1989, we were chosen by Leeds City Council to represent the City of Leeds, on an eight-day concert tour of Dortmund, its twin city [in Germany].

In 1989 Dudley moved to Leeds and tutored and led New World for many years thereafter, while working as a music teacher within the Leeds City Council Music Service until 2010. In 1990 Geraldine Connor, a world renowned ethnomusicologist, took up a post at the Leeds College of Music, where she promoted steel pan music and assisted with New World's development. Geraldine taught at Bretton Hall, University of Leeds until 2004. Her work on Carnival Messiah earned her a PhD from Leeds University in 2005. She died, aged 59, in 2011, leaving a huge hole in Carnival culture. The Geraldine Connor Foundation, with support from the Lascelles family, continues to develop art and culture, rooted in the African diaspora, in her name. Generations of young people in Leeds and beyond are in debt to Arthur, Dudley and Geraldine for developing their musical skills and appreciation of the art of pan.

By 2011, New World was fully established. It set out its multicultural mission as follows:

- to encourage the participation of local young people to come together to enjoy the indigenous music of Caribbean culture
- to express themselves through sound
- to be creative
- to allow young people of Caribbean heritage to stand proud and to learn, understand and appreciate their Caribbean heritage
- to allow young people of British heritage to learn, embrace, adopt and enjoy a cultural product not belonging to them that draws them together in a common pursuit.

Once more, we should note the seamless merger of the creative arts with a transformative social and political mission that embraces active multiculturalism. Arthur France, Geraldine Connor and others who did this intellectual, artistic and political work shaped this steel band, developing a new form of music that could only have been originated in Trinidad. New World Steel Orchestra's members were tutored by Geraldine Connor and played at all three British performances of her 'Carnival Messiah', in 1999 and 2002 at West Yorkshire Playhouse and

L-R: Susan Pitter, Cllr Bernard Atha (Lord Mayor of Leeds), Dudley Nesbitt, 2001. © Max Farrar

in 2007 at Harewood House, the Lascelles' family seat. Just as Leeds West Indian Carnival is led by people of African descent, so is New World. Both organisations have always welcomed people from every other ethnic group into their midst, as New World's aims show. My own life-long friendship with Hughbon Condor began when he invited me into Carnival in 1973. Carnival is a cultural bridge.

Leeds West Indian Carnival: 50 years and counting

For most of its life, it was called Leeds West Indian Carnival because Arthur and his team wanted to place the positive mark of West Indian life and culture on the city of Leeds. Despite changes in terminology in the 1980s, it did not call itself an 'African-Caribbean' Carnival. 'West Indian' embraces many heritages, including Asian, and Carnival in Leeds is inclusive. It is fitting that in recent years it has embraced the title The Leeds Carnival: this reflects its place as a central part of the city's cultural programme. The full year-by-year story is told, mainly in photographs, in a book titled *Celebrate! 50 Years of Leeds West Indian Carnival*, because that is how the city now responds: in celebration.

Arthur was quite properly at the centre of the celebratory events in 2017. Susan Pitter, a member of the Carnival committee from the mid-1970s, was highly instrumental in raising the profile of Carnival in the city. The first stage in its ascent in recent years was to move the Queen Show from the Leeds West Indian Centre in Chapeltown into the city centre, first to Millennium Square and Leeds Town Hall and then to West Yorkshire Playhouse (now Leeds Playhouse). The latter provided both the back-stage facilities and the auditorium – with its professional sound and lighting – to showcase the costumes properly, and a proper stage for the supporting acts.

Susan's presence and skill as MC, and her relationship with the comedians Robbie Gee and Eddie Nestor, along with the development of King costumes and performances, meant that each show got better and better. By 2017, the presentation was at its peak. Arthur's speech, in the presence of Vicky Cielto, the 1967 Carnival queen, and Carnival pioneers such as Mr and Mrs Samlalsingh, Willie and Rashida Robinson and Calvin Beech provided a fitting showcase for the Leeds Carnival. The Carnival parade was the largest and most spectacular in all its 50 years.

Acknowledging Arthur's roots in St Kitts-Nevis, Shelagh James, who grew up in Chapeltown and now works for the government of Nevis, organised a large delegation from the country of Arthur's birth to attend the 2017 Carnival, including Vance Amory, Premier of Nevis, Abonaty Liburd, the Director of Culture for Nevis, and Keith Scarborough from the Premier's Ministry.

Susan Pitter also fund-raised and co-ordinated a huge exhibition of Carnival photographs and artefacts, curated by Sonya Dyer, beautifully exhibited at a premiere location in the city centre, The Tetley Centre for Contemporary Art and Education, from 12th August to 5th November 2017. The Tetley had the space to display costumes made by Arthur and others, including Hughbon Condor's magnificent 'Man on Hos' Back' that won the competition in 2007.

Another of Susan's projects celebrating 50 years of Carnival was the commissioning of four new headpieces for Carnival masqueraders, exhibited at Leeds City Museum, including the beautiful work of up-and-coming young Carnival designers Renata Gordon and Lorina Gumbs. In the same year, Dr Emily Zobel Marshall organised a major international Carnival conference at Leeds Beckett University. Emily, who is a member of the Harrison Bundey Mama Dread Masqueraders and a leading academic, was generously supported by the research centre in cultural studies and humanities at the university.

The conference provided a rare opportunity for academics and Carnival practitioners to share their knowledge, and for the Carnival founders – Arthur France, Calvin Beech, Rashida and Willie Robinson – to tell their stories and answer questions. Dr Marshall also raised funds for me to make a pop-up Carnival exhibition of my Carnival photos, stretching back almost 50 years, which has toured the city. A lasting tribute to the work of Arthur and his team is the *Celebrate!* book. My brother Guy raised sufficient funds for this to be sold at a reasonable price and to be provided free to every school and library in Leeds – ensuring that resources are available to subsequent generations who want to find out about the history, the art and the politics of Caribbean Carnival culture.

Arthur reflects on his life in Carnival

Arthur's Carnival costumes always have a political story attached to them. In his Foreword to the *Celebrate!* book he said:

> My whole feeling with Carnival is that it's the only way to remember who we are and where we came from. Long ago I realised that Carnival was something you could use to show the story of our history. You cannot tell people too

much – you might switch them off if you're always giving them lectures. But Carnival is a more entertaining way of capturing some of the stories people need to know, always connecting them to Africa ... [In 2016] my costume for the King and Queen Show was Ashanti, and it included all Ghanaian features ... One year I did King Jaja. Some youngsters were in [Leeds Carnival] HQ where I was constructing it and they asked what was going on. I explained, and they went on their smart phones to get the history in Nigeria. And then they gave me new information, things I didn't know. This is the fourth generation of British-Caribbeans, doing their research on the web, and they are genuinely interested in this history.

Again, for Arthur, the key issue is education. Carnival is another mode in which people can learn important things that are so neglected in the British Schools National Curriculum.

"It's quite a queer thing. For most people, it's either politics OR Carnival, but for me, they're inseparable. I'm very passionate

Members of the Nevis delegation to the 2017 Carnival celebrations in Leeds Civic Hall, including the Premier, Vance Emory, Abonaty Liburd (Director of Culture), Keith Scarborough (Premier's Ministry), Vernon Richardson, Dis and Dat (Calypso King), Nevis Cultural Group including the Sugar Hill String Band, Cllr Jane Dowson, Cllr Angela Wenham, Cllr Alison Lowe, Cllr Mohammed Rafiq, Rehana Minhas, Rashida and Willie Robnson, Calvin, Hyacinth, Angela and Karen Beech, Veronica and Tyrone Samlal Singh. Arthur France is in the back row. Photo © Sylvester Meade about my roots. I am fortunate to have been brought up in the Caribbean so I could see what the celebration of emancipation was all about." When the pioneers – Arthur, Calvin Beech, George Archibald and their exuberant Jamaican friend from Leeds University, Tony Lewis – travelled across England to go to a Carnival function in another city, they would talk politics and argue fiercely with each other all the way there and back. "But when we got there, we just dropped all that and concentrated on being polite to everyone. They weren't very interested in our politics."

Darcus Howe was a notable exception to this 'apolitical' rule, and the magazine he edited, *Race Today*, wrote extensively about the Notting Hill Carnival in radical terms. In Leeds, the Harrison Bundey Mama Dread Masqueraders have, for more than 20 years, integrated Carnival with politics, taking up a contentious theme in each year's troupe. In 2017, their theme was All Ah We Ah Migrants, and they created King David Oluwale and his one hundred migrant masqueraders. As we saw in Chapter 7, David Oluwale was a British Nigerian who arrived in Leeds in 1949 and was hounded to his death by two policemen in 1969. Mama Dread masqueraders handed out postcards and leaflets telling the Oluwale story and calling for everyone to support the migrants of the world as they paraded around Harehills and Chapeltown. Ruth Bundey, a white solicitor, who started the troupe with the late Athaliah Durrant (Mama Dread) and Guy Farrar, was invited into Carnival by her Kittitian neighbour, the late Edris Browne, in 1970, and has participated every year since then. Yet again, Carnival includes everyone, whatever their backgrounds.

Over the years, Arthur has come to the conclusion that "You can't move forward unless you work with people in the council and the police, whether you like them or not." He has special praise for George Mudie. "When he was leader of Leeds city council, he understood the importance of Carnival." They went for years with no financial support from Leeds council. At first, some time in the mid-1980s, George Mudie gave them a small grant of £5000. "I went on the radio and said it was rubbish." Then he bumped into George in Morrisons supermarket. "He pulled me up and complained about what I'd said. I replied 'It's true, £5,000 is nowhere near enough'." George appreciated plain speaking and he knew he had to keep Arthur on board. "Things started to improve from then on. If it wasn't for that support we wouldn't have got where we are."

When Brian Walker was Labour leader of the council, he allocated the Carnival the building they now use as their HQ, at the south end of Chapeltown, near the West Indian Centre. Keith Wakefield, when he was leader of the Labour group, made sure that the Conservatives continued to fund Carnival while they were in charge of the council. That's how they were able to put the marquee into Millennium Square for the Queen Show. Another Labour leader, Judith Blake, now Baroness Blake of Leeds, was equally supportive. It's Arthur's charisma, powers of persuasion, and people-skills that have brought about these changes.

Standing up to racism: Arthur France and Calvin Beech in 2017. © Christian Høgsbjerg

Another crucial supporter was Dave Williams, Arthur's boss at Technorth education centre. At the same time as he was forging his relationship with George Mudie, meeting Dave was something of an eye-opener. He still marvels at how much he could have had in common with a white man. "We had no place to make costumes. Dave said use a vacant unit at the back of Technorth. If anything goes wrong, I don't want to know." This was a turning point for Carnival.

Calvin told Arthur that someone had come up to him and said 'I don't understand Arthur. He preaching Black Power to us and I see him down the road with this white man, hugging up.' Calvin said 'I don't think you understand the system'. Arthur turned to Malcolm X's final years as an example. "Malcolm recognise this as well," Arthur told me. Like Malcolm, Arthur can combine his religious belief with his advocacy for radical social and political change. (Even though, back in days when he went to church in his Afro and badges, "Some people think I'm with the devil." It still makes him laugh.)

"I have pride and pleasure in what we have achieved but I'm worried about the long-term future of Carnival in Leeds. I'm not confident that enough people understand the way that politics, race and culture work together." A clear knowledge of that complex interface is the key to driving Carnival forward. He says that the Notting Hill Carnival is now more of a jamboree than a proper Carnival, with all the different camps fighting each other for a slice of the grant income. In Leeds, he fears that "the main ethos of Carnival, a celebration of emancipation" might be compromised. "You have to have the right balance of people with the passion and knowledge of what Carnival is and how it must continue."

Over the years he's found that some people want to join the Carnival committee without any knowledge of how hard the struggle has been over the years, so they have no clear vision of what Carnival actually represents. That's why Carnivals in some other cities have collapsed. On the other hand, "We've got more costume designers in Leeds than anywhere else in the country, and we have the momentum." The big challenge is to ensure that Leeds does not become a jamboree. Arthur describes Trinidad's Carnival nowadays as a "bikini thing", introduced by the mas camp called Poison. Lots of people there are fed up with this 'pretty mas' Carnival, and Arthur was pleased to see that St Kitts-Nevis Carnival won the Carifesta prize because it has stuck to its traditional roots. With so much still to do, and now in his mid-80s, Arthur should be relaxing more, but he's finding it's hard to take a back seat in Leeds Carnival. "You've got to bring everyone with you, not leave anyone behind," is his mantra, and he looks like developing the art, the thinking and the emancipatory politics of Carnival for quite some time.

References in this chapter

Geraldine Connor and Max Farrar, 'Carnival in Leeds and London, UK: Making New Black British Subjectivities' in Milla C Riggio (ed.) *Culture in Action - The Trinidad Experience*, London and New York: Routledge, 2004.

Geraldine Connor, *Pan! The Steelband Movement in Britain*, GBAKHANDA Publishing, 2011.

Geraldine Connor's many achievements are set out in her obituary here https://www.theguardian.com/stage/2011/oct/31/geraldine-connor Accessed 7.4.2020.

Guy Farrar, Tim Smith and Max Farrar, *Celebrate! 50 Years of Leeds West Indian Carnival*, Huddersfield: Northern Arts Publications, 2017, provides a detailed history of the Leeds' Carnival combined with hundreds of colour photographs.

Max Farrar, 'A Dream Come True', interview with Ian Charles and Arthur France about the first Carnival in Leeds in *Leeds West Indian Carnival 21st Anniversary Magazine*, 1988. Available at http://www.leeds Carnival.co.uk/wp-content/uploads/Dream-Come-True-1988-mf.pdf Accessed 6.4.2020.

Max Farrar, 'George Hendrickson – King of Carnival String' in *Leeds West Indian Carnival 23rd Anniversary Magazine'*, 1990.

Karen Fog Olwig, *Global Culture, Island Identity – Continuity and change in the Afro-Caribbean community of Nevis*, Reading: Harwood Academic Publishers, 1993. Republished by Routledge in 2017.

Arthur France was a key-note speaker at 'Power, Performance and Play', 19-21 May 2017, an international conference on the Caribbean

Carnival, organised by Dr Emily Zobel Marshall and Professor Max Farrar, supported by the Centre for Cultural Studies and the Humanities at Leeds Beckett University, UK. LBU's research stream on Carnival is online at https://www.leedsbeckett.ac.uk/caribbean-Carnival-cultures/ Accessed 13.8.20

Colin Grant, *Homecoming – Voices of the Windrush Generation*, London: Jonathan Cape, 2019.

Errol Hill, *The Trinidad Carnival*, London: New Beacon Books, 1997.

Emily Zobel Marshall, Max Farrar and Guy Farrar, 'Popular Political Culture and the Caribbean Carnival' in *Soundings,* Issue 67, Winter 2017. This article, and much more research on Carnival, including video interviews with the founders of the Leeds West Indian Carnival, is available here http://www.leedsbeckett.ac.uk/Carnival/#Carnival-research Accessed 7.4.2020.

Novelette Morton-Henry, *History of St Kitts and Nevis Carnival* at https://www.sknvibes.com/islandfacts/sitepage.cfm?p=163 Accessed 23.7.2021

M A Katritzky's book *Healing, Performance and Ceremony*, (Ashgate 2012) is the source of the verses from the 1605 Shrovetide play, quoted in the Wikipedia entry 'Carnival'.

Michael La Rose, 'The City Could Burn Down, We Jammin' Still – The History and Tradition of Cultural Resistance in the Art, Music, Masquerade and Politics of the Caribbean Carnival', *Caribbean Quarterly*, special issue edited by Dr Emily Zobel Marshall, Vol. 65, No. 4, December 2019.

James W Sutton, *A Testimony of Triumph: A narrative of the life of James Sutton and family in Nevis and St Kitts, 1920-1940*, Scarborough, Ontario, Canada: Edan's Publishers, 1987

Chapter 9

ONE LOVE, ONE STRUGGLE

I n our last interview for this book, in the Leeds West Indian Carnival HQ at the south end of Chapeltown, Arthur wore a mask. Not, unfortunately, a carnival mask: he had one of the disposable surgical masks that, as the Covid19 pandemic ravaged populations all over the world, we were all being urged to wear. He looked a bit worn, and this thin piece of fabric took all of the normal animation out of his face.

Our topic was "family". It was striking how often his comments on the family he has created with Tattra, his children and their children, took him back to his own mum and dad and his grandparents. This bond of love, now stretching across so many decades, is a source of immense joy, and it clearly sustains him in this difficult time. As David Lascelles says in his Preface to this book, Arthur often signs off with the Rastafarian expression, "One Love". While there is hardly a drop of Rastafari in Arthur's make-up, love is a burning force in his life.

The Beatles sang "Love is all you need" but as Arthur looks at the world in 2020, there are more tears than smiles. He knows that Love alone won't beat Covid19, still less the rampant murder of unarmed Black people by American police officers. When George Floyd was killed on 25th May 2020 in Minneapolis, USA, Arthur cried for three days. I heard of two Leeds Black women in their 60s who were so disturbed by that killing that they referred themselves to a National Health Service counselling unit.

But Arthur is nothing if not resilient. His strength comes from his birth family, and it is sustained by the family he's created in Leeds. He draws further strength from knowing his roots and drawing from them. Another famous, strong person with heritage in St Kitts-Nevis is Spice Girl Melanie Brown. Her father, Martin Wingrove Brown, who (as mentioned in Chapter 5) laboured at the Copper Works in Leeds for 35 long years, often said to Melanie: 'Remember who you are, and where you came from'. That's Arthur's message too.

If Covid-19 is a biological killer, racism is a social killer. Both search out Black people as their target. During the 2020-21 pandemic, I wondered if we could coin the term 'Kkkovid'. To survive, you have to be super-strong. There is a beam of hope in the upsurge of the Black Lives Matter movement promoted by the murder of Mr Floyd: stretching across the whole of the USA, with support demonstrations all over the world, these huge manifestations remind us of the Civil Rights struggles that Arthur took a leading part in during the 1960s.

They led to major reforms in America which, while arguably developing a Black middle class and leaving the Black working class behind, changed America for the better. The 2020 upsurge has an advantage over the earlier struggle for civil rights: this round of militant protest included far more white people than we saw in the 1960s giving their solidarity to the freedom marchers.

As ever, hope lies with the young. Arthur and Tattra's children are not so young, but they have children of their own, making their own contributions. Arthur has a strong memory of taking his three home, with Tattra, to Nevis in December 1990. Mahalia had been born in 1976, Asha in 1980 and Vinod in 1982. "They changed my life. But three was enough – I declared my innings." The children were growing up fast, and in 1990 they were very excited at seeing the islands their dad had said so much about – and meeting their fabled grandmother. (Sadly, Ebeneza had died by then.)

It was an amazing journey because at the airport they bumped into Arthur's good friend Arif Ali, the journalist and publisher based in London (originally from Guyana), on his way to Antigua. Naturally, Arif knew the pilot so the children were invited into the cockpit to see how the plane worked. From Antigua, the Frances took the small plane to Newcastle airport, near Mt Lily in the north of Nevis. "The children for the first time saw a Black person flying an aeroplane – they'd never witnessed Black people in such responsible jobs in Leeds."

Uncle Claudy, other family members, and his friend Rudolph (Spoon) greeted them at the airport and took them to his brother Samuel's new, fully-equipped house. (Samuel was on the nearby island of Tortola, where he was working.) He remembers the sun coming up the following morning and ten year-old Asha being delighted to look out of the window and start finding out what Nevis was like.

"When mum arrived I couldn't believe the magnet there was between her and the children." They insisted that Grandma Olga shared their bed each night of their stay, and she was more than happy to oblige. After a few days they crossed over to St Kitts to see other family members, with the children making sure that grandma came too. "It made me feel so good to see this strong bond." The captain of the Caribbean Queen ferry that tackled the fast-running straight between the two islands was the son of the captain Arthur had known many years before, so the children were invited to join him in the bridge to steer the ship – even more excitement.

For their three days in St Kitts Arthur was drafted in to help with the Sports – Carnival – because everyone knew he was a carnival man to his core. To head off the complaints from the Nevisians that he was participating in St Kitts' masquerades, he put Mahalia, Asha and Vinod into the St Kitts' Sports in costumes that represented his very own Nevis.

Grandma sat in a pickup serving the food and drinks as the revellers passed through – as always, Arthur was the butt of his sister Hyacinth's joke that he was working their mum so hard she might drop down dead, such were the crowds and commotion of carnival.

Word was out that Arthur was home, so Nevis Prime Minister Sim Daniel came by to try and persuade Arthur to settle in Nevis and contribute to the development of the island. Instead, Vinod, aged eight, suggested they took Grandma back with them to Leeds. Olga said she'd like to make the trip. Arthur's sister Marjorie was living in Leeds and, when the Frances got back to their house, Tattra phoned Marjorie to say she must come to see Arthur, because he was ill. When she arrived, to find Arthur perfectly well and her mother ensconced in the house, she was so surprised she almost fainted.

"The children were so attached to their grandma. More than to their parents! It's a funny African/Caribbean thing – it's because the grandparents have more time." Vinod would take his grandma her cup of tea every morning and the girls were forever giving her a bubble bath.

His mother's presence in Leeds had a big impact on Arthur, too. "I was so radical I had abandoned religion for a while, but I had to take mama to Roscoe Methodist Church while she was in Leeds. Vincent Smithen said 'Out of evil comes good – if Mrs France hadn't come here we would never have seen Arthur again'." Arthur wasn't offended – he just laughed. By this time, the church was much more engaged with carnival and local politics so Arthur was happy to rejoin the congregation.

Mahalia and Asha had picked up the politics bug and while they were doing well at school they became more radical. (In 2020 Mahalia and Asha played an important role in the Black Lives Matter groups in Leeds and organised big events furthering the struggle for full rights and freedom.) As we saw in Chapter 4, education is central to Arthur's worldview. He always stressed the importance of education to his the children. "I never missed a parents' evening and I always made sure I had a good relationship with their class teachers and the school as a whole."

As Arthur's reputation grew, in 1995 the Frances were picked out by Channel 4 TV's Breakfast Show to be featured as its 'Family of the Week' – they were put up in London so they could be filmed in the studio for six days in succession. In 1997 he was invited to Buckingham Palace to be honoured with the award of the MBE (Member of the Order of the British Empire). Mahalia and Asha accompanied Arthur and Tattra to the Queen's Garden Party that year.

June 2002 was the Queen's Golden Jubilee and Arthur France, one of the Leeds's pre-eminent advocates of Black Power and a fierce critic of Empire, was happy to be involved in the celebrations. Again, the family played its part: both Mahalia and Asha wore their carnival costumes in the pageant created for the Queen's Jubilee visit to Yorkshire – and they were "very chuffed" to be featured in the TV films that covered the event, with Asha speaking positively about the Royals.

At the special dinner at Harewood House for the Queen, the Earl placed Arthur close to the Queen. Like so many Caribbean people of his generation, Arthur says: "I was brought up to admire the Royal Family and I still feel loyal to the Crown." What might seem a paradox somehow fades away as we recognise that Arthur can criticise a hierarchical and exploitative system but not entirely blame the people who sit at the top of the pyramid. A photo of him with Prince Charles was featured in the press. "I first met Prince Charles at Technorth. He has an amazing memory. He saw me at Harewood House years later and came over and said 'And how is Prime Minister Bradshaw?' I said 'He died some years ago.' We both burst out laughing and the photographer captured the moment."

This man of incredible energy and fortitude, who never smoked or drank alcohol, was diagnosed with prostate cancer around 2010 (no one seems to know exactly when it was). Tattra was terribly upset. Arthur however was optimistic . "Some people see the glass as half empty. I see it as half full. I never feared for my future." The symptom was that he couldn't pass water. Tattra immediately got him into St James's Hospital where he had the operation that saved him.

"I cried a few times, but not for me, for my Dad." Ebeneza had had prostate cancer. "I understood what he went through." Arthur was upset at the knowledge that his father's cancer was not diagnosed and operated on as it would be today, as it was for him. "People don't know that one-third of men over 55 have prostate problems." In the UK, about 1 per cent of men between 64 and 74 have prostate cancer – it's the leading cause of deaths of British men. It's worse for Black men: 25 per cent of them will get prostate cancer. There's a lot of resistance. As Arthur put it: "Black men don't want nobody to mess with their behind." But Arthur says they've got to pay attention and get the test. For Arthur, it was a struggle, but he pulled through, and he didn't miss a single carnival.

"People don't believe it, but I cry regularly." Through this difficult period the love and support of his family was even more important than ever. And the extended family is very large. "I am a very family-oriented person. I have quite a few nieces and

Tattra, Vinod, Mahalia, Arthur and Asha France at Channel 4 TV, 1995. Photo courtesy Arthur France

Vinod, Arthur, Tattra and Asha France after Arthur's MBE ceremony, 14th June 1997. Photo courtesy Arthur France

nephews all over the world. In our culture, I'm the uncle, and they have grandchildren themselves, but they still phoning me and asking for advice. We're very much old-fashioned in that way." One of his nephews talks to him "in a very old-fashioned, respectful way, and I like that."

Arthur and Tattra have several grand-children of their own and Arthur took out the note from his wallet of their names and dates of birth. "I see a lot of them and I love them. They bring back a lot of my memories." Asha's first, Iamini, tragically died in child-birth in 2001. Then Mahalia had Halima in the same year. Asha had Alisia in 2003, then Cassius arrived for Vinod in 2004 (the name is an homage to Muhammad Ali), Lina for Mahalia in 2007, Zayn for Vinod in 2011 and Mahalia gave birth to Eve in 2012. Asha had Aston in 2013, Jacob in 2016 and Alaia in 2019 – giving nine youngsters for Arthur and Tattra to enjoy.

"Me and my brother and sisters used to love to climb up the sides of the big four-poster bed to cuddle up with our

Grandma and Grandpa in Nevis, so I love it when our little ones get into bed with me and Tattra. Some people lose touch with their grand-children – they don't realise the love that you get with them – that's very sad." Arthur's glad he has WhatsApp on his phone. No longer does he have to pay a fortune on phone cards – the free wi-fi calls to all his family and friends are a bonus.

"Having grand-children is a blessing, being able to have direct connection with them is a double-blessing. Every fortnight we have them in our house and I like to watch them play and carry on, and it brings back a lot of memory of my childhood days. It makes me think how Daddy and Mama would have loved them, and it would have brought joy to them."

These deeply personal feelings stem from his passionate nature – and that passion can quickly shift to world affairs. The day before this conversation, Arthur had watched an American football match on TV that was called off as part of a Black Lives Matter protest. "One of the players said 'You don't know what it's like being a Black man in America'. He was so right. We are living in some shocking times that really piss me off, you know."

Then we remembered something entirely positive – his grand-daughter Halima's poem about him, published in 2018:

Mr Carnival

She'd watch him as a little girl,
Jammin, singing, smiling,
Always smiling,
Mr Carnival,
Father of Carnival,
He was just grandad to her,

She'd watch them,
All the vibrant, warm colours dancing by,

Some of the family in 2003, L-R (back row) Fritz, Vinod, Modassa, Asha. L-R (front) Cathy, Tattra, Arthur, Mahalia with baby Halima. Photo courtesy Arthur France

People laughing and smiling so was he,
Always smiling,
Mr Carnival,
Her grandad,

She was done watching,
She was there,
On the road in her reds and her golds,
Dancing and joking,
Laughing and smiling,
Enjoying the atmosphere that came only with carnival,

Carnival day 2013,
She was there with NWSO behind the instrument whose history connected with hers,

In such a way that it is a part of her and everyone here
    today,
She remembers,
All the sore feet and pains and groans,
And the toilet races from the truck to Pablo's,

She's been there,
Witnessed the stress of the last minute costume making,
Stayed the long nights of gluing and sticking,
She laughed after the glue gun burns,
After the shouts of 'ah me mudders dot dot dot',
And streams of language more colourful than the
    costumes,

She had also thought,
About the issues going on in today's society,
Terrorism, Brexit, racism just to mention a few,
She had seen each and every year the masses of people,
Of all ages races and religions celebrating emancipation
    together,
All brought together by a small group of ordinarily
wonderful people that create carnival,
No politician, world leader, king or queen could do that,

My grandad,
Mr Thomas Arthur Benjamin France,
A man with a great woman behind him,
Nanny,
They had a daughter,
Mum,
Who married a man,
Dad,
They had me,
Halima France Mir,
And then Lina and then along came Eve,

And we are a part of one big carnival story,
And we will continue to tell it,
Continue the tree and one day it may be my children
telling your children the story of carnival,
And then their children will turn over the page to write
    another chapter,
Carnival is my past, present, and future,
Our past, present and future,

And it all started with a boy in Nevis who came to
    England,
A boy who never thought that the day he set off would be
the last time he saw his father,
A boy who is now a grandfather,
Mr Thomas Arthur Benjamin France,
Mr Carnival
Father of carnival,

I watch him,
Jammin, singing, smiling,
Always smiling,
Mr Carnival
Father of Carnival

Halima knows that grand-dad Arthur, his family, and carnival
are all branches of a tree called Emancipation, a tree now
festooned by people 'of all ages, races and religions'. Almost
always smiling, Arthur is the father of Carnival and the rest of
us will follow, with NWSO (New World Steel Orchestra,
described in Chapter 8) playing our tune.

This is a family that embraces diverse heritages, and
celebrates that diversity. There's no petty nationalism in the
Frances. Arthur would agree with another famous son of St
Kitts-Nevis, the writer Caryl Phillips, who said this in an
interview with Professor Bénédicte Ledent:

Arthur and Tattra France's Family Tree

What you have throughout the [Caribbean] islands, is people thrown together from different backgrounds who have been forced to get on in some way. And it's been – and it continues to be – problematic. It's involved genocide; it's involved huge amounts of prejudice and racial and social inequality ... [Nevertheless], I think there is a lot we can learn from the Caribbean about people coexisting and making new cultures; making new forms.

That is what Arthur France has brought to Leeds, and to the UK: a lifetime of struggle to make 'new cultures', to make 'new forms' of living together, in strident opposition to racism, in utter dedication to removing social inequality.

At the close of our final interview for this book, Arthur turned back to British history. "Can you imagine, the Church of England kept slaves, and had them branded, like animals?" Then he looked forward. "I can't control yesterday but I have a moral responsibility for the future." As always, Arthur speaks of the betterment of humanity. "We can all make a difference." The struggle must go on. And on. Education is the key, for Black people as well as white. "I say this to my friends: You can't be sitting on the fence."

References in this chapter

Melanie Brown (with Louise Gannon), *Brutally Honest*, London: Quadrille, 2018.

Halima France Mir, 'Mr Carnival' in *Any Change? Poetry in a Hostile Environment*, edited by Ian Duhig, London: Forward Arts Foundation. Available here https://www.strixleeds.com/any-change

Caryl Phillips in conversation with Bénédicte Ledent, 'Encountering Chapter One', the First Eccles Centre Plenary Lecture at the 43rd Annual *Conference of the Society for Caribbean Studies* held on 3 July 2019 at the University of Central Lancashire. London: The British Library's Eccles Centre for American Studies, 2021. bl.uk/eccles-centre

NEVIS AND ST KITTS: A HISTORY OF REBELLION

WHENEVER ARTHUR FRANCE IS ASKED TO SAY something about carnival, which is pretty often, since he's been organising the carnival in Leeds for more than 50 years, he says two things. Firstly, I am an African, and I am extremely proud of my heritage. Secondly, carnival is about Emancipation. These roots, and Black people's impulse for freedom, dignity and rights, are central to Arthur's life; to really understand Arthur, we need to understand Nevis, the tiny Leeward island in the Caribbean, inextricably linked to a slightly larger island, St Christopher (St Kitts), but separated by a two mile stretch of choppy sea. To understand Nevis, we need to know its history; in particular we need to understand the enslavement and forced labour of Africans.

It's true that, in general, the winners write history, and so we know very little about the losers. When it comes to the Caribbean, for far too long its history has been 'white': written by white people justifying the role of the white capitalists who owned the people and the land they were forced to work on. Thanks to radical scholars who are highly critical of the winners, more 'history from below' has been written, acknowledging the point of view of those who lost out. So there are histories available that expose the amorality and avarice of the white ruling classes and speak up for the poor. But it's wrong to position all the Black people of the Caribbean today as losers.

The birthplace of Arthur France, Mount Lily, is in the north
of the island of Nevis (Niévès)

There's now a class of people who are doing very well, and the
role of the new Black ruling classes is sometimes exposed.

This chapter takes a slightly different point of view. It's
written – by a white man – with the Black rebels constantly in
mind. St Kitts and Nevis have a proud history in which poor
people have continually confronted their rich exploiters. The
Arawaks and the Caribs rebelled, so did the enslaved Africans,
and, in the transition to independence there were even some
whites who took the side of Black workers, resisting both the
white colonists and the emerging brown middle classes. While
this chapter attempts to be comprehensive, it is deliberately
slanted in favour of those who struggled against oppression and
exploitation.

* * * * *

My T-shirt, bought in the market in Basseterre in 2016 just before I crossed to Nevis for the first time, says "St Kitts Est. 1624 West Indies Limited Edition". T-shirts are no better a guide to history than the curriculum Arthur received in his primary school in Nevis. As he often says, he knew more about Britain than he did about the Caribbean until he left school and educated himself.

1624 *was* an important year in the history of St Kitts and Nevis. It's when the white colonists arrived. But it wasn't the first year of the life of the people of these islands. Arawak Indians had settled St Kitts around 1,000 BC, arriving from South America. The Ciboney people then arrived in St Kitts around 800 AD. These were a branch of the Arawaks known as the Taino, who had developed their culture, including pottery, farming and trade, in the part of Cuba known as Ciboney. These were the people who met the Italian explorer Christoforo Colombo (known to English speakers as Christopher Columbus) when he arrived in Cuba in 1492. (Columbus found them to be very friendly and thought they would make good servants.) The Caribs reached St Kitts from the Orinoco region of South America some time after the Arawak/Taino people, perhaps around 1200 AD, and they seem to have been more aggressive, trading with and overcoming the Taino by the time the whites arrived.

So it was on 28th January 1624 that 15 English settlers, led by Thomas Warner, landed on St Kitts, arriving in a place discovered, and settled, nearly 2,500 years before he got there. They set up camp on the edge of what is now called Old Road Bay. Warner had first spotted St Kitts in 1622, on a voyage back from Surinam under Captain Roger North. He stayed there for several months and, Chris Birch has observed, became friendly with the Carib leader Tegramond (or Tegreman), while noting that the island would be a suitable place to grow tobacco.

According to an account by a contemporary, Captain John Smith, published in 1630, the Caribs were helpful to Warner's group, even if the weather was not:

At their arrival, they found three Frenchmen, who opposed Captaine Warner, and set the Indians upon us; but at last we all became Friends, and lived with the Indians at Moneth, then we build a Fort, and a House, and planting Fruits, and by September we made a crop of Tobacco; but upon the 19th of September came a Hurricane and blew it all away.

Warner's party did not discover St Kitts; they weren't even the first Europeans to reach that beautiful island. Columbus had arrived there, funded by the Spanish monarchy, in 1493. At some time in the 17th century it acquired the name St Christobal and Warner's people then called it St Christopher's Island. As Kitt was a common nickname for Christopher, it became known as St Kitts.

The Arawaks (Tainos) were twice the losers (first to the Caribs, and then to the Europeans) and their name for the island, Liamuiga, was erased by the British. Liamuiga roughly translates as 'fertile land'. If the occasional tourist reaches the top of St Kitts' highest peak, Mount Liamuiga, we hope she or he pays homage to the Arawaks who arrived there, 2,500 years before Columbus 'discovered' these islands. (There's evidence of an even earlier settlement of the islands from around 3,000 BC.)

The 17th Century

The French also settled on St Kitts from 1625, and the British and the French partitioned the island. The indigenous Caribs – a grouping known as the Kalinago, led by Tegremond – may have begun to resist these intruders who were bent on taking control of their island. The Wikipedia article on St Kitts says that Thomas Warner was tipped off by an 'Indian woman' that a

Kalinago attack was imminent, prompting Warner to invite them to a party, ply them with alcohol, and then have his people kill 120 of them while they slept.

Wikipedia's account of the circumstances of these murders is questionable. The rationale given by the Wiki author is that there was an impending uprising by the Caribs. But John Cordy Jaeffreson, using documents left by Warner's contemporaries, including those of his forebear Colonel John Jaeffreson, Warner's friend, has an entirely different account of this event. In a book he published in 1878, John Cordy wrote this, based on his research in his family archive:

> Short work was made of the Caribees on St Christopher's island. Having learnt, or imagined themselves to have learnt, that the natives had prepared a scheme for their destruction and were on the point of putting it into effect, the European settlers took stern and perhaps needless measures for their self preservation. Falling on the Caribees by night, they slew 127 of their stoutest men; having selected a few of their comeliest women for domestic service, they ordered the remainder of the aboriginal population to quit the island. This painful affair took place in 1625 or 1626.

The true horror of this massacre of people who up to that point had helped Warner's party is revealed by Jeaffreson's clear sense of shame. He wrote that the whites 'imagined themselves to have learned' of an uprising. These murders were 'perhaps needless'. Only 'the comeliest women' were spared.

There was worse to come. Despite the differences between the French and the English, the Europeans decided they had a common enemy in the Caribs. In 1626 a joint Anglo-French force rounded up 2,000 to 4,000 of the Kalinago Caribs at the place known today as Bloody Point, near Challengers village and Palmetto Bay, where they killed 2,000 of them. The Caribs fought back and killed about 100 settlers. But the gun is mightier than the spear.

Here we have yet another example of the genocide that accompanied European domination of the global south. No doubt keeping more of the 'comeliest women' for their domestic service, most of the surviving Kalinago were expelled to Dominica, where some of their descendants remain today in the part of that mountainous island where the original Caribbean people still live. If anyone should wonder why Arthur France can be searing in his criticism of the white elites of the world, an example like this, in the history of his own islands, of what the British will do, even to their friends, should be born in mind.

The Anglo-French occupation was then supplanted by the Spanish, who defeated them in battle in 1629 and took 600 to work in their South American colonies' mines. Four shiploads sent by the Spanish to Britain returned to St Kitts as soon as the Spanish departed; in 1670 the Spanish handed the islands over to the British. The French weren't happy and, having fought the British in 1635 (when they armed 250 slaves to fight for them) and again in 1667, further Franco-British wars broke out in 1689-90. Violent conflict went on between 1701 and 1713, when Britain finally gained control (though the French briefly took power once more in 1782-3). Each time the French won, the British retreated to Nevis, re-grouped and attacked again.

Any visitor to St Kitts has to spend only a few minutes in the Brimstone Hill Fortress, built from 1690, to feel the strength of British resolve to win those wars and maintain control over 'their' property. Fire and brimstone certainly rained down on the French settlement below Brimstone Hill. Fittingly, that fortress is close to Bloody Point. This island knows much about blood and power as the Europeans fought among themselves to dominate the slave trade and exploit their colonies' resources.

Power relations on these islands were complex. When the French defeated the British in Nevis in 1706, taking 3,400 enslaved people from British ownership, those who escaped then formed their own army on Maroon Hill and fought off the French. The British had been utterly routed by the French who had burned their homes and sugar factories to the ground. Further research is needed to explain why the Africans on Maroon Hill did not take advantage of the British humiliation and press for full freedom. Presumably they did not feel sufficiently powerful to take over the whole of Nevis and then expel the British from St Kitts.

Warner's party had arrived with some enslaved Africans, and it is the steady increase in the number of these shackled people that stamped the character of the islands of St Kitts and Nevis after the elimination of the Kalinago Caribs. The French brought 40 Africans from Senegal in 1626. By 1635 there were 5-600 Africans on St Kitts. The number of whites expanded between 1654 and 1685, when 118 white women and 496 men sailed from Bristol to St Kitts and Nevis.

St Kitts' economy was originally based on tobacco, the growing and selling of ginger root, and the extraction of the dye from the indigofera plant, all in the area around Old Road and the Wingfield river. (Romney Manor's Caribelle Batik emporium, near Wingfield River, is a contemporary reminder of the island's indigo trade.) But stiff competition from the north American colony led to a halt in tobacco production in 1639, and the introduction of sugar cane from Brazil in 1643. The new, deadly trade in sugar was about to take off.

Both islands were found to be highly fertile due to their volcanic origins and thus favourable to the planting of sugar cane. The Africans on St Kitts were large enough in number, and so bitterly hostile to their condition that they revolted in 1639 – it took 500 French soldiers to suppress them. By 1671 there were 1,739 Africans enslaved on plantations in Nevis; by 1677 there were 3,849, far more than the 1,436 recorded in St Kitts in the same year. (The number of Africans on Nevis was larger than on St Kitts because the smaller island at this point had neither slave revolt nor Franco-British violence to impede the sugar plantations' development.) Nevis's Black population in 1677 consisted of almost equal numbers of men, women and children (1,422 men, 1,321 women, and 1,106 children).

Thomas Warner had allowed Anthony Hilton and about 100 others from St Kitts to settle Nevis in 1628. (Estimates of the numbers vary. One source says 80. Another account, in *The True Travels of Captaine Smith*, cited by June Goodfield, says there were 100. Christine Eickelmann has reputable sources which give the number as 150. History is not an exact science.) The people in charge did their best to suppress bad behaviour. Charles Rochefort published a book in 1666 which referred to his visit to Nevis in the 1650s. Karen Fog Olwig (1993) quoted Rochefort's observation that 'Swearing, Thieving, Drunkenness, Fornication, and all dissolutions and disorders are severely punish'd' on that island.

Other British colonials spread to neighbouring Antigua and Montserrat in 1632. Like St Kitts, Nevis had acquired a European name; only Oualie Beach (and its hotel) retains the memory of the indigenous people's name for their island: Oualie. It meant 'land of beautiful waters'. The British seem to have derived their name for Nevis from the Spanish *Nuestra Señora de las Nieves*, meaning 'Our Lady of the Snows'. As you make the short boat journey from Basseterre, the capital of St Kitts, to Charlestown, the capital of Nevis, you can see that the high point of this conical island is often surrounded in cloud. It's thought the Spanish used 'Nieves' because this cloud reminded them of the snow that, as narrated in a Catholic miracle of the 4th Century, fell on the Esquiline Hill in Rome.

Warner had obtained a royal patent to colonise the Leeward Islands in 1620 and he formed a company – the Society of Adventurers – to raise the cash he needed. In 1664 he merged it with the Royal African Company (its title tells us so much about the monarchy's role in the slave trade). It transported around 100,000 Africans into slavery in the Caribbean between 1672 and 1689. Between 1674 and 1688, in Charlestown, Nevis, the Royal African Company auctioned over 6,000 Africans for slave labour. The visitor today can, if she searches hard, visit the plot of land at the western edge of Charlestown where this barbarous trade was made.

Sugar was a miracle for those British people who were running the plantations and investing in the trade from the comfort of their homes in the UK. By 1652, Nevis was the most profitable of all of Britain's Caribbean colonies. Around 1675, there were 3,595 whites and 5,132 enslaved Africans, making Nevis's total population 8,727. The Spanish and Portuguese influence meant that there were four Sephardic Jewish families registered in Charlestown, Nevis, in the 1667-8 muster roll, rising to seventeen families at the end of the century, with their own synagogue. The Sephardic cemetery in Nevis has 19 stones for the period 1669 to 1730, inscribed in Hebrew, Portuguese and English, and research in 1957 by Rabbi Malcolm Stern and his wife Louise documented 60 individual Jews who lived in what was called 'Jew Street' in Charlestown. Joan Robinson has pointed out that anti-Semitism was to some extent by-passed: 'Originally England prohibited Jews from owning land but these laws were often overlooked, so Jewish people seem to have been plantation owners and merchants'. (In 1740 the British parliament passed legislation to encourage Jews to settle and trade in their Caribbean islands.)

Nevis seems to be unusual in providing cultivatable land specifically for the Africans, no doubt because the need for home-grown food was pressing. Olwig (1993) has drawn attention to the crop-related disorder that is mentioned in the preamble to a 1682 law: 'Many thefts and rebberyes committed on this Island by negroes have been for the greatest part occasioned through their masters not planting or allowing them any provision or some Exceeding little that they are not able to subsist on it'. The law mandated the planting of 'one thousand plants Ground in provision' for every slave, though this might not have been enforced. Much later, Africans were able to buy land for themselves.

The British demand for sugar was insatiable, rising from 4 pounds per person in 1700 to 18 pounds in 1800. By 1776, St Kitts was Britain's richest colony, measured by per capita income of the whites. Making sugar was fine for the whites but hell for the Africans. Work on the sugar plantations was, literally, killing. On average, they survived only 8-12 years the field. In the 18th century, two-thirds died within a year of arrival. Nevertheless, their numbers rose inexorably with the ever-increasing demand in Europe for sugar.

The 18th Century

The death rate among the first enslaved Africans was very high because their diet was so bad, and they had the most arduous tasks of clearing all the forests and undergrowth and ploughing the land to make it ready for planting cane. The horrifying death rate meant that Africans continued to be imported as chattel labour throughout the 18th century. In 1724, the population of St Kitts was 4,000 white and 11,500 Black, while Nevis was 1,100 white and 4,400 Black. By 1774, the population on St Kitts was 1,900 white and 23,462 Black, while Nevis was about 1,000 white and 10,000 Black by 1780.

Olwig (1993) quoted a 1730 description by Reverend Robert Robertson (of St Paul's Anglican Church in Nevis) of the newly-arrived Africans' attitude towards their white masters. He identified a mix of admiration, fear and hatred:

When the *newer* Negroes observe that we can read and write (or, as they word it, *make paper speak*) and do many other things above their comprehension, they seem to take us for a sort of Superior Beings, made as it were to rule over them; they both admire, and fear and hate us.

Bearing in mind that this is a colonial master's account, we may read this as the transmission into Nevis of acceptance among the Africans of the hierarchical order (where some rule and others follow) that they knew from their home countries, combined with the Africans' inherent hatred (and fear) of the overwhelming power and merciless cruelty of their captors and their owners. Acceptance of white superiority did not, of course, last for long.

Robertson certainly provided a white-washed portrait of the Africans' situation in this account, quoted here by Joan Robinson:

> The Field Slaves ... were kept hard at Work all the week, many of them have Saturday Afternoon, or some other the like space of Time, or (by some Masters) the whole Saturday, allow'd them to plant Corn, Potatoes, and other Provisions for themselves which they may sell, and convert the Money to what Uses they think good, and that they hold their Markets in or near several Towns on Sunday ... whatever Orders may be made again it diverts themselves with Singing, Playing and Dancing After their several Country Modes, and such as can afford it Feast, Dance and Carouse, either in their Masters plantations, or at the Graves of their deceased Kindred.

In 1776 John Pinney offered a disparaging description of the majority of the whites who had been born on Nevis. Not only were they drunk and debauched, 'the Creoles in general are a set of lazy indolent people and some of them will not scruple to go to any lengths to save appearances and serve a turn. In short, int[erest] and self-preservation are their only objects, but there are a few really sensible and good men'.

There is one famous son of Nevis who defied the laziness and indolence attributed to the whites by Pinney. Alexander Hamilton, who became a leading figure in the revolt against the British in America, and a founder of the new republic, was born in Nevis around 1775. His mother, Rachel Faucette (of English and Huguenot heritage) had previously married Johann Lavien (who was either German or Danish) on the island of St Croix, but she left him in 1750 and took off to St Kitts, where she settled with James Hamilton.

She and Hamilton then moved to Nevis, where she had been born and had inherited a house from her father, and they had two children, James and Alexander (but they never married). (Their house is now the site where the Nevis House of Assembly stands today.) Alexander went to a school where the headmistress was Jewish and, as well as becoming an avid reader, he learned the Hebrew alphabet. James Hamilton then left her, and in 1765 she took her two sons back to St Croix, where she died three years later.

Ten year old Alexander Hamilton got a job as a clerk in a St Croix import-export firm that was trading with New York, and in 1772 he was taken under the wing of Reverend Hugh Knox, who recognised his talents and arranged for him to sail to America, where he enrolled at the Elizabethtown Academy in New Jersey. By 1774 he had graduated from King's College in New York (now Columbia University). In the same year he published his first pamphlets attacking British rule and supporting the American claim for independence.

Joan Robinson attributed Hamilton's radicalism to his early experiences in Nevis and St Croix. In particular, he seems to have recognised the injustice and barbarity of slavery. He lived close to the slave market in Nevis and his mother owned three slaves. This might well have shaped his attitudes, firmed up, perhaps, by his mentor in St Croix. Robinson wrote that Hugh Knox had tutored Hamilton's writing style, and instilled in him 'a strong work ethic, religious piety, a distaste for slavery' and opposition to alcohol. In 1779, witnessing slavery in America, he wrote that the idea that Black people were inferior to whites was refuted by reason and experience, and he advocated that the Negroes should be armed to fight against the British in the war of independence.

The whites in Nevis were a small minority of the population and, according to Pinney, their talent was in short supply, but

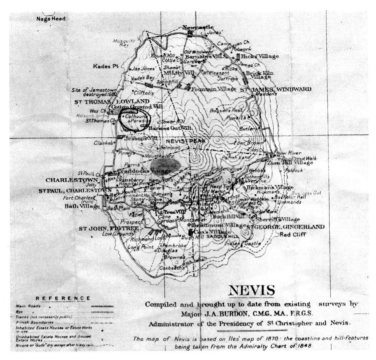

The map of Nevis in 1870, showing Mt Lily Village in the north. Maroon Hill (unmarked) is very close to Dunbars, on the south side of the Nevis Peak

they were able to stay in control. They had two tactics. They intimidated the majority of Africans by selling off recalcitrant slaves to America or other islands, and they used their whips, manacles and guns whenever they felt they needed to control those they kept on their land.

The importation of additional Africans during the 18th century was reduced because the roughly equal numbers of men and women meant that, with the encouragement of the slave owners, the birth-rate was high: 65 per cent of all Africans were born in St Kitts or Nevis by the end of 1700s. Being born into an enslaved family and experiencing no other mode of existence probably further reduced the likelihood of open revolt.

The Africans lived in nuclear families in clusters of houses. From the age of four or five children were put to work feeding the animals or weeding. The communal social structure of the enslaved meant that African culture and its oral traditions, such as the Anansi trickster stories brought to the Caribbean from West Africa, were spread among them. (James Sutton referred to listening to Anansi stories told by his mother and her friends in St Kitts in the 1920s and 1930s.)

Emily Zobel Marshall has explained how Anansi stories fertilised rebellious ideas. The Africans elected their own leaders and organised everyday resistance, such as stealing food, tools and animals from the owners, 'misunderstanding' orders and finding other ways of avoiding work. (These are some of the tricky ways of the shape-shifter Anansi.) Some escaped to the remaining forests. They were pursued, and, between 1765 and 1783, John Pinney had 30 of those who had fled his Mountravers plantation on Nevis recaptured, branded and fettered in blocks of wood. Knowing that his slaves persistently resisted him, Pinney had bought, on 21st February 1767, six 'negro necklocks'.

Slavery: some numbers and some profits

The extent of this evil buying and selling of Africans, and the profits made, cannot be described too often. From 1761 to 1807, European traders forced 1,428,000 African captives to cross the Atlantic Ocean from Africa to America and the West Indies – this is the 'middle passage' of the triangular trade. Combining the traffic in human cargo by the British, Portuguese, Spanish, French, Dutch and Danish traders it is estimated that 11 to 13 million Africans were transported across the Atlantic to the Americas and the Caribbean during the 400 years of slavery. Olaudah Equiano, a freed slave, described his experience in the hold of the slave ship: 'The shrieks of the women, and the groans of the dying, rendered the whole scene a scene of horror almost inconceivable'. About one fifth of these Africans – maybe two million people – perished on their ships during the middle passage. When a party of Africans from Nigeria arrived in Basseterre in St Kitts in March 1737 on a Bristol ship called *The*

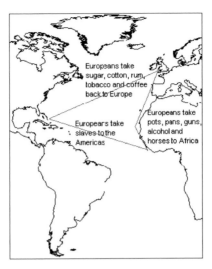

The 'triangular trade', where two million Africans died in the
'middle passage' from Africa to America and the Caribbean

Prince of Orange, more than 100 of them threw themselves into
the sea in despair after their voyage and in fear of their
presumed fate on the plantations. Thirty-three drowned.

Between 1630 and 1807, those British men and women who
had invested in slavery made a profit of about £12 million on the
purchase and sale of African people (about £1.6 billion in today's
pounds sterling). Overall, the merchants' profit from slave sales
was about £60 million – around £8 billion in today's money. Upon
abolition in 1833, the 3,000 or so British investors in the slave
trade were reimbursed (for the loss of their 'property') by the
government to the tune of £16.5 billion in today's money.

One of the beneficiaries of slave ownership in Nevis, George
Pollard, received £2,416 in compensation under the 1833 Slave
Abolition Act (around £230,000 in today's money). Pollard was
the first manager of the London Joint Stock Bank which, after
mergers, is now part of the global giant bank HSBC. Pollard got
his compensation after a claim he made against Charles Pinney,
the owner of Colhoun's estate (or Windmill) on Nevis. Charles
Pinney could afford to pay up: his pay-out for the loss of his
chattels was £25,136 (just over £3 million today).

Of Charles Pinney's 1,655 slaves at the time of emancipation, 74 were on West Farm in St Kitts, and the rest were on Nevis, spread across Stoney Grove, Stoney Hill, Clarke's, Golden Rock, Bachelor's Hall, Dasent's, Mt Sion/Symond's and New River. His relative John F Pinney had 597 slaves in British Guiana, Monserrat and St Vincent, Nevis and St Kitts. These earned him £12,620 in compensation (equivalent to £1.5 million today). The Africans got no money at all, of course. Spiritually, there is no price on freedom, but the material imbalance here – the whites getting huge amounts and Black people nothing at all – deepens the bloody wound of slavery.

Karen Fog Olwig provided a sociological analysis of the transformation of the position of the enslaved Africans in her book about Nevis published in 1993. She pointed out that, when the first Africans were shipped to the island in the 17th century, the English settlers' ideology justified 'an hierarchical patriarchal socioeconomic order'. They believed it was natural that white men were at the top of the hierarchy and that it was natural that the economy would be run for their benefit. At the end of the 18th century, a new idea was emerging in northern Europe: equality. Crucially, in Nevis, the achievement of 'equality' required strict conformity to the norms and values of the emerging English middle class, summed up in the term 'respectability'. The Christian churches were the principal means through which this notion was promulgated across the island. (Olwig argued that both hierarchical and egalitarian tendencies were intertwined in the slaves' African cultures, too.)

As time went by, these principles of hierarchy and equality operated to change the status of the African-Caribbean people. At first, they were incorporated into society, with a social status below the indentured white servants. Later, even that status was denied: they were 'virtually excluded from the human ranks of society and reckoned to be part of the plantations' stocks'. At first, the Africans were regarded with curiosity and incredulity; later that were 'increasingly condemned as immoral and animal-like'.

Olwig made the crucial point that, whatever the whites tried to impose, the Africans created spaces of their own, outside the control of the plantocracy. Specifically, their ability to grow their own food gave them a certain amount of autonomy. But, after Emancipation, equal rights were a long time coming, and still only available to those who conformed to English notions of respectability, as they attempted to move up the social ladder.

To these important observations I would add that, as much as the white owners described Africans as bestial, open-minded travellers who observed them in their homes noticed how intelligent they were. Baron de Wimpffen visited San Domingo (now Haiti) in 1790 and is quoted by C L R James as follows:

One has to hear with what warmth and what volubility, and at the same time with what precision of ideas and accuracy of judgement, this creature, heavy and taciturn all day, now squatting before his fire, tells stories, talks, gesticulates, argues, passes opinions, approves or condemns both his master and everyone who surrounds him.

As these witty and analytical Africans learned to read and write, many developed a critique of acquiring English 'respectability' as their first step on the ladder of hierarchy, adopting instead the more radical principle of equality (developed in the late 18th century's so-called Enlightenment). These Black radicals believed in economic equality, as well as social and legal equality, campaigning for increased wages and the right to run the economy themselves, outside of white colonial rule. (San Domingo's Toussaint L'Ouverture is the most famous of the first Black revolutionaries.)

Slavery was not only a system in which Black bodies were degraded and dehumanised in pursuit of white wealth. It had a moral and psychological effect on the whites that was memorably set out by the enslaved African-American Harriet

Jacobs in 1861. After describing the sexual grooming of teenage Black women and, if bribes didn't work, the use of the lash or starvation by white male owners in order to gain 'submission to their will', Harriet Jacobs wrote this:

> I was twenty-one years in that cage of obscene birds. I can testify, from my own experience and observation, that slavery is a curse to the whites as well as to the blacks. It makes the white fathers cruel and sensual; the sons violent and licentious; it contaminates the daughters and makes the wives wretched.

We can assume that many, perhaps most of the whites on Nevis and St Kitts were similarly cursed, and that they imposed their stunted humanity on all the inhabitants of those islands.

Pero, a slave born in Nevis, servant to John Pinney

We can learn a lot more about slavery on Nevis by examining the life of John Pinney and his African named Pero, as told by Christine Eicklemann and David Small. Pinney moved with Pero from Nevis to Bristol. Slavery marks several British coastal cities. Dr Eric Williams, Prime Minister of Trinidad and Tobago from 1962 to 1981, famously suggested in his pioneering work *Capitalism and Slavery* (first published in 1944) that we should see the magnificent buildings in Liverpool's port as cemented with the blood of Africans. There's a trace of slavery in St Kitts-Nevis in Bristol, where there is a bridge named after Pero, Pinney's man.

Pero was born in Nevis around 1753. He was purchased, aged about 12, by the Englishman John Pretor Pinney in 1765. Pinney was born in Chard, Somerset, in September 1740. He acquired the plantations and buildings on Nevis that had been established by his ancestor Azariah Pinney, who had escaped execution or life imprisonment by sailing to Nevis after fighting for the Duke of Monmouth in his failed uprising against King

James II in 1685. (Eight hundred other white rebels were sold into slavery in the West Indies in punishment for supporting Monmouth.) John Pinney had inherited 141 slaves along with the family properties in Charlestown and the sugar plantations on the island. We saw above that John Pinney regarded most of the white Creoles who ran the plantations as lazy and self-interested. All the property and land he inherited was run-down and laden with debt, while a third of the slaves were infirm or 'good for nothing', according to his estate manager, William Coker. Pinney's estate was on the north east of Nevis.

Pinney described his favourable first impression of the geography of Nevis in a letter to Mrs Williams, a friend in England:

> It is small but very pleasantly situated and commands a full and clear prospect of no less than seven neighbouring islands; it has a very high mountain in the middle covered with trees on the top, on the North and South sides there are a few high hills covered with trees also on the top. The plantations ascend gradually from sea to mountain and you may see at one point of view, land preparing, others just holed for planting, adjoining young cane just upspringing out of the earth, near that canes almost ripe and often the next piece cutting and carrying to the mill and pieces of potatoe and intermixed which with the sea and shipping, etc. I think it affords a very pleasing prospect.

As Eicklemann and Small point out in their web publication 'The Mountravers Plantation Community, 1734 to 1834', Pinney neglects to mention that this transformation of a natural wilderness into cultivated plantations had been undertaken by enslaved Africans.

Pero, his sisters Nancy and Sheeba, and a 25-year-old African woman called Harriott (all purchased for £115) initially seem to have worked on John Pinney's Gingerland plantation, but by 1767 they worked on his main estate, Mountravers, in the parish of St Thomas Lowland. As we have seen, cutting and processing the cane into sugar was extremely hard work: between 1765 and 1775, of his 250 slaves on Mountravers, 40 died. But Pero was more fortunate: he soon became Pinney's personal servant, working alongside a ten year-old white boy named Tom Peaden, whom Pinney took on as an indentured servant in Dorset before he set sail for Nevis.

It is not known if Pero lived in Pinney's house or in the village with the other Africans. He had access to the master's food, but he also grew his own vegetables to supplement the plantation allowance of salted herrings, corn, potatoes, rice and yams. There is a record of him selling sheep to Pinney, so he must have kept livestock, too. By 1771, Tom Peaden had become an overseer on the plantation, and Pero was a skilled barber; Pero also learned some dentistry skills, much needed because of the teeth decay brought on by sucking sugar cane.

The North American war of independence (1775-1783) caused extreme hardship in St Kitts and Nevis. The French, taking the Americans' side, attacked the British Caribbean colonies, disrupting the food supplies from America on which the islands depended. Between 300 and 400 slaves had died from starvation by March 1778, but Pinney planted vegetables in place of cane on parts of his estate, which seems to have saved the Africans on his plantation from extreme hunger. Pinney's proposal that Nevis should surrender to the French was agreed by the Nevis Island Council on 9th January 1782, and, having boarded the *Ville de Paris* on 14th January, moored off Charlestown, with his wife's father William Burt Weekes, the British capitulation was accepted.

The French took St Kitts later that month, after a sea battle in Frigate Bay. A combination of battles with the French, the effect of the hurricanes that swept the island, and interruptions in trade meant that by the close of the 18th century, the economy of Nevis was in decline. One manifestation of this was that the number of Jewish traders dropped to only three, and the synagogue ceased to function.

Pero left Nevis on 5th July 1783, accompanying the Pinney family on their voyage to England. Mrs Pinney's maid was the African Fanny Coker, freed in 1778, aged about 8. Fanny was the daughter of Black Polly or Polly Pinney and William Coker, Pinney's estate manager. Polly was about 14 at the time she gave birth to Fanny, and, carefully evaluating the evidence, Christine Eickelmann concludes that Coker had raped her. Pinney denied Polly's claim that he was the father of another of her children, Billey Jones, but Eickelmann thinks it quite likely that he was. Pinney regularly gave her money, which she put to good use, and Polly became something of an entrepreneur in rum and fabrics. She also invested in animals, which she reared and sold.

Arriving in Dover on 15th August 1783, the Pinneys and their staff initially lived in London, where Pero and Fanny would have met some of the 10,000 or so Africans settled in the English capital. (There were an estimated 14-15,000 Black people across England at this time.) Most of them were free, but Pero was still enslaved. The famous Mansfield judgement of 1772 had ruled only that escaped slaves could not be returned to the West Indies; they could still be bought and sold, and those that escaped in England could still be hunted down. Pero might have hoped to be set free, since Pinney had manumitted Fanny and one or two others, but there's no evidence that he was. In March 1784 the Pinneys took him to their new home in Bristol, where Pinney had set up in business as a merchant in sugar, sending ships back and forth between Bristol and Charlestown. One of his ships was called *Nevis*.

Pero sent gifts to his family in Nevis, and revisited the island with Pinney in 1790 and in 1794. As Pinney's valet, and staff member with the longest service, he should have been head of the male household in Bristol; being still in slavery, that role was probably denied him. But it was an intimate job he did, shaving his master, powdering his wig, looking after his hair, helping him dress and undress as well as waiting at table. Being literate, he would have attended to all sorts of Pinney's important affairs. The Pinneys had their Nevis plantation manager send them mangoes, ginger, guava marmalade, tamarinds, pineapples, pickled pepper, yams, cassava bread, sugar, rum and even, for special occasions, turtles. The delights of the West Indies were already part of a rich English family's gastronomic pleasure.

Pero seems to have lost favour with Pinney after the 1794 visit to Nevis – Christine Eickelmann and David Small, in their fascinating pamphlet on Pero, speculate that his relative wealth and his experience of some autonomy (compared to field slaves) may have led him to rebel against the Pinneys by working less hard. It seems he developed a taste for alcohol, too, and enjoyed time in the company of what Pinney described as 'abandoned characters', who may have been escaped slaves and abolitionists. They say he would have heard about Toussaint L'Ouverture leading the 1791 slave uprising in San Domingo, read Equiano's own book, and followed the newspaper reports of the abolition movement, all of which would encourage disaffection with his master. Additionally, he might well have read in the newspapers about the north American revolt against British rule, and the revolutionary concepts of Life, Liberty and the Pursuit of Happiness, embedded in its new Constitution (1787), in which Nevis's Alexander Hamilton had played such an important role. Pero died in 1798, and Mrs Pinney sent his possessions to his sisters, his father and his nephew in Nevis. Pero's was a life of servitude and, it seems, resistance.

Fanny Woolward and Lord Nelson

Frances Herbert Woolward, born in Nevis in 1758, is often mentioned in the official histories of St Kitts and Nevis because she became the wife of Lord Nelson. Her connection to the Pinney family (and her varying fortunes) are not so well known. Her mother was a descendant of the Earl of Pembroke and a relative had been the President of the Council of Nevis until 1768. Hers was a wealthy family, and she had a personal slave called Cato. But, having fallen on hard times, she returned to England as a young woman where she was reduced to being the guardian of John Pinney's children (whom he disowned when he returned to England in 1783). Fanny then returned to Nevis, living with her uncle John Richardson Herbert at his grand house in Montpelier (Richardson was President of the Nevis Council).

In 1784, Horatio Nelson was in command of a ship enforcing the Navigation Acts that promoted English trade interests against American and European rivals in the sea around Antigua. (Nevis merchants actually supported the Americans.) Nelson, confined to his moored ship while a court case against him was being mounted, met Fanny on Nevis. Fanny was described by one of Nelson's friends as 'pretty and sensible', while another said she had 'a freshness of countenance not common in that climate', but she was not at all clever. Nelson became enamoured – particularly when John Herbert offered him a large amount of money to marry her – and the marriage took place in 1787 on the Montpelier estate. They then settled in Norfolk, in England. By 1789, however, Nelson had become infatuated with Lady Emma Hamilton, and he abandoned (but did not divorce) Fanny. (Hallie Rubenhold has pointed out that Lady Hamilton, formerly Amy Lyon, began her career as a harlot in Covent Garden, London.)

Lord Nelson's views on slavery came into public focus in the UK after the 2020 campaign to remove statues in British cities that celebrated men whose wealth was based on their slave holdings. Nelson was denounced in 2017 by Afua Hirsch as a white supremacist. The evidence cited was a letter he wrote to his slave-owning friend attacking William Wilberforce (one of the leaders in Nelson's time of the effort in Parliament to make slavery illegal). The letter, published in 1807 after Nelson's death, included his commitment 'to launch my voice against the damnable and cursed doctrine of Wilberforce and his hypocritical allies'.

Martin Downer, a Nelson scholar, then alleged that Nelson had written 'cruel', not 'cursed', and that all he meant was that anarchy would result if slaves were freed. Nelson supporters also say he made several humanitarian gestures which indicate some distance from the proponents of slavery. The fact remains he had slave-owning friends, his wife was from a Nevis family that owned slaves, and he opposed Wilberforce's campaign. His effigy stands on a huge column in Trafalgar Square, in the heart of London, and his dubious history was conveniently forgotten until the much-needed campaign against British slave-owners on plinths erupted in 2020.

The 19th Century rebellions

The British House of Commons discussed the situation in St Kitts in 1811. The quality of the white people who were running St Kitts and Nevis in the 19th Century was poor. Chris Birch quoted Hugh Elliott, Governor of the Leeward Islands, who had stated that the rich men who owned the St Kitts' estates had, in the main, left the islands. Those that remained:

> managers, overseers, self-created lawyers, self-educated physicians and adventurous merchants [had] little real capital and scanty credit ... The acquirements of education among many of this description of persons, are very unequal to taking a share in the governments ... Individual interest – personal influence – animosity of party feuds, weigh down the scale of justice, and divert the course of the legislative authority into acts of arbitrary and unjustifiable power.

Thus the representatives of this motley crew were incapable of running the economy of the islands. Birch reported that in 1817 their leaders wrote to the Governor of St Kitts, Nevis, Anguilla and the Virgin Islands stating that there 'was nothing short of famine' and 'extreme distress' on their island. They pointed out that 'a state of tranquillity' among the enslaved Africans is only preserved if they receive 'the necessaries of life'. Without them, they 'become irritated and discontented to an alarming degree'. A 'Humble Address' to King George IV a few months later said that the situation was 'calamitous' and the island could only 'join in the policy adopted by the Mother Country' if relief was provided. This plea proved successful and in June importation of provisions (including bread, biscuit, flour, beans, peas, wheat, rice) from British dominions was permitted.

Chris Birch's relative James Berridge landed in St Kitts in 1794, aged 20. He came from a village near Nottingham in England and arrived in St Kitts without a penny to his name. As a newcomer, he perhaps wasn't as inept and nefarious as the men denounced above by the Governor. His skin colour and his wits made him a successful merchant. By 1817 he owned 21 slaves, whose roles allow us to imagine what kind of life he had. Some served him in his large house in Pall Mall Square in Basseterre (now Independence Square) where he was waited on by a valet, a butler, a cook, a washer/ironer, a nursery maid and three general servants. Another African was a stable boy, managing his horses and fine carriage. One was an infant.

The others worked in his businesses: four were porters, six were sailors. He had a cooper who manufactured barrels, casks, buckets and the like – it's not clear if this was another business, or these were made for domestic purposes. Seventeen were listed as black, but three were described as 'sambo', which Birch reads as 'the offspring of a black and a mulatto', but which is sometimes used to identify a person with a mix of various heritages – indigenous (Carib), African, European, Asian. Of the 21, five were born in Africa. Perhaps Berridge's fine style was not well-founded: by 1820 he declared himself to be in serious debt.

From time to time, punishment of slaves went beyond the norms that some of the white people adhered to. Chris Birch provided some examples. In 1810 (perhaps 1812) Edward Huggins, one of the richest plantation owners on Nevis, had 32 of his slaves tied down in Charlestown and given 200 or more lashes apiece. The unwritten law was that the maximum number of lashes was 39. Huggins was arrested but a jury of his peers found him not guilty. The Nevis Assembly then passed a resolution condemning Huggins' action as 'cruel and illegal'. The infliction of 242 lashes on one African and 291 on another was described as 'an act of barbarity, altogether unprecedented on this island'. The fact that the punishment of only two was described as barbarous, and that the newspaper that printed the resolution was found guilty of libel, gives an indication of the mentality of the slave owners of Nevis. (Thomas Southey published full details of Huggins's crimes, and his acquittal, in 1827. This account included reference to the Africans Huggins had murdered, and noted that there had been five attempts to poison him, further evidence of African resistance.)

The Reverend William Davis beat a slave to death on St Kitts in 1813; in 1818 the Reverend Henry Rawlins killed by flogging one of his slaves who had run away. In 1826 Colonel Charles Maxwell, Governor of St Kitts, said, in a speech to the legislature, that the island's Africans were a 'degraded class in the moral scale of creation'. Perhaps this falsehood explains the fact that two clergymen could kill Africans without punishment of any kind.

Maxwell retired as Governor in 1827. For the past twelve years he had been prevaricating with those in the British Parliament who were advocating 'amelioration' of the conditions under which Africans were in bondage in St Kitts and Nevis. Since he believed these men and women were a 'degraded class' we can assume he took the side of the planters and their agents who opposed all efforts to undermine their wealth and power.

The Honourable Stedman Rawlins, a prominent slave and plantation owner, took over as Governor. In January 1828 he steered a bill through the St Kitts' Council that became 'An Act for Further Improving the Condition of the Slave Population on St Christopher'. This 'further improvement' allowed for female domestic slaves to be whipped, but abolished the use of the 'cart-whip' in the fields. Rawlins died in Nova Scotia in 1830.

By 1826, 11 per cent of the African population on St Kitts was free. Chris Birch quoted a St Kitts Act of 1802 regretting that 'serious inconvenience' had recently arisen from the fact that slaves from 'other Colonies' were being brought to St Kitts and manumitted soon after. These 'free negroes and free persons of colour' were 'very suspicious and improper characters' who were 'turning loose among the Public'. Others were the offspring of white masters and Black slaves who had either bought their liberty with their earnings (as lawyers' clerks, shop-keepers, masons or carpenters, for instance), or they had been freed by absentee and local plantation owners.

The children of white fathers and African mothers also had more freedom than the field slaves. Some of the free Africans went to neighbouring islands to earn higher wages; one or two became merchants. A new social class was clearly emerging among the people of colour. Their freedom was a source of worry for the whites and inspiration for those still in bondage. St Kitts' population at this time was 22,700, of which only 7 per cent were white and 82 per cent were enslaved.

Legal freedom after the 1833 Abolition Act did not remove racial discrimination, but the introduction of wage labour changed the way that the employers controlled their workers. Very few plantations on St Kitts and Nevis were making much money by this time. Nevis was less profitable than St Kitts – other sources of sugar were becoming available, the once extremely fertile land was over-exploited and increasingly less able to produce the top-quality sugar that had made the island so valuable – so the wages offered to farm labourers were lower than those offered on St Kitts.

While we don't know how rebellious Pero became, we do know that Africans in Nevis and St Kitts were by no means passive in the face of white domination. (Whites on St Kitts who supported abolition included the Attorney General, the Chief Justice, the Dean of St George's church in Basseterre, and three former Lieutenant Governors.) No doubt the near starvation of 1817 fuelled their anger. An African rebellion erupted for a couple of years after Britain's Parliament finally emancipated the Africans. The slave owners in St Kitts and Nevis tried to circumvent the new law by utilising in 1834 a type of apprenticeship for Africans that was effectively another form of bondage. In protest, and no doubt influenced by the fact that the Earl of Romney had actually freed 300 of his slaves, a group of Africans in St Kitts in July 1834 took to the hills or refused to do the work in the fields allotted to them.[1]

At the end of the month, Africans on twelve to fourteen estates refused to use their 'hoes and bills' any more, while a few days later 'on a great many estates' workers refused to 'throw meat' or look after the cattle. ('Meat' referred to the grasses and cane tops that were thrown on the ground to feed the animals.) Across the island, resistance was almost total. On four estates, around 800 people were described as being 'in a riotous way'. Hundreds took off completely into the mountains, joining others who had been on the run for three or four years. One of them, 'Markus, King of the Woods,' was described as being very skilful in the use of his musket. 'No order may be expected in the country unless he is taken', wrote one of the militia.

---

1. There is a Leeds connection to this campaign to abolish the apprenticeship system. The actor, writer and historian Joe Williams, of Jamaican heritage, born and resident in Leeds, has called our attention to the Leeds merchant Thomas Harvey: 'Thomas Harvey had his own shop on Commercial Street, [in Leeds' City Centre] and when he heard about the injustices of the apprenticeship system in Jamaica which replaced slavery [in 1833] but was actually much worse than slavery, he took the trouble of travelling four thousand miles to the West Indies to investigate and bring back evidence to present to Parliament who then abolished the apprenticeship system [in 1838]. I just think that is phenomenal, because I am not sure that I today, with the ease of travel, would travel four thousand miles to the Congo, let's say, to report on the atrocities that are going on there, in the name of international trade. But he did that, in times when it would take months to get from one place to the other, and not very comfortably either. I just think that's phenomenal, so Thomas Harvey has a place in my heart.'

This is a 'bill', the instrument used by enslaved and 'free' Africans to cut cane.

Solicitor General Raymond Claxton lamented that the careful organisation of this rebellion had 'hitherto remained undetected'. 'Incendiaries', he wrote were 'peregrinating the land'. On 6th August 1834, Evan Murray Macgregor, governor of the Leeward Islands, introduced martial law in St Kitts and soldiers from Barbados attempted to enforce it. Despite the leaders being rounded up and whipped, the revolt stayed solid. Raymond Frucht has described this as 'an organised event [that] constituted the first stage of the development of a working class-for-itself'.

The whites' counter-attack was ruthless. Speaker of the Assembly G H Burt, a plantation owner in St Ann Parish, 'cordially co-operated' with the men sent to burn the homes of those on his estate who escaped or refused to work. This punishment had already been administered on another estate. Soldiers were sent to burn the resisters out of their camps in the mountains. The revolt was suppressed, and sixteen were whipped and imprisoned or expelled from the island. Martial law was lifted on 18th August but the workers remained 'sulky, insolent' and reluctant to work. The revolt nevertheless taught the owners a lesson and full legal freedom was introduced in 1838, following the example of Antigua.

Starvation reappeared at the end of the 19th century. In 1896 Africans with empty stomachs set fire to cane fields in yet another rebellion, this time against the injustices of capitalism, rather than the abomination of slavery. When Arthur France tells us of his pride in his African heritage, it is this fine tradition of resistance and revolt that he has in mind.

Economic difficulties resulted in the Nevis landowners introducing sharecropping. Black people were allowed to develop their own smallholdings, but were required to give some of their produce to the owner of the plantation on which they lived. (By 1900, there were smallholdings on 61 estates on Nevis – St Kitts only had two.) This gave the Africans on Nevis a modicum of control over what was planted, and many of them thus were able to plant vegetables and fruits for their own consumption. As we saw in Chapter 2, Arthur France's father, Ebeneza, was one of those, who, in addition to his main job, had a smallholding whose eggs, chickens and other products not only sustained his family but were shared with the poor.

It is well established that slavery was not abolished simply because a majority of British legislators belatedly came to see that this system of enforced labour was immoral. The bogus claim that dark-skinned people were a lesser species than the white-skinned actually gained ground as 'racial science' was promulgated from the mid-19th century. Nevertheless, profits from sugar were dropping, rebellion was increasing and it came to be understood that an economy based on free labour would be more efficient and productive than one based on enslaved or indentured labour.

It was capitalist economics and slave revolt, with some help from humanitarian conscience, that drove emancipation. Economic competition remained brutal and it hurt the British Caribbean. When German sugar extracted from beet came to be cheaper than Caribbean cane sugar at the end of 1800s, the St Kitts-Nevis economy was badly hit and plantations cut their labour force, wages dropped and, as we have seen, starving

Africans rose up. Freedom under the law meant that Africans could migrate, and many Kittitians and Nevisians, perhaps lacking smallholdings, moved to other islands, especially Trinidad, in search of work.

The 20th Century

Modernisation was one response to capitalist competition from the class in power, and the St Kitts' Sugar Producers Association centralised the industry into one factory in 1912; it started building a railway on the island in the same year. Telephones were introduced in St Kitts in 1896, and some Nevisians got their phones in 1913. But electricity didn't arrive there until 1953. Efforts to develop a cotton industry during World War One were then foiled by the boll weevil in the 1920s.

The Nevis government bought up the land bankrupted during that decade's Great Depression. Karen Fog Olwig explained as follows:

When the sugar plantations finally collapsed in the early twentieth century, the British crown purchased the old estate land and sold it to the local population in a major land-settlement programme that aimed to create a population of peasant proprietors. The land sold ... has been described as 'worn out' ... the land settlement programme had come way too late.

But, as pointed out in Chapter 2, owning and farming this land, even though it was not as fertile as it once was, raised Black people's standard of living and helped them establish a respectable life.

St Kitts' population declined by 43 per cent in the first three decades of the 20th Century, while Nevis lost 9 per cent of its people. (The lower percentage in Nevis might be because the government's ownership of much of the land preserved its labour force.)

Hard labour in the cane fields of St Kitts, 1903.
Source: USA Library of Congress

The fact that the people, mainly of African descent, on Nevis and St Kitts were working for a wage, rather than merely subsisting on small plots of land, meant that a labour movement would develop in response to the lowering of wages and rising unemployment in the 1930s. The Workers' League, formed by Thomas Manchester of Sandy Point in St Kitts in 1932, was instrumental in spreading the news of the strikes breaking out in various Caribbean islands.

In British Honduras there was a strike in February 1934 (ending in a riot in September); in Trinidad in the same year 15,000 Indian labourers on sugar estates created disturbances from May to July; and in January 1935 the St Kitts sugar workers went on strike, no doubt taking advantage of their conglomeration in the single sugar factory. This developed into a general strike of all agricultural labourers. (The Buckley's Estate protests have been described in more detail in Chapter 6.) Significantly, with violent protests erupting in Harlem in May 1935, a 'St Kitts Defence League' was formed in New York at that time to (as Margaret Stevens put it) 'defend an entire island – an incipient and would-be nation – rather than just one or two pre-eminent figures' who were arrested after the demonstrations by the St Kitts' sugar workers.

James Sutton wrote that, soon after the 1939 Trades Union Act was passed, the St Kitts-Nevis Trades and Labour Union was formed, with an Executive including Thomas Manchester, Matthew Sebastian, Joseph France, E O Challenger and Joseph Nathan. 'On Sundays especially these men went from village to village throughout St Kitts ringing The Union Bell', calling the public to their meetings. James Sutton and his friends 'were enthused by what we heard', and many labourers joined the union. His brother Oliver, a worker at Spooner's Cotton Factory, was 'very impressed' by Sebastian and France and became an 'outspoken and apparently fearless' advocate of the advantages of union membership, despite reprisals from the estate managers.

Paul Foot, discussing the history of profit for the whites and revolt by Black people in the Windward Islands, wrote:

Trade union leaders were bullied, threatened, even murdered. But nothing could stop the unions, and, gradually they formed themselves into political parties ... Nowhere in the West Indies were the planters more resistant to change than in St Kitts. Consequently perhaps, nowhere were the sugar workers more courageous in their support for their trade union and labour leaders.

(Foot went on to explain that Mr Bradshaw did not advance the workers' cause as well as he might, but Foot supported Bradshaw when the white planters attempted to organise a coup against him in June 1967. Foot also supported Bradshaw's position (as did the American CIA) when Anguilla tried to break away from the St Kitts-Nevis-Anguilla confederation in 1967.)

In Chapter 2 we saw that Arthur France's uncle, Sir Joseph France KCMG, CBE, JP was one of the Workers' League organisers of the 1935 strike. In 1940, he became General Secretary of the St Kitts and Nevis Trade Union. He served in the Legislative Assembly and was the Minister of Social Services when Paul Southwell was Chief Minister of St Kitts-Nevis-Anguilla in 1960. Robert Bradshaw succeeded Mathew Sebastian as President of the union in 1943 (according to Wikipedia; Sutton wrote that Bradshaw was Vice President in 1943). In 1945, Bradshaw became President of the St Kitts-Nevis-Anguilla Labour Party, which had been recently formed out of the Workers' League.

In January 1958, St Kitts-Nevis-Anguilla became a constituent part of the West Indies Federation, a self-governing entity established by the British government. It was composed of ten islands that were part of the British Empire, with a population of three to four million people. Based in Trinidad and Tobago, Sir Grantley Adams of Barbados was Prime Minister and Robert Bradshaw of St Kitts was its Minister of Finance. Disputes among the leaders of the various islands led to its demise in May 1962. Arthur France is one of many who regret this failure to overcome the rivalries between the islands; the disunity the English-speaking Caribbean offends him to this day.

This was the period when Arthur decided to migrate to Britain – he had been formed inside the African population of Nevis and St Kitts, but was now seeking greater opportunities in what he had been unreliably informed to be the Mother Country. His lifelong commitment to the rights of Black people and the cause of social and economic equality stems from his admiration for Uncle Joseph and the St Kitts and Nevis union activists.

In 1967, after many other islands had become fully independent of Britain, St Kitts-Nevis decided instead to become an Associated State of Britain. It became a separate entity in 1983, with Robert Bradshaw as Chief Minister and Joseph France as his close adviser.

For the year 2013, the population of St Kitts and Nevis was described on the Afro-Kittitians and Nevisians Wikipedia site as follows:

- 92% African-Caribbean (subdivided as 75% black, 5.3% mulatto [partially of Irish origin] and 12% Afro-European [European of African descent])
- 8% of other origin (subdivided as 5% Indian and Afro-Indian, and 3.3% from other parts of South Asia)
- 1% white (of British, French, Portuguese and Lebanese descent)

(I don't know why this adds up to over 100%.)

Given the widespread belief in God among Caribbean people, it is useful to note the religious affiliations in St Kitts-Nevis were listed in 2001 as:

- Protestant 74.4 per cent (includes Anglican 20.6 per cent, Methodist 19.1 per cent, Pentecostal 8.2 per cent, Church of God 6.8 per cent, Moravian 5.5 per cent, Baptist 4.8 per cent, Seventh Day Adventist 4.7 per cent, Evangelical 2.6 per cent, Brethren 1.8 per cent, other 0.3 per cent)
- Roman Catholic 6.7 per cent
- Rastafarian 1.7 per cent
- Jehovah's Witness 1.3 per cent
- Other: 7.6 per cent (none 5.2 per cent, unspecified 3.2 per cent).

Since sugar – rooted in slavery, producer of huge profits for the white owners, and source of militant opposition by Black workers – is at the heart of the story of Nevis and St Kitts, this chapter concludes by noting that 300 years of history came to an end on 22nd July 2006 with the closure of the St Kitts Sugar Manufacturing Corporation (SSMC) factory. 1,500 workers were made redundant, and given some encouragement to find new work in farming, fishing and other small businesses. It was the end of an era; but its legacy marks the islands, and the city of Leeds, UK, to this day.

References in this Appendix

Chris Birch *The Milk Jug Was a Goat – Two Families, Two Caribbean Islands, 1635-1987*, Cambridge: Pegasus Publishers, 2008. (E-book available via GooglePlay, published 2011.) The St Kitts quote from Captain John Smith *The True Travels of Captaine Smith*, 1630, and other material, including the quote from Governor Hugh Elliott, comes from Chris Birch. Birch was born on St Kitts and is related to the 'two families' in his title. These were Colonel William Burt (deputy governor of Nevis in 1685-6) and James Berridge, who arrived in St Kitts in 1794.

Olaudah Equiano (c. 1745-31 March 1797), one of the Eboe people enslaved by the British, known in his lifetime as Gustavus Vassa, published his autobiography, *The Interesting Narrative of Olaudah the African* in 1789. During his lifetime the best-selling book was published in nine editions and various languages. He campaigned for his fellow African John Annis, who had been illegally taken to St Kitts, to be freed, to no avail. Equiano's book is available today in several editions.

Paul Foot, 'Twenty Years of Pirates, Profits and Blood', *Socialist Worker*, 19.04.1969. https://www.marxists.org/archive/foot-paul/1969/04/windies.htm (Thanks to Christian Høgsbjerg for this article.)

Sir Joseph France: Some of this information comes from my interview with Prudence and Erikson France, Sir Joseph's children, in Basseterre, St Kitts, on 7th March 2017. See also Prudence France's article 'A Humble Leader – Sir Joseph Nathaniel France' in *St Kitts & Nevis Visitor*, Volume 2, 1997-98, p. 27.

Richard Frucht, 'Emancipation and Revolt in the West Indies: St. Kitts, 1834'. *Science & Society,* 1975, 39 (2).

June Goodfield's *Rivers of Time* (Leicester: Matador, 2008) has some of interesting factual information about Nevis, as she tries to uncover the story of Philippa, starting from the lonely gravestone on Saddle Hill, shown to her by Roland Archibald. The stone says that Philippa Prentis Phillips, who died on 11th August 1683, had been the wife of Clement Prentis and later of William Phillips. Much of the book is fictional. But Phillips plantations were established on both St Kitts and Nevis.

Simeon Hill, *Nevis Heritage Sites (St George) – Story Map of the Heritage Sites of Nevis*. This provides fascinating information about key sites on the island of Nevis, including the location of Maroon Hill. Available at https://storymaps.arcgis.com/stories/e85ad1ef2b544eb792af6703264de89e Accessed 16.12.2021.

John Cordy Jeaffreson (ed.) *A Young Squire of the Seventeenth Century – from the papers Christopher Jeaffreson of Dillingham House, Cambridgeshire*, Hurst and Blackett, England, 1878, p. 39. (Researched for my book about Chapeltown, Leeds: Max Farrar, *The Struggle for 'Community'*, Lampeter and New York: Edwin Mellen, 2002.)

Harriet Jacobs, *Incidents in the Life of a Slave Girl*, New York: Dover Publications, 2001 [first published in Boston, USA, in 1861].

Jews of Nevis: see the leaflet 'A Brief History of the 17th and 18th Century Sephardic Jewish Community, Nevis, Leeward Islands, Easter

Caribbean', prepared by Michelle M Terrell, Ph. D, 2003, available from the museum in Charlestown, Nevis.

Jasper Jolly, 'Barclays, HSBC and Lloyds among UK banks that had links to slavery', *Guardian*, 18.6.20, https://www.theguardian.com/business/2020/jun/18/barclays-hsbc-and-lloyds-among-uk-banks-that-had-links-to-slavery Accessed 19.6.20.

On Toussaint L'Ouverture, see CLR James, *The Black Jacobins*, New York: Vintage Books, 1989; and Charles Forsdick and Christian Høgsbjerg (eds.) *The Black Jacobins Reader*, Durham: Duke University Press, 2017.

Emily Zobel Marshall, *Anansi's Journey: A Story of Jamaican Cultural Resistance*, University of the West Indies Press, 2012.

Karen Fog Olwig, *Global Culture, Island Identity – Continuity and change in the Afro-Caribbean community of Nevis*, Reading: Harwood Academic Publishers, 1993. Republished by Routledge in 2017.

Karen Fog Olwig, *Caribbean Journeys – An ethnography of migration and home in three family networks*, Durham & London, Duke University Press, 2007.

Pero: Much of the information on Pero and John Pinney comes from Christine Eickelmann and David Small, *Pero – The Life of a Slave in Eighteenth-Century Bristol*, Bristol: Redcliffe Press in association with Bristol Museums and Art Gallery, 2004.

John Pinney: Christine Eickelmann has done an immense amount of additional research relating to John Pinney and all the people on his estate. See: Christine Eickelmann 'The Mountravers Plantation Community, 1734-1834 https://seis.bristol.ac.uk/~emceee/mountravers plantationcommunity.html The direct quote from Pinney, with his first impressions of Nevis, comes from that website.

Profits from slavery: *Legacies of British Slave-ownership*, constructed by University College London, provided George Pollard's and Charles Pinney's profits. Accessible at https://www.ucl.ac.uk/lbs/

Bonham C Richardson, *Caribbean migrants: environment and human survival on St. Kitts and Nevis* (1st ed.). Knoxville: University of Tennessee Press, 1983, as cited on the 'Afro-Kittitians and Nevisians' Wikipedia page https://en.wikipedia.org/wiki/Afro-Kittitians_and_Nevisians Accessed 27.12.2020.

Joan Robinson, *Alexander Hamilton: Nevis in the time of Hamilton, his contribution to his adopted country and Nevisian legacy*. Arnold Printing, New York, 2014. (Pamphlet)

Hallie Rubenhold, *The Covent Garden Ladies*, London: Penguin Random House, 2020.

St Kitts-Nevis history: Some of my history of St Kitts and Nevis has been derived from web-pages published by Wikipedia and other history sites, including the St Kitts-Nevis government's site and the BBC's.

St Kits-Nevis population and religion statistics for 2001 are from Ben Cahoon "Saint Kitts and Nevis". WorldStatesmen, at https://www.worldstatesmen.org/Saint_Kitts_and_Nevis.html Accessed 12.2.20. This site also includes an extensive list of all the colonial and post-colonial leaders of St Kitts and Nevis. I have used the terminology for the population statistics as used on the 'Afro-Kittitians and Nevisians' Wikipedia page.

'Sugar Industry in St Kitts Closes' SKN web http://www.sknweb.com/sugar-industry-in-stkitts-closes/ Accessed 18.3.2020.

St Kitts photo in early c20 from this USA Library of Congress website https://www.loc.gov/pictures/search/?q=%22st.+kitts%22&fa=displayed%3Aanywhere&sp=1. Re-printed here with their permission.

Thomas Southey, *Chronological History of the West Indies: In Three Volumes (Volume 3)*, London: Longman, Rees, Orm, Brown and Green, 1827.

Margaret Stevens, *Red International and Black Caribbean – Communists in New York City, Mexico and the West Indies, 1919-1939*, London: Pluto Press, 2017.

James W Sutton, *A Testimony of Triumph: A narrative of the life of James Sutton and family in Nevis and St Kitts, 1920-1940*, Scarborough, Ontario, Canada: Edan's Publishers, 1987.

Joe Williams, interviewed by Christian Høgsbjerg, 'The Leeds Black History Walk', *African Studies Bulletin*, No. 78, 2016-7. Available at https://lucas.leeds.ac.uk/article/the-leeds-black-history-walk-an-interview-with-joe-williams/#_ftnref3 Accessed 15.3.2020. (Referring to Leeds businessman Thomas Harvey.)

Eric Williams, *Capitalism and Slavery*, Chapel Hill: University of North Carolina Press, 1944/1994.

Fanny Woolward and Horatio Nelson information comes from their Wikipedia entries. Afua Hirsch's remarks on Nelson and monuments to slavers were in the Guardian newspaper (22.8.2017) https://www.theguardian.com/commentisfree/2017/aug/22/toppling-statues-nelsons-column-should-be-next-slaveryhttps://www.theguardian.com/commentisfree/2017/aug/22/toppling-statues-nelsons-column-should-be-next-slavery Accessed 17.10.2020. Martin Downer's defence of Nelson was in the Daily Mail newspaper (12.10.2020) https://www.dailymail.co.uk/news/article-8832743/Expert-proof-Admiral-Horatio-Nelson-did-NOT-support-slavery.html Accessed 17.10.2020.

Index